Public Services and Financial Austerity

Public Services and Financial Austerity

Getting Out of the Hole?

Roger Latham
Visiting Fellow, Nottingham Business School,
Nottingham Trent University, UK

Malcolm Prowle
Professor of Business Performance, Nottingham Business School,
Nottingham Trent University, UK

With a Foreword by

Margaret Wheatley

palgrave
macmillan

First published 2012 by
PALGRAVE MACMILLAN

Palgrave Macmillan in the UK is an imprint of Macmillan Publishers Limited, registered in England, company number 785998, of Houndmills, Basingstoke, Hampshire RG21 6XS.

Palgrave Macmillan in the US is a division of St Martin's Press LLC, 175 Fifth Avenue, New York, NY 10010.

Palgrave Macmillan is the global academic imprint of the above companies and has companies and representatives throughout the world.

Palgrave® and Macmillan® are registered trademarks in the United States, the United Kingdom, Europe and other countries.

ISBN: 978–0–230–29650–3

This book is printed on paper suitable for recycling and made from fully managed and sustained forest sources. Logging, pulping and manufacturing processes are expected to conform to the environmental regulations of the country of origin.

A catalogue record for this book is available from the British Library.

Library of Congress Cataloging-in-Publication Data

Latham, Roger, 1950–
    Public services and financial austerity : getting out of the hole? / Roger Latham, Malcolm Prowle.
        p. cm.
    Includes index.
    Summary: "The authors suggest that some of the problems of the public sector are self-inflicted and that current policies may only
deliver partial success "at a price we cannot afford". It proposes a radical alternative and discusses practical ways it could be implemented. It also explores the threats and opportunities that such an approach might face" – Provided by publisher.
        ISBN 978–0–230–29650–3
    1. Municipal services – Great Britain. 2. Public utilities – Great Britain. 3. Budget deficits – Great Britain. I. Prowle, Malcolm. II. Title.
HD4645.A5.L38 2011
363.606891—dc23   2011043802

10 9 8 7 6 5 4 3 2 1
21 20 19 18 17 16 15 14 13 12

Printed and bound in the United States of America

Contents

About the Authors

Roger Latham is a visiting fellow at Nottingham Business School where he collaborates on a number of themes with Malcolm Prowle. He has a first-class honours in Economics and Statistics and a Master's in Monetary Economics. He qualified as a CIPFA (Chartered Institute of Public Finance and Accountancy) member through the CIPFA's senior officer's scheme.

Roger has held various senior finance posts in local government subsequently becoming County Treasurer at Nottinghamshire County Council and later its Chief Executive. He is well known and well connected in local and central government and was once described by the *Local Government Chronicle* as 'a complete one-off' with a powerful intellect and was placed in their informal 'Top Ten' treasurers. He has been involved in various government task forces, including being chair of the Local Government Task Force, developing the 'Rethinking Construction' idea; chair of the East Midlands Improvement Partnership; and a member of the Chief Executives' Task Force, advising on the wider efficiency agenda. He also led the Local Government Association task group, preparing the local government response to the Simms sustainability agenda. He has held many positions of esteem and was the president of the CIPFA from 2009 to 2010.

Malcolm Prowle is Professor at Nottingham Business School and Visiting Professor at the Open University Business School and has held several academic posts in UK universities. He has more than 40 years of experience of public services (in the UK and overseas) in central government, local government, health and education. He is a member of CIPFA and ACCA and has held senior financial management posts in public service organisations. He had many years of consultancy experience with two international consulting firms (KPMG and PWC), involving clients in the UK and overseas.

He is an active researcher and has led and/or participated in a many funded research projects on public sector themes which have led to published research reports and papers. He has more than 50 publications to his name. This includes five books, numerous research reports and papers in both academic peer refereed and professional journals. This is his sixth book.

He has worked at the highest levels of government and has advised ministers, ambassadors, senior civil servants, public service managers and service professionals on a variety of public policy and policy implementation issues. He has had several periods of secondment to Whitehall departments of state and has also been financial adviser to a House of Commons Select Committee, adviser to two shadow ministers and a consultant to the World Health Organisation.

Foreword

Margaret Wheatley

Einstein is credited with saying that insanity is doing the same thing twice and expecting different results. If we would look truthfully at our behaviour as leaders, we'd have to admit that we're fast becoming insane. As the stakes get higher, as citizens get angrier and more impatient, as politicians make increasingly unreasonable promises, as experts compete and clamour for attention, as problems grow more complex and become more intractable, our default response is to keep applying the old solutions over and over again. The only things that change are the speed with which we apply them, and the names of the leaders tasked with making them work.

In our frantic and desperate attempts, we rarely step back and question our approaches or the assumptions that underpin them. Yet if we don't, we can't expect anything to change. Here are three assumptions about leadership that are largely outdated but commonly accepted these days especially in governmental circles:

- Leaders have the answers. They know what to do.
- People do what they're told. They just have to be given policies, plans, and instructions to implement them.
- High risk requires high control. As situations grow more complex and challenging, power must shift to centralised control (to the leaders who know what to do).

These beliefs give rise to the models of command and control revered in organisations and governments worldwide. Those at the bottom of the hierarchy submit to the greater vision and expertise of those above. Leaders promise to get us out of this mess; then the public complains bitterly and grows more cynical when they don't.

The only predictable consequence of leaders' attempts to wrest control of a complex, even chaotic situation, is that they create more chaos. They go into isolation with just a few key advisors, and attempt to find a simple solution (quickly) to a complex problem. And people pressure them to do just that. Everyone wants the problem to disappear; cries of 'fix it!' arise from the public. Leaders scramble to look like they've taken charge and have everything in hand.

But the causes of today's problems are complex and interconnected. There are no simple answers, and no one individual can possibly know what to do. We seem unable to acknowledge these complex realities. Instead, when the leader fails to resolve the crisis, we fire him or her, and immediately begin searching for the next (more perfect) one.

And yet in the midst of this growing insanity, there are a few leaders who see clearly and who understand the deeper dynamics that explain why governments and their leaders have become so impotent. This provocative and clarifying book is just such a work. It invites us to contemplate the historic watershed that Britain is in, and offers a well-grounded, experience-based set of choices that would end the impotence and provide genuine opportunities for local governance that would work. It's an ambitious and clear call that is issued here; we cannot ignore it if we are to find our way out of this current negative spiral of insanity.

Margaret (Meg) Wheatley is an internationally renowned and respected writer, speaker, consultant and teacher on organisational development, focussing on how we can accomplish our work, sustain our relationships, and willingly step forward to serve in this troubled time. Meg Wheatley was thrown into the public spotlight in 1992 with the publication of *Leadership and the New Science* which challenged our standard ways of thinking in organisations. *Industry Week* called it 'The best management book of the year' in 1992 and it went on to become a bestseller. A story in *National Journal* described how it even found its way into the White House where several members of the Clinton staff apparently took its message to heart. Since then, Meg has become one of America's most sought-after and influential management philosophers. She is co-founder and President emerita of The Berkana Institute, a research foundation working on the design of new organisations and has authored six books, including the classic *Leadership and the New Science*, and, most recently, *Perseverance* (2010), and *Walk Out Walk On: A Learning Journey into Communities Learning to Live the Future Now* (2011).

Preface and Acknowledgements

The former UK Chancellor of the Exchequer, Denis Healey, famously formulated his first law of holes as 'when you're in one, stop digging!' There can be little doubt that the present-time public services in the UK, along with many other countries, are probably in the biggest financial hole that they have ever experienced. Certainly, when we look for periods in which there had been an absolute decline in public expenditure, we can only find two modern examples, and both of those were associated with changes from a wartime to peacetime economy after the two world wars of the 20th century. At a recent CIPFA conference, a former US comptroller and auditor general, David Walker, stated that developed nations are facing a 'tsunami of spending' because of changing demographics that governments are failing to address. He argued that the developed world needed to act on the demographic trends facing them or face economic catastrophe.

This book is about the challenges facing public services for many decades to come. In doing this we have focussed largely on the UK situation but the content and lessons from this book are applicable to other countries, many of whom find themselves in a similar situation. As we began to write this book our principal concern was that the only debate that seemed to be going on was about financial restructuring and, to use the 'hole' metaphor, the discussion seemed to be about what size of spade to use and how fast we should be digging. Our concern was that there were a whole range of other extremely important issues to do with the environment, social change, demographic change, and so on, which have huge implications for public services and community well-being, but which were not getting discussed.

Our concerns have not diminished as we have been writing this book. In addition we feel that important alternatives to the traditional approach of determining the size of the public sector and its delivery mechanisms are being overlooked in a rush towards an urgent financial restructuring. We feel that the current approach and policies may well be successful, but it will be 'at a price that we cannot afford' in terms of losses to important public services, the impact on communities, the consequences for future generations, and ultimately the sustainability of the Western democratic ideal that has been dominant in the world thinking over the past hundred years.

A book like this cannot be written without, as Newton put it, 'standing on the shoulders of giants'. We are aware of a vast number of commentators and writers who have already contributed much to this agenda. We have tried in all cases to credit them throughout this book. However if we have overlooked any acknowledgement of contribution, we apologise, and will put it right if it is pointed out to us. You may find that this book makes controversial statements, and makes claims that are speculative and not completely proven. We make no apologies for that. If this book starts a debate about the wider agenda and alternative ways of meeting our future needs then we will have done our job.

We wish to acknowledge all who have contributed to the writing of this book by contributing ideas and suggesting improvements. To students, professionals, politicians, and academics who have heard earlier versions of some of this thinking, we offer our thanks for their insightful comments and questions which have helped to hone our thoughts. To the distinguished management philosopher, Dr Meg Wheatley, we offer our thanks for writing a foreword to this book. To our families and spouses who have had to put up with distracted authors, and drafts and redrafts, we ask forgiveness, and we hope that they will think that it has all been worthwhile.

As always, any errors and omissions are entirely our own fault and we take full responsibility.

Tables

Figures

Boxes

Part I
Issues and Alternatives

1
Introduction

In all countries public services are of great importance to a wide range of people and organisations such as:

- Clients or recipients of public services
- Taxpayers who fund public services
- Employees who work in public services
- Managers who plan and manage public services
- Politicians whose constituents may have concerns about public services
- Companies which provide goods and services to the public sector
- Non-governmental organisations of various kinds

All of these constituents, whether they realise it or not, have a clear interest in the way in which public services are planned and managed since these matters will ultimately impact on the public services organisations themselves and the services delivered.

For several decades, in many countries, the process of planning and managing public services largely concerned the distribution of growth monies which were the fruits of economic growth. The impact of global economic recession and the credit crunch was to create havoc with the public finances of many countries, with the consequence that growth monies for public services disappeared and were replaced by an environment of austerity. This new financial economic climate has meant that many of the traditional approaches to the planning and management of public services have come under scrutiny and new approaches are being considered. This book concerns the position of public services and the way in which they are planned and managed in a time of fiscal austerity.

We are where we are

The UK, along with many other countries, such as Greece, Spain, Ireland, Portugal etc, is in the midst of a major financial and economic crisis which will have profound implications for public expenditure and public services for the foreseeable future. The contextual situation is discussed more fully in Chapter 2 but in summary the UK faces the following challenges:

- A record UK public sector budget deficit
- The highest public sector budget deficit of any OECD country
- Record UK Government borrowing
- An escalating national debt
- An economy struggling to achieve reasonable levels of economic growth

Many other countries also face similar sets of circumstances.

Over the last century the UK has actually had a number of serious financial crises. For example at the outbreak of the First World War in 1914 there were strong fears of financial collapse both in the UK and across Europe. The period between the First and Second World Wars was also a period of financial turmoil with such events as the 1929 Wall Street crash and the Great Depression. However, the harbinger of the current situation was the financial crisis of 1976, which many people today will still remember. In 1975 Tony Crosland, the then Secretary of State for the Environment, commented:

> For the next few years times will not be normal. Perhaps people have used the words 'economic crisis' too often in the past. They have shouted 'wolf, wolf' when the animal was more akin to a rather disagreeable Yorkshire terrier. But not now. The crisis that faces us is infinitely more serious than any of the crises we have faced over the past 20 years... With its usual spirit of patriotism and its tradition of service to the community's needs, it is coming to realize that, for the time being at least, the party is over... We are not calling for a headlong retreat. But we are calling for a standstill. (Crosland 1975)

The phrase 'the party is over' still resonates today as a warning that the good times in the public sector are over once again. In 1976 the UK economy was in a mess. The left wing of the Labour Party had just defeated the Public Expenditure White Paper in the Commons in March 1976 and a few months later Harold Wilson resigned as Prime Minister, allegedly 'burned out', and James Callaghan took over. Around this time, investors became convinced that the pound was overvalued and that the Government might devalue it again. A large-scale sale of sterling began, which rapidly lost value against the dollar. The world's financial markets were losing confidence in sterling as the British economy stumbled. The Treasury could not balance the books while, at the same time, Labour's strategy emphasised high public spending which it appeared could no longer be paid for. Sounds familiar?

Despite further efforts to reduce inflation, the pound continued to lose value, reaching a record low against the dollar in June 1976. Prime Minister Callaghan was told there were three possible scenarios:

- A disastrous freefall in the value of sterling
- An internationally unacceptable siege economy
- A deal with key allies to prop up the pound while painful economic reforms were put in place

The third scenario was adopted. The US Treasury Secretary agreed with officials in the International Bank of Settlements that the pound was undervalued. He offered to partially fund a stand-by loan of $5.3 billion to support the pound. The Americans were very concerned that a collapse of the UK economy could lead to the UK having to substantially cut back on its defence expenditure and its nuclear deterrent, which was a matter of some concern to it as the UK was the key NATO ally and this was the depths of the Cold War. Some of these issues still resonate today.

As pressure on the pound continued, the UK Government approached the IMF for a loan of $3.9 billion in September 1976. This was the largest amount ever requested of the Fund, which needed, in turn, to seek additional funds from the US and Germany. The IMF negotiators demanded heavy cuts in public expenditure and in the budget deficit as a precondition for the loan. The then Chancellor of the Exchequer, Dennis Healey, had put forward proposals for a cut of around 20% of the budget deficit and these proposals were hotly debated in Cabinet. Eventually the Cabinet acceded to this level of cuts, as it seemed likely that the refusal of the loan would be followed by a disastrous run on the pound.

Following the agreement with the IMF, the overall economic and financial picture improved. Interest rates were soon reduced and the pound quickly appreciated in value. By the end of 1977, partly as a result of new oil revenues, there were improvements in the balance of trade. Britain did not need to draw the full loan from the IMF. Nevertheless, the IMF crisis reinforced a change in policy orientation away from full employment and social welfare towards the control of inflation and expenditure. It marked a 'sea change' for the public sector, and set the pattern leading to our current situation.

As this book will discuss, public services in the UK now face substantial real terms reductions in funding, which is unprecedented in modern times. When talking about the planned cuts in public expenditure, many people often refer to the 'cuts' in the era of Margaret Thatcher, but the cuts in public spending imposed under her premiership were a myth. Under her premiership, public spending actually grew at a healthy average of 1.1% a year. Only during two years did public spending actually fall in real terms: 1985/6 and 1988/9. During her time in office, although she was a fiscal hawk she only managed to put a brake on the growth of the state. Even then she *planned* to freeze spending increases, not cut. Public spending only fell because of lower-than-expected social security outlays.

There are only two examples of sustained real terms cuts in public spending in the UK. One is the sustained public spending squeeze which took place after the Second World War – the era of post-war austerity as the economy adapted from wartime to a peacetime footing, but perhaps the nearest parallel to the present situation is the Geddes cuts of the 1920s just after the end of the First World War.

After the First World War, Britain was gripped by enormous debts and a growing sense of panic that Government spending was hugely wasteful. The national debt had risen dramatically. A vast civil service, that had come together to administer the war effort, was still operating at full capacity, while spending on education had increased substantially. Many of the middle classes complained how their tax bills had shot up. Again this resonates today.

The Government was under pressure to do something. *The Times* newspaper noted in 1922: 'There are signs of an astonished realisation of the alarming bill for civil pensions that in a few years will be a millstone on the taxpayer's neck.' David Lloyd George, the prime minister, acted by appointing a businessman Sir Eric Geddes to head a new Committee on National Expenditure, which was soon dubbed 'The Great Axe'. It highlighted waste in all areas of public spending, including details such as there being a ratio of one cleaner for every vehicle in the Army. Between 1921 and 1922 it recommended economies totalling £87 million, a huge sum of money at that time.

Though the Cabinet only agreed to £52 million of cuts, these were enormous for the time and, in the end, total cuts were larger than either of these figures. Geddes was hailed a 'superman' by one leading businessman, but the axe hit some people very hard and led to a large reduction in social benefits, particularly secondary education.

The biggest cuts were in the Army and Navy. The defence budget was cut by 42% in the space of one year. Civil service numbers were cut by 35% – mostly female staff hired during the war.

At the close of 1921, wage cuts had been imposed on 6 million workers, leading to growing anger against the government. The cuts were driven partly by a Treasury desperate to keep a control of its debts and partly by the disastrous executive decision of the then Chancellor, Winston Churchill, to restore the Gold Standard system of exchange rates and retain the pre-war sterling/dollar parity. The overall economic impact required to balance the books under the principles of 'sound money' was to require a 20% reduction in economic activity. These decisions were widely criticised and Keynes wrote a book *The Economic Consequences of Mr Churchill* (Keynes 1925) to express his criticisms. They substantially added to Britain's woes in the

1920s – a period of far greater economic trouble for the country than it ever experienced during the 1930s. The General Strike in 1926 can, in part, be explained by the mounting resentment caused by the cuts, though some economists argue it helped Britain exit the vicious recession of 1919–1921 more quickly than it might otherwise have done.

What are the implications?

We need to be clear about the implications of the situation we now face. This is important since there is strong evidence that many politicians, some public service managers, and the public are in denial about the current situation.

When in power and subsequently, the former Chancellor Alistair Darling put forward a plan to halve the size of the UK budget deficit over a four-year period. He has indicated quite clearly that the public expenditure cuts proposed by him as a consequence of this plan would be deeper and tougher than the supposed 'cuts' of the Thatcher era. Clearly the impact of the much more ambitious plan of the Coalition Government to eliminate the deficit in four years will be even tougher.

Yet in the 1976 crisis when the IMF was called in to provide support to the UK economy, what Dennis Healey, the then Chancellor, was proposing at that time amounted to only a 20% reduction in the budget deficit at a time when the total annual deficit was approximately 7% of GDP. Today, the budget deficit is nearer 12% of GDP. Not surprisingly some have suggested (Bundred 2009) that even the dark years of the mid-1970s and the early 1990s 'may look like days of wine and roses' quite soon compared with the current situation.

Overall we see two overarching questions that will be addressed in this book:

- *Real Economy* – where countries such as the UK have large public sector budget deficits, how should those deficits be reduced in such a way as to minimise the damage to the real economy and factors such as economic growth and employment?
- *Public Services* – where the reduction in the public sector budget deficits involves large-scale reductions in public expenditure, how should those reductions be planned and managed in such a way as to minimise the damage to public services?

The dangers of orthodoxy

There is always the danger that financial and economic crises like the one we now face are dealt with by orthodox methods without clear thought about their applicability at the current time. This is a bit like the comment about all generals fighting the present war using the tactics of the previous war. Such a mentality has huge dangers.

An excellent book by Liaquat Ahamed (Ahamed 2009) charts the history of the economic and financial crisis after the First World War as seen through the eyes of the four main central bankers. Although the technical economic and financial problems of that time are substantially different from those of today (in 1929 it was the problems of over-inflated asset prices on Wall Street while today the problems are those of sovereign debt), there is an eerie sense of there being a parallel of using orthodox methods blindly with catastrophic consequences. Indeed the great economist Maynard Keynes seems to have spent a large proportion of his life arguing against the prevailing orthodoxy and being proved right almost every time. To quote just one example, as noted above, in 1925 the then Chancellor of the Exchequer, Winston Churchill (against his own better judgement and that of Keynes), was persuaded that the UK should return to the Gold Standard because that was the orthodox thing. The implications of this policy are generally regarded as disastrous for the UK. Other catastrophic policy errors concerning the timing of interest rate changes were also made by the US Federal Reserve.

At the time of writing, in 2011, the rate of inflation is increasing in the UK and there is the usual clamour from the City of London for the Bank of England to increase interest rates because this is the usual remedy. But is this the right thing to do in the current circumstances? It is clear that much of this inflation is self-inflicted (e.g. the VAT increase) or a consequence of external trends (e.g. oil price and food price increases). Average earnings growth in recent months has been negative so it doesn't seem that we are over-paying ourselves. The UK economy is in a very fragile state with very low confidence levels among business and the public. The economy needs all the help it can get. Raising interest rates to follow economic orthodoxy could be catastrophic for the UK economy and the future of public services. The respected economic commentator Anatole Kaletsky (Kaletsky 2010a) said in March 2010:

> Without a commitment from the Bank of England to keep interest rates near zero for the next four or five years, it is almost impossible to imagine how the British economy can return to a growth rate of around 3 per cent in the next Parliament. Without such a return to normal growth rate it will be impossible for the next government to keep a promise to halve public deficits, regardless of whether Labour or the Tories are in charge.

These examples show that we need to be very cautious about using the so-called tried and tested orthodoxy in the current situation we find ourselves in.

What this book is about

As its subtitle states, this book is about the planning and management of public services and, as such, it is inevitable that it will touch on other related issues such as the organisation and financing of public services, and general economic policy. However, the book is also concerned with how we should address these tasks in an environment of unprecedented financial austerity. It aims to highlight the inappropriateness of the current approaches and the need for alternative models if public services are not to be destroyed.

The book is organised in three parts:

- **Part I** will review the current circumstances faced by public services in the UK. One of the clear conclusions will be that whilst we are currently obsessed with dealing with the economic and financial issues, there are a wide range of demographic, environmental, and social issues which have long-term consequences and which remain to be dealt with. Briefly looking at the ways in which other countries faced with public sector finance difficulties have dealt with the issues (primarily Canada, Sweden, and the Republic of Ireland), we will conclude that the UK is facing a unique set of circumstances and that the experience elsewhere may not be a sound guide to future policy-making. We will, however, draw out the important distinction that elsewhere public sector adjustments have not attempted to protect any specific part of the public services. This will make the UK economic experiment in modern public service delivery, upon which we are about to embark, both high risk and a model which others will look to in the light of their own circumstances. Finally, this part will look at a strategic options analysis for evaluating change options for the public services which will provide an academic underpinning for the critique that follows.
- **Part II** turns to look at the practical issues around the traditional change model adopted by UK public services and assesses how likely it is to be successful in achieving the objectives. We begin with a brief overview of the development of public services which draws the key conclusion that with UK public services, change has rarely been dramatic but has largely been incremental, and that the constitutional weaknesses and centralised model have led to a process of 'muddling through' rather than a visionary and revolutionary change. We will then look at the traditional UK public services model and its strengths and weaknesses. Subsequently, we discuss, at some length, previous attempts at reform of UK public services and the extent to which they have succeeded.
- **Part III** of the book will propose some radical alternatives based on new thinking around the way the social/economic system actually works in practice. We will suggest that adopting these new approaches will

radically redefine the pattern and role for the state. We then go on to look at organisation and delivery arrangements for public services based on alternative models of organisation. We will suggest that this new thinking will significantly alter the pattern for public services delivery, and has significant constitutional effects for the political governance of the UK. At this point we will have hopefully convinced the reader that we are facing a truly unique situation in terms of the demands for change, and that the traditional approach is not likely to lead us towards long-term success and a more radical approach is called for. However, we do not underestimate the barriers to making a radical change, though we believe that the final outcome will be worth the inevitable turmoil of working through to a new set of arrangements. In Part III we will conclude that the real obstacles to change are unlikely to be technological, or structural, and are much more likely to be cultural and threats to the existing power arrangements. In this respect we will suggest that the simplest thing to do, and the hardest to accomplish, will be to effect the change of mind that is required to embrace and implement radical alternatives.

The book finishes with references and a suggested reading of other books to which the interested reader may turn for reference.

2
The Current and Future Challenges Facing Public Services

Charles Handy, the management guru, used an illustration of a frog to describe the relative inertia to change within organisations (Handy 1989). Put a frog into hot water, he said, and it will certainly jump out again. Put the same frog into cold water and heat it up gently and the frog will simply sit there until it cooks. Whether this is actually true or not is not the point. The fact is that certain issues that become 'hot water frog' and provide the stimulus to make sudden and often dramatic changes. On the other hand 'cold water frog' issues have a habit of creeping up on one until the point at which they become sufficiently hot and we have to do something about them. In his book *Collapse,* Jared Diamond (Diamond 2005) concludes that it tends to be the 'cold water frog' issues that remain unaddressed which create the conditions under which societies, communities, and civilisations finally collapse, and this collapse is often a sudden, rather than a gradual event. In this chapter we discuss the current 'state of play' regarding public services by considering the various contextual factors in which public services need to be viewed. These contextual factors include both 'hot water frog' and 'cold water frog' issues.

In truth the hot and cold water frog issues need to be dealt with simultaneously. Maslow (Maslow 1943) in proposing his 'hierarchy of needs' distinguished between those needs which were essential to individual well-being and those which needed to be secured before the higher level 'self-actualising' needs could be fulfilled. The lower needs represented necessary but not sufficient conditions for human well-being while the self-actualising factors represented sufficient but not necessary conditions. Taken together they created the 'necessary and sufficient' conditions that were required. In an equivalent way the current 'hot water frog' issues need to be dealt with, but it would be a grave mistake to pay so much attention to them that we did not address some of the important, and ultimately critical 'cold water frog' issues.

There have been significant turning points in the development of public service organisations which have tended to be based on 'hot water frog' issues which have overwhelmed the preceding arrangements and have made change inevitable. We now need to see whether the current contextual factors that face the public services at present represent one of those key turning points.

While other factors discussed below (e.g. ageing populations, energy price rises) have the characteristics of the 'cold water frog' in that they have been dealt with in public services by gradual changes, it seems to us that the 'hot water frog' issue which is likely to promote major changes in the delivery of public services concerns the catastrophic state of the public finances and the legacy of public debt, in the UK and many other countries, which will take decades to resolve.

This chapter provides a comprehensive analysis of the various factors which present formidable challenges to the organisation, delivery and financing of public services for the remainder of this century. Figure 2.1 shows

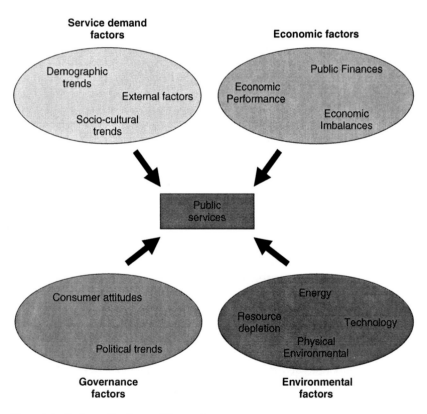

Figure 2.1   Factors affecting public services

diagrammatically the key contextual factors which impact public services, grouped together into four principal areas. All countries will be impacted, to some degree, by all of these factors but the balance between the various factors will vary from country to country. As we consider each of these issues in turn, we would progressively move from the 'hot' towards the 'cold' end of the spectrum, but given what we have said the public sector needs to be addressing the whole spectrum of issues, not just one part of it.

Economic factors

Under this heading there are three themes to consider.

Economic performance

The longer-term future of public services in any country is inextricably linked to the longer-tem performance of its economy. On the one hand, economic growth will drive the volume of personal and corporate income and wealth and, in turn, the level of tax receipts which will provide the funds for public expenditure purposes. On the other hand, poor economic performance will also have consequences in a number of areas such as unemployment and social dislocation which in turn will impact on their demands for public services and expenditure.

During the period 2007–2009, the world suffered a major economic downturn. In some countries such as India and China this meant a substantial drop in the previous high levels of economic growth, while in other countries such as the UK, Germany and the USA their economies suffered a formal economic recession with negative economic growth. Such recessions are seen as an inevitable part of any normal business cycle which take place every seven to ten years or so. However this latest recession had some distinguishing characteristics from other recessions. First, there was the impact of the associated credit crunch which did not exist in previous recessions. This is a squeezing of business credit and a contraction in banks' liquidity positions. It has as its genesis the losses incurred by several US and UK banks in the US sub-prime mortgage market with the consequent and uncertain exposure to risk of financial institutions worldwide. The underlying problem was the poor business model that underpinned the 'sub-prime' market. The model was based on the assumption that continuing economic growth would lead to inflation in property asset values so that even if the lender was unable to repay mortgages from income, they could afford to do so from increased equity, or, in the last resort, foreclosure would mean that the lender would recover the loan. This assumption, together with an extensive derivatives market which 'collateralised' these debts by spreading them and mixing them with good value loans meant that lenders believed that they were buying good quality assets, and in some cases had no knowledge of what the underlying asset base was. When it became clear that the risk model could not cope with the uncertainty of a general downturn and loss in asset values, individual banks, though deeming their own loan books satisfactory, recognised the riskiness of the holdings of others. In these circumstances they denied them the normal pattern of rolling credit in the market, thus creating the so-called credit crunch and bringing the normal operations of the financial services market to a dead stop. The consequences of this credit crunch in the UK were extensive and have involved runs on some banks and a general reluctance by banks to lend to businesses and individuals, as well as to other banks. As a result the initial crisis in the financial markets ricocheted into the real economy and resulted in a significant sectoral downturn in manufacturing, other services, investment, and personal consumption. The only sector that remained relatively stable was in exports, and the only sector that could act counter cyclically was the public sector, where the downturn automatically increased the public sector deficit, a fact exacerbated by deliberate government counter cyclical policy, and incurring of significant public sector debt liabilities in order to stabilise the banking sector.

The second feature was the global impact of the recession. It used to be said that '*When America sneezes, the rest of the world catches a cold*' recognising the predominance of the American economy within the overall world economy. But having said that, until fairly recently, the impact of a recession on one country on other countries was often fairly limited. However, the globalisation of business and finance has significantly altered that. Today we have huge international trade flows between countries, large-scale movements of populations and global movement of capital. Thus a recession in one country, particularly if it is a large country, will have impacts on other countries. The highly integrated nature of global manufacturing, the rise of significant new players in the global economy, particularly China, together with the development of derivative, collateralised, debt instruments meant that individual country elements of the wider global economy were both interlinked and held the assets and liabilities of other international trading entities in a complex arrangement of transactions.

As most countries have suffered, at least, some economic slowdown in recent years, their governments are implementing austerity policies and these could be accompanied by changes in foreign policy and aid policy from rich countries and the possibility of 'beggar my neighbour' policies as countries, more and more, try to look after their own economies and populations. Furthermore, a survey of the global financial community (e.g. hedge funds, investment banks) showed that 60% believe corporate profit margins and/or returns on capital will not return to pre-crisis levels for at least five years (EIU 2007). So with this pattern of the international economy, and particularly the financial generation of the recession of 2008, it was perhaps inevitable that wherever the collapse began it would be transmitted swiftly across the world's economies. Indeed, no part of the world was exempt from its impact, although in the Western-style economies with high levels of debt, deregulation, and open financial systems, it was inevitable that the impact was greatest.

In 2008, the UK economy formally entered a period of economic recession defined as a reduction in economic output for two successive quarters. Such recessions are characterised by a variety of phenomena such as reduced consumer demand, falls in house prices, and increasing unemployment. The end of a recession is defined as the point when contraction in GDP ceases and the issue sometimes being missed here is that since the UK recession has resulted in a sharp drop of around 7% in GDP, it would take many years to recover the ground lost.

After six quarters of declining economic output the UK came out of recession in the last quarter of 2009 with weak growth in GDP of 0.4% for the three-month period. Subsequently, this has been followed by further periods of weak growth tipping sometimes into negative growth. At the time of writing there is real concern about the future prospects of the UK economy. There is often a substantial degree of optimism expressed, particularly among politicians, the media, and the financial sector, that the UK economy will quickly bounce back to pre-recessionary levels of economic growth and this is sometimes reflected in official forecasts. Some commentators argue that we should take a much more realistic view of the future of the UK economy since research among a range of companies suggests limited optimism among UK-based companies about the future prospects of the UK economy (Lowth, Prowle, and Zhang, 2010).

Although similar economic problems were encountered in many countries there are several specific factors in the UK which may hamper a strong economic recovery including high levels of personal and corporate debt, a continued inability or reluctance by banks to lend to businesses, and instability in the housing market. The recovery from the economic recession in the early 1990s following the withdrawal of the UK economy from the ERM was largely financed by the debt arrangements outlined above. The current recession gives no opportunity to use debt any further, and the reduction by all sectors in their 'overleveraged' positions imparts a significant drag on economic recovery.

In these circumstances with most sectors of the economy attempting to pay down their debt levels, and the government having an inability to finance a recovery through borrowing, it will need to be the manufacturing sector that provides the primary source of recovery through exports. The rapid depreciation in the sterling exchange rate will significantly assist in this. However, it will be the growth of global demand that will be critical. The global nature of the recession has already been referred to, and ongoing growth world demand would help those countries, such as the UK, more significantly affected by the downturn, to recover. However, linked to this are the fiscal and economic problems of the Eurozone of which the UK is not a member. These problems seem likely to stall economic growth in Europe and, as a significant exporter to the rest of the EU, the UK recovery would be hindered. Furthermore, at the time of writing we are seeing major political instability in the Middle East, a part of the world which provides a third of the world's oil supply and economic disruption in Japan as a consequence of a major earthquake.

In addition, if we look much deeper we see over the last two decades a steady shift of global financial and economic power away from the West towards other nations, principally the Islamic states and China and the consequent relative weakness of large European economies (especially the UK economy) in relation to these new economic powers. In the past this has largely been the result of the demand from Western economies for more materials, principally oil, and the rapid development of the Far East, particularly China, as a low-cost source of manufacturing for Western-based companies. The impact of the pattern of surplus and deficits on the holding of Western financial assets has already been commented on. With this recession, however, it is likely that a rapid recovery of growth in the so-called BRIC economies (Brazil, Russia, India, and China) will be matched by a slower and much less dramatic recovery in the Western economies, so that by the time the Western economies have recovered from the current recession the gap between them and the developing economies in terms of overall absolute economic performance and GDP per head will have significantly narrowed. This recession may therefore prove the turning point in great power status within the world.

National economic imbalances

Two intrinsic imbalances that can be associated with any national economy are:

- the imbalance between different regions of the country
- the imbalance between different sectors of the economy of a country

Both these factors are particularly profound in the UK.

Regarding geographic imbalances, there exists within the UK strong asymmetries between London/South East and the rest of the UK. This is a phenomenon that has existed for many years prior to the large growth in the financial services sector but the situation has worsened over the past 20 years.

Consider first the demographic picture as shown in Table 2.1.

Only in the UK does the largest city dominate demographically to such an extent and furthermore, in some of the countries shown the capital city is not even the largest city. This provides some sort of balancing effect between two centres and it is only in the UK that the capital city dominates demographically and politically. But London (and the South-East) also

Table 2.1   Demographic comparisons of countries

	UK	USA	Germany	Italy	Netherlands
Total population	60.3	293.0	82.4	58.1	16.3
Capital city	London	Washington	Berlin	Rome	The Hague
Largest city	London	New York	Berlin	Rome	Amsterdam
	million	**million**	**million**	**million**	**million**
Capital city population	8.1	3.4	3.4	2.7	0.5
Largest city population	8.1	17.8	3.4	2.7	0.8
Largest city as percentage of population	13.4%	6.1%	4.1%	4.6%	4.9%

Source: United Nations

dominates the country economically as well. Table 2.2 outlines Gross Value Added (GVA) in the UK economy.

The GVA from the London economy is much greater than its population share would suggest and the GVA per capita for London (and to a lesser degree the South-East) is much higher than for the rest of the UK. In turn, this is reflected in gross average earnings which are much greater in London and the South-East. In other words not only does London dominate the UK demographically and politically but it is also much richer on average. It has been suggested that this 'North/South' divide is in fact the result of the geographical spread of wealthy and poor communities. So, it is argued, there are many wealthy 'South East style' communities in the North, just as there are some pockets of severe deprivation in London and the South. This 'within region' variation is undoubtedly true, but it does not mask the very significant geographical 'between region' variation that is the most significant characteristic pattern. In the light of this situation, one of the authors of this book once wrote an article entitled 'The Problem is London'.

When we turn to sectoral imbalances we see imbalances between the different sectors of the UK economy and, to a large extent, this reflects the geographic asymmetry discussed above. Consider the data shown in Table 2.3.

Between 2000–2007 there was a large overall growth in the total GDP of the UK (44%) but a significant contraction in the contribution to that GDP from the manufacturing sector. In fact, over that period the monetary contribution from manufacturing hardly increased at all and the bulk of the GDP growth came from the financial and real estate sectors much of which is concentrated in London and the South-East. Furthermore, the

Table 2.2   UK regional analysis of Gross Value Added

Region	GVA £bn	GVA %	Population million	Population share %	GVA/capita "£000
North East	40.9	3.2	2.6	4.19	15.9
North West	120.7	9.6	6.9	11.20	17.6
Yorks and Humber	89.1	7.1	5.2	8.49	17.1
East Midlands	80.0	6.4	4.4	7.22	18.0
West Midlands	94.5	7.5	5.4	8.82	17.5
East of England	111.6	8.9	5.7	9.34	19.5
London	265.1	21.0	7.6	12.42	34.8
South East	181.8	14.4	8.4	13.66	21.7
South West	97.8	7.8	5.2	8.48	18.8
Wales	45.6	3.6	3.0	4.88	15.2
Scotland	103.8	8.2	5.2	8.42	20.1
Northern Ireland	28.7	2.3	1.8	2.89	16.2
Total UK	1259.6	100.0	61.4	100.0	

Source: ONS

Table 2.3   Trends in UK GDP by sector, 2000–2007

Sector	2000 (%)	2007 (%)	Change (%)
Agriculture	1	1	0
Mining and quarrying	3	3	0
Manufacturing	17	12	−5
Electricity, gas and water supply	2	2	0
Construction	5	6	1
Non-financial services (including public sector)	45	44	−1
Financial services	5	8	3
Real estate activities	22	24	2
Total %	100.0	100.0	0
Total value of GDP	£864bn	£1246bn	

Source: ONS

contraction in the manufacturing sector in the UK is somewhat worse than in comparable countries as shown in Table 2.4.

What are the implications of these imbalances? For some time now the UK has a two speed economy with very strong reliance on the financial

Table 2.4 Sectoral analysis of GDP by country (in %)

Sector	UK	France	Germany	Italy	EU	Japan	USA
Manufacturing	11	12	17	15	14	21	12
Financial (including real estate)	29	30	28	26	26	28	31
Other (including public sector)	60	58	55	60	60	51	57
Total	100	100	100	100	100	100	100

Source: OECD

services sector of the economy (which is strongly focussed on London) to the detriment of other sectors which are more broadly based and which results in the bulk of the wealth being generated in London/South-East. Does this really matter? Space does not allow a full description of the consequences but these are described briefly below.

- It leads to relative poverty and deprivation in the rest of the UK. Many statistics can be produced to show the wide inequalities in income, wealth, health status, housing standards and so on that exist across the UK.
- The asymmetries in London/South-East lead to asymmetries elsewhere. For example, certain parts of the UK are over-reliant on public sector employment because of the lack of private sector jobs.
- The excess of demand over supply in the South-Eastern housing market leads to inflationary pricing bubbles which eventually burst. The bursting of these bubbles has contributed to the 'credit crunch'.
- The UK outside of London and the South-East suffers disproportionately as a consequence of economic recession even though this recession had its genesis in the London-based financial sector. When we look at insolvency rates, unemployment levels and household financial stress across the UK for the period 2008–2010 in all cases, we see the same skewing of recessionary pain and hardship towards regions of the UK other than the South-East.
- UK economic policy gets distorted because it is often geared to economic conditions in London and the South-East but which end up having damaging impacts on regional economies elsewhere. For example, in the past rising national inflation caused by pay increases in London was often met by interest rate hikes which have a negative impact on other regional economies.
- The overdependence in the UK economy on the London-based financial services sector (coupled with the implicit guarantee within an *open* financial services sector) leaves the UK holding considerable financial risks.

- Although the UK manufacturing sector now comprises just 12% of GDP it does provide 50% of UK exports. The lack of domestic confidence and demand means that the development of export-led growth is critical to the future of the UK economy.

We see this catalogue of problems as being very serious and we are amazed that no UK Government in the past has ever tried, *seriously*, to address them. To some extent the social problems involved have been mitigated by high levels of public spending consequent on the buoyancy of the financial services sector, but the collapse of this sector and the loss of tax revenues mean we now face large-scale cuts in public spending. There are real concerns that this might lead to social unrest, as has already happened in some countries, and we see it as imperative that the underlying economic asymmetries are addressed urgently.

Making these sorts of changes are long-term and there are many exceedingly strong vested interests to overcome. In the short-term, implementation of the above may actually lead to a lower rate of economic growth. However, the recent financial crisis should have taught the dangers, in any country, of over dependency on a single sector and a more balanced economy should lead to a more stable, equitable, and ultimately more economically secure society.

Public finances

Figure 2.2 shows the impact on UK public finances of changes in economic activity since the Second World War.

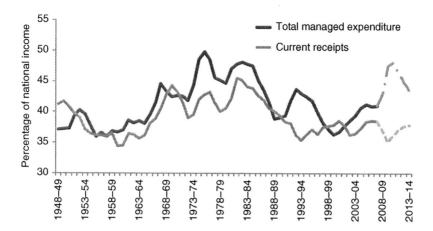

Figure 2.2   UK Government expenditure and receipts
Source: CIPFA/SOLACE/IFS

The chart shows that it was the primary impact of the economy on public finances which has created the current crisis, rather than any specific issues to do with the recapitalisation of the banks. We need to see whether the nature of the economic crisis was so global as to make the UK simply an individual country case of what was an international economic crisis.

The state of a country's public finances has a major bearing on the policies of its Government and the amount of public expenditure it can incur. Currently there is seen to be a crisis in the public finances of many countries including the UK. The basic problem is that in recent years many governments have got themselves into a situation where government expenditures far exceed government revenues (from taxes and so on) such that governments incurred large financial deficits which can only be financed by new borrowing. Keynesian economics legitimised the policy of governments running fiscal deficits in times of economic recession to be compensated for by running budget surpluses in times of economic growth but in recent years the scale of Government deficits have become alarming as illustrated in the international figures shown in Table 2.5.

The problem of the UK's public finances is well known and currently dominates Government policy in the UK since the current UK budget deficit is the one of the largest of any OECD country. In 2010, the UK Government generated a budget deficit (excess of Government spending over Government revenues) which required it to borrow some £155bn or 11.3% of national GDP. It is sometimes claimed this situation was a consequence of global economic forces which were largely outside the control of the UK Government, but this is not true. While global forces had an impact on the public finance situation, the seed of the problem was planted many years previously. As shown in Table 2.6, the UK Government was already

Table 2.5 Government budget deficits

Country	Forecast government budget deficit 2010/11 as a % of country GDP
Australia	–2.4
China	–2.2
France	–7.9
Germany	–3.7
Greece	–9.5
Spain	–9.6
UK	–10.4
USA	–9.0

Source: The Economist

Table 2.6   UK public finance trends

Year	Growth/Contraction in GDP[1] (%)	Government financial balances as % of GDP[2] (£bn)
2009	–5.25	–11.0
2008	0.55	–5.5
2007	2.53	–2.7
2006	2.85	–2.7
2005	2.15	–3.3
2004	2.98	–3.7
2003	2.80	–3.7
2002	2.13	–2.0
2001	2.45	0.6
2000	3.90	3.7
1999	3.70	0.9

Source: [1] http://www.tradingeconomics.com/Economics/GDP-Growth.aspx?Symbol=GBP
[2] http://www.oecd.org/dataoecd/5/51/2483816.xls

running budget deficits during a period of significant economic growth in the years prior to the start of the economic recession. The impact of the recession was to make things very much worse.

There were two main reasons for this. Firstly, there was a substantial decline in Government tax revenues as illustrated in Table 2.7.

Secondly, economic recession inevitably leads to greater demands for public expenditure. At the direct level this is a result of the need to pay additional social benefits as a consequence of increased unemployment. At the indirect level it is often claimed that economic recession and associated unemployment place greater demands on public services such as the NHS.

The budget deficit figures contain an element which is termed a structural deficit which needs some explanation. With any budget deficit, part of that deficit may be regarded as being cyclical in that it is incurred during the downswing of a normal business cycle and will be compensated for by a budget surplus generated during the upswing of the business cycle. However, a structural deficit, by definition, is not cyclical and is not something which will be eradicated by movement through the normal business cycle. Hence Government action, through increased tax revenues and/or reduced public expenditure, is needed to eradicate that structural deficit. Estimating the size of a structural deficit is not easy and the latest estimate (OBR 2010b) was that the structural deficit amounted to around 8% of GDP.

Table 2.7 Collapse in UK tax revenues

Tax source	% fall in tax revenues 2008 (HI)–2009 (HI)
Income tax	−6.5
Corporation Tax	−25.4
VAT	−15.5
National Insurance Contributions	−3.5

Source: Office for National Statistics, Statistical Bulletin, Public Sector Finances June 2009

To finance budget deficits it is necessary for governments to borrow money and the sums now being borrowed are enormous and are adding to the national debt at an alarming rate. As noted in 2009/10, the UK Government borrowed a record sum of £155 billion (11% of GDP) and this took the national net debt to a figure of £771bn.

Some have argued that the UK borrowing and debt levels are not the highest in international terms but there are three concerns here.

- Firstly, the reality is that the cost of servicing such high levels of debt is very significant. The National Institute of Economic and Social Research has estimated that costs of servicing government debt will rise from £25.6bn in 2009/10 to £50.7bn in 2013/14 which would exceed the entire budget allocated to the defence programme (Institute of Commercial Management 2009). This warning underlines the cost facing taxpayers as Government debt rises at the fastest rate in peacetime history.
- Secondly is the fact that by failing to reduce the level of national indebtedness, all we are doing is passing the problem to future generations. Consequently, our children and grandchildren will be responsible for incurring debts incurred during our lifetime. There is an important issue here of inter-generational equity.
- Thirdly, there is the crisis in the financial markets over sovereign debt. In past recessions, when the attractiveness of private sector equity and debt was lessened, the markets tended to go to a sovereign government backed debt as a safe haven notwithstanding the fact that it had lower returns. However, in this recession such is the level of public sector indebtedness across most of the Western economies that questions are being raised about the ability of governments to finance and rollover their borrowing. When doubts are held about the value of sovereign debt interest rates will rise very sharply, as the experience of Greece within the Eurozone arrangements has shown. Unless countries show themselves are willing to undertake significant reductions in public sector deficits this can result in a flight from the debt of that particular country into those who are more

secure with a significant rise in the level of interest rates for the country, which only serves to make the debt problem worse, and the adjustment sharper. At the time of writing, the UK possesses the prestigious triple-A rating but the situation is being kept under review by credit ratings agencies such as Standard and Poor. A ratings downgrade or a shift to 'negative watch' could be very serious for the UK since it could imply either that the Government being unable to borrow to finance its budget deficit, and thus relying on extra market from being from the IMF or EU, or being forced to pay much higher interest rates at yet higher interest, thus exacerbating the debt position. Such a threat of a credit rating downgrade should not be dismissed lightly since Standard and Poor have downgraded ratings in many countries including, most recently, the Republic of Ireland and the USA.

- Fourthly, the figures for UK national debt are arguably large understatements of the true future total liabilities which are, in reality, much higher. As well as conventional debt discussed above, other types of public liability include: outstanding liabilities on such items as the public sector pension schemes and Private Finance Initiative contracts as well as any losses arising from the bank bail outs. If we add in these items the overall public future liability could more than double.

In the UK the Coalition Government elected in May 2010 adopted a policy to eliminate the budget deficit over a four-year period. This policy involves a mixture of 20% tax increases and 80% public expenditure cuts. Their belief is that this policy will satisfy the financial markets who lend funds to the UK and that the reduction in Government spending will stimulate the private sector economy and lead to enhanced economic growth. However, the UK will still have large borrowings for several years to come as shown in Table 2.8.

An alternative view is that the pace of deficit reduction is too quick and should be addressed over a longer time period. The concern is that the current scale of deficit reduction will damage the performance of the UK economy and that financial markets will be scared more by this than the size of the budget deficit. It also suggests a more appropriate deficit reduction approach with

Table 2.8   Projected UK borrowing

Year	Borrowing requirement (£bn)
2009/10	155
2010/11	149
2011/12	116
2012/13	89
2013/14	60
2014/15	37

more emphasis on tax increases and less on public expenditure cuts. However, whichever model was adopted the reality is that the scale of spending cuts means that the UK is in an unprecedented situation and, over a period of time, probably needs to address a number of fundamental questions including:

- What should be the role of the state and what should be its limits?
- What should be individual and collective responsibilities in relation to public services?
- Should public policy be more or less authoritarian?
- What should be the balance between incentives and sanctions?
- How should public services be paid for?
- How should public services be organised?
- In public policy terms, what should be the balance between sticks (sanctions) and carrots (incentives)?
- Because of the shortage of resources, must public policy become more authoritarian in outlook?
- What should be the balance between the private and public sectors of our economy?
- What should be the balance between the private and public sectors of our economy in the delivery of public services?

Governance

If the current financial position represents the hottest of the 'hot issues', then issues to do with the state of the body politic, whilst less hot, are nevertheless significantly 'warm', to extend our metaphor. Dealing with serious financial issues requires a level of stability in politics, and an underlying element of trust. We now look at two issues included in this category.

Consumer attitudes

A key issue concerns the attitudes towards public services of users of those services and the general public at large.

Degree of satisfaction with public services

There are significant variations between countries regarding the degree of satisfaction with public services. Using health as an example, available data shows high degrees of consumer satisfaction in countries such as Denmark, Austria and Sweden and low degrees of satisfaction in countries such as Italy and Greece (Cabinet Office 2001).

In the UK, in spite of the various public service reforms that have taken place over the past 30 years and the substantial growth in public service funding, there still appears to be a considerable degree of dissatisfaction among UK citizens with public services in general (Cabinet Office 2001). Interestingly, there appears to be something of a paradox in that while dissatisfaction with public services exists widely among the general public there is a greater degree of satisfaction from those individuals who have recently made use of certain public services. Thus, for example, while there are still widespread concerns about the NHS, those people who have actually been in hospital tend to be satisfied with the services received. Surprisingly, the exception to this rule appears to be the police service!

Willingness to pay more tax

With increasing levels of globalisation in the world economy, countries found themselves in a virtually competitive market over business taxation. Consequently, over the past two decades, the emphasis in taxation has tended to shift from business to personal taxation. Polls suggest the UK public now has a strong aversion to paying higher levels of taxation even though the UK is not the highest taxed population in the developed world. In the minds of most UK politicians this translates as a wish not to impose higher rates of income tax and no political party is now likely, in the foreseeable future, to raise the basic rate of income tax. However, as noted above, in reality the tax burden on UK citizens has risen sharply in recent years through a combination of new taxes and changes to existing taxes (other than raising the basic rate of income tax). Part of this reluctance to pay higher taxes seems to derive from a strongly held view that much of public expenditure is 'wasted' expenditure coupled with the level of dissatisfaction with public services referred to earlier.

Political trends

A number of themes can be considered under this broad heading and have great relevance to public service provision.

Politicians and the growth of the managerialist model

A fairly recent phenomenon is the growth of the managerialist model in Government. No longer, in the UK, are politicians prepared to provide a political or ideological lead and leave the details to civil servants, professional managers, or administrators. Instead politicians have become quasi-managers having sometimes a detailed operational involvement in a wide range of policy issues.

The three circles in Figure 2.3 represent the different contributions of politics, professionalism, and managerialism to public services in particular, and to the community in general. Politics handles the big and difficult questions for any community – the definition of who is 'us' and who is 'them', defining the community identity. Politicians must take the key questions about the use of force if necessary to defend that community identity. Politicians, when enacting legislation, must determine the difficult dividing line between those restrictions on individual freedoms necessary to maintain community cohesion, and the maintenance of individual liberties. Professional bodies act as guardians of the body of technical knowledge in admitting suitable candidate to the profession only after extensive training. Although professionals tend to see themselves as being above politics, in fact

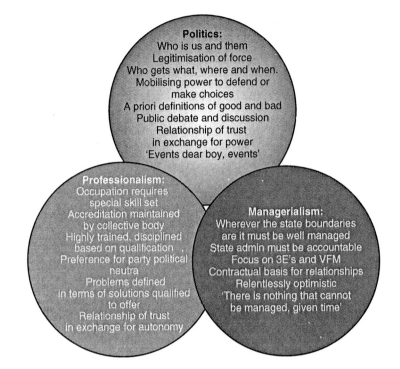

Figure 2.3 The interaction of politics, professionalism, and managerialism

they are often deeply involved in key political issues, and in the past there has been a considerable tendency for professional groups to define community problems in terms of the solutions that they are able to offer, sometimes finding it difficult to 'think outside the box', and thus have tended to be a force of conservatism. For two of the three groups – politicians and professionals – the basic relationship with the community is one of trust. Within any complex market economy individuals will be placed at a disadvantage in terms of information and capacity to act against those who have elected authority, or specialist knowledge. The deal is that in return for exercising collective activity on behalf of the public, in the public interest, politicians and professionals are given the ability to be self-regulating and to determine within their private groups the admission, discipline, and dismissal criteria, together with any necessary qualifications and training for individuals operating within those groups. There are clear downsides to this arrangement, there may be abuses of trust and corruption, and there may be tendencies to define problems in terms of solutions that people have available to offer rather than solutions that are needed, but overall we have tended to have faith in these relationships. However, over the past 20 or 30 years these relationships of trust have been eroded by creeping managerialism that utilises the needs of efficiency, control, and accountability and transparency, to spread a different relationship. However, the nature of the relationship is that obligations are limited in time and scope; loyalty is not specifically rewarded; and pragmatism, rather than principle, is the governing factor. Under these circumstances the philosophy of 'what works' has become prevalent together with the 'command and control' structures that support it. The inefficiency of these arrangements and their impact on standards of ethics and governance (Sennett 2003) are the significant downside with which we are now coping.

Trust in politicians

Trust in politicians would seem to be an attribute important in assuring the general public about the future of public services since lack of trust can inhibit the implementation of certain public policies. Unfortunately, in many countries, trust in politicians is low. This is especially the case in the UK and prior to the 2010 expenses scandal the UK was in the lowest quartile of EU countries in terms of confidence in its national Parliament. Also, electoral turnout in the UK was among the lowest in Europe and the job of MP had one of the lowest levels of public esteem. What would the picture be like today? The MPs expenses scandal has reduced public esteem still further. A recent poll suggested that only 13% of the general public trust our politicians to tell the truth.

Patronage and the client state

Despite the rise in the contractual relationship implied in the growth of managerialism, patronage has always been a part of political life in most countries. In the UK the Prime Minister has sole discretion in making ministerial appointments and in making recommendations to the Queen for honours. Other Ministers are able to appoint chairs of QUANGOs, non-executive directors of NHS Trusts and so on. In recent years the term client state has been used to describe the wide range of individuals and organisations that have become strongly dependent on state patronage. These include charities, lobbying firms, think tanks, management consultants, representative organisations and sorts. The concern is that many of these organisations, who might be expected to have independent views on topical issues, are reluctant to do so because of their financial dependency on the government

The rise of the professional politician

Nationally (and to some degree locally) politics is becoming largely professionalised. In practical terms entry into Parliament is, effectively, not an option for the 98% of the population who are not members of one of the main political parties. Even for those who are party members and who wish to enter Parliament the road is not easy. In recent years the selection process of the two main parties has become more centralised with reduced discretion for local party members to choose their candidates. It is not surprising, therefore, that more and more Parliamentary candidates of the main parties come from a fairly limited background of having worked for an MP, been a party official and so on without ever having had experience of business, the professions, the public services, trade unions etc. An examination of the members of the previous Labour cabinet will show that the vast majority have either been solely employed in professional politics (or had close connections with the higher reaches of the Labour Party) whilst also having had some limited experience of the law or journalism.

Thus we see the rise of the professional politician who enters Parliament, often at a young age and with only limited work experience outside politics, with the intention of it being a lifetime occupation hopefully combined with promotion up the Ministerial ladder. This leads them to having two main objectives – getting re-elected (by impressing their constituents with their level of activity) and getting promotion (by impressing the Whips with their loyalty to the Party line). Not surprisingly, many concerns are frequently being expressed about the poor calibre of persons becoming MPs, and ultimately Ministers, and the potentially negative impact this is having on public policy decisions.

Changing political ideologies

Political ideologies have always had a strong influence on a Government's attitude towards public services. Traditionally, it is suggested that the impact of political ideologies would be as shown in Figure 2.4.

The classical ideological picture suggests, for example, increasing enthusiasm for higher levels of public spending as we move from the political right

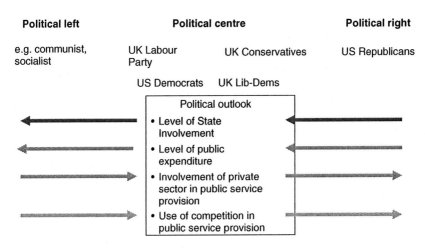

Figure 2.4   Political ideologies regarding public services

to the political left and increasing enthusiasm for competition and private sector involvement as we move from political left to the political right.

While these may have been traditional political ideological views regarding public services this is not necessarily the case today. Consider, for example, the following examples:

- The use of markets and competition in public services by a Chinese communist government.
- The high levels of public spending by the Republican Bush administrations in the USA.
- The enthusiasm of the previous UK Labour Government for the PFI.

Thus although political ideologies will have an implication for public service reform, the correlation of policy with ideology may not always be as clear as in the past.

The collapse of deference

As a consequence of many of the themes described above, people have become far more sceptical about professionals and politicians and no longer defer to their views or decisions. This has implications for the implementation of public policy. Take for example the situation, a few years ago, with MMR vaccination rates. The lack of belief by the general public that political and professional leaders would tell the truth meant that many individuals would not accept Government assurances about the safety of the vaccine and refused to have their children vaccinated. Another example was the heavy rejection, by voters, of road pricing plans for the city of Manchester. Voters just did not believe Government assurances about the benefits the policy would generate but they did understand that it would involve a tax which would cost them an extra £100 per annum. This rejection was thought to have put back pay as you drive road pricing schemes by a decade.

Service demands

This section concerns the main cultural, community and environmental factors which drive the demand for public services. The three issues we consider here are:

- Demographic trends
- Socio-cultural trends
- External factors

Demographic trends

Demography is the study of human populations and the key aspects are the size and structure of populations. Over the past 100 years, human populations have grown across the globe as illustrated in Table 2.9.

Table 2.9 Population trends

	1950 million	2000 million	2025 million	2050 million	% change over 100 year period %
China	545	1267	1453	1417	160
Germany	68	82	79	70	3
India	372	1043	1431	1614	334
Indonesia	77	205	263	288	274
Japan	82	127	121	102	24
Pakistan	41	148	246	335	717
Russia	102	147	132	116	14
USA	157	288	359	404	157
UK	51	59	67	72	41
More developed regions	812	1195	1277	1275	57
Less developed regions	1717	4920	6735	7875	359
World	2529	6115	8012	9150	262

Source: United Nations: World Population Statistics, http://esa.un.org/unpp/

These figures show increases in population in all countries but clearly there are huge variations between developed countries and developing countries. In global terms a rapid increase in population can be unsustainable, bringing with it the spectre of Malthusian shortages, conflict between communities, and competition for resources that degrades the environment and has international effects between individual countries. Population growth has several implications for the economy and public services:

- Increased demand for public services deriving from a growing population taking account of such factors as the age structure of the growing population and the level of employment and economic activity of the growing population.
- The potential for greater economic growth to be derived from having a larger labour pool in the country. Such increased economic growth can, in turn, fuel increased public spending.

There is no simple answer here since it depends on such factors as the source of the growing population, the age and skill base of the people involved and their potential for aiding economic growth. For example, in the UK, until recently population growth was fuelled by immigration from other countries and such immigrants often brought much needed skills to the UK economy. However recent evidence suggests that population growth is now fuelled by increasing birth rates in certain parts of UK society. This is a very sensitive political and social issue but, in these circumstances, it does seem possible that the demands of this growing population for public services may not be compensated for by increased economic growth deriving from population growth.

However, the key demographic change concerns the ageing of the population. In the UK and most other countries the population is getting older as more and more people live into their 70s, 80s, 90s and beyond. This phenomenon is illustrated in Figure 2.5

It can be seen clearly that across the globe the percentage of the population represented by elderly people is growing substantially, particularly in the developing world. This presents issues of increasing demand for public spending on health, social care, and pensions, whilst at the same time the increasing imbalance between economically active and inactive populations places additional pressures on tax revenues to support the expenditure. Less obvious is the impact on inter-generational and cultural values. Within developed economies there has traditionally been an assumption of wealth inheritance between generations, which can be significantly undermined if capital that has been accumulated during a lifetime of economic activity has to be dispersed in paying for social care. Further, in developed economies increased economic and social mobility often means that there is a decreasing level of local family care, which puts increasing pressure on public service provision. Additionally, the increasing complexity of social and medical issues that comes from increasing longevity, such as dementia and frailty, mean it is increasingly difficult for non-specialised family carers to cope, even if they are available, thus putting increased pressure on professional social caring services.

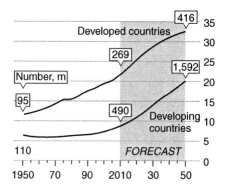

Figure 2.5   The ageing population
Source: The Economist
Note: Population aged 60 and over, % of total

So, although the impact of the ageing population on public services is well known it is perhaps the case that the *magnitude* of the impact is not fully appreciated. This is starkly illustrated in Figure 2.6.

This graph shows, starkly, that in all countries (to varying degrees) the financial impact of the recent (hot water) financial crisis is dwarfed by the longer-term (cold water) impact of the ageing population.

Socio-cultural trends

There are a variety of socio-cultural trends which have serious implications for public services. These will vary between countries but some themes which are important in the UK, and in some instances to other countries, concern:

- loss of family/community cohesion
- attitudes to immigration
- the dysfunctional family/community
- employment trends

Loss of family/community cohesion

In the UK, the collapse of deference from the 1960s onwards was paralleled by an increasing loss of community cohesion. The sense of upward mobility

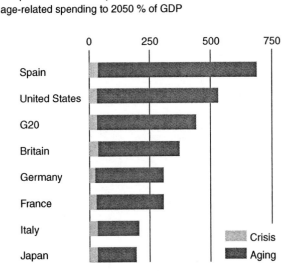

Net present value of impact on fiscal deficit of recent crisis and age-related spending to 2050 % of GDP

Source: IMF

Figure 2.6   Financial impact of ageing
Source: The Economist

created by a more meritocratic society; an enormous upsurge in communications (particularly with the advent of the microchip), a demand for much more flexible working in the economy; and the downturn in traditional patterns of belief resulted in an increasing fragmentation of the traditional structure of society. With the rapid growth of new housing the travel to work areas of local economies became greater, and people tended to live in one geographical community and work in another. The geographical sense of community gave way to a functional sense of community, with individuals identifying with other groups with which they were not necessarily connected in a physical or geographic sense. Organisations which asked of their member's adherence to a set of beliefs or values gave way towards organisations whose membership was of a more contractual nature. Instead of being part of a single community, individuals increasingly saw themselves as being members of multiple communities split by time of day, day of week, specific sub-interest or activity. This fragmentation has increasingly been picked up by polling and marketing organisations which have increasingly subdivided the population into smaller groups based upon economic, social, and value characteristics. These increasingly have been important both in the pattern of policy initiatives from political parties and in the delivery of public services.

This general fragmentation is demonstrated in a number of specific areas:

- *Family breakdown* – The UK has seen a large-scale increase in marital and relationship breakdown and a decline of the conventional family of two parents and their children. Consider the data on marital breakdown shown in Figure 2.7.

Over the past 30 years or so, we have seen a huge increase in the rate of divorce among married couples. In addition, there is also the issue of non-married cohabiting couples who break up. These trends of marriage and relationship breakdown have led to major changes in family structures. As a consequence, children in the UK are increasingly likely to live in single-parent families with nearly a quarter (24%) living with just one parent in 2007 compared with 8% in 1972. The figure has crept up from 21% a decade ago and from 22% in 2001. (ONS 2008a)

- *Loss of the extended family* – the UK used to have high levels of what was termed the 'extended family', meaning three generations (children, parents and grandparents) living under the same roof. Similarly there used to be a high prevalence of family members living in close proximity to their siblings and having regular contact with them. A report by the ESRC (ESRC – undated) stated that the classic extended family model, already rare in 1960, was now all but extinct. Also, the prevalence of brothers and

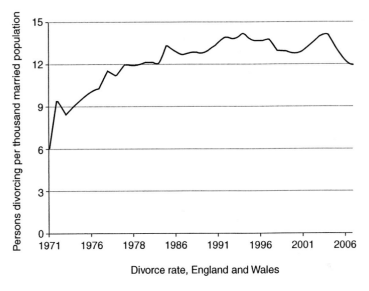

Figure 2.7   Marital and relationship breakdown
Source: ONS

sisters living nearby and remaining in close contact had showed a marked decline. Clearly these trends suggest a marked change in extended family structures and one which has significance for public services, particularly around childcare issues.

- *Persons living alone* – more people now live alone than ever before, and by 2021, it is estimated that more than a third of all households is expected to consist of just one person (BBC 2005). Although a large proportion of these involve the elderly, younger people are also involved and 15% of men aged 25–44 (compared to 8% of women) now live alone. These numbers are expected to rise.

These changes are linked to the demographic changes already discussed and the impacts are expected to show in demand for housing units, particularly social housing, and the consequent impact on environmental public services.

Attitudes to immigration

Immigration (and emigration) has always been a facet of UK society and in modern times we have seen waves of immigration from the Caribbean, the Indian subcontinent and most recently from Eastern Europe. However, in recent years (and at the 2010 general election) immigration became a key political debating point with concerns about the impact of high levels of immigration on the economic and social fabric of UK society. Similar concerns have also arisen in other developed countries such as France and Holland.

Levels of immigration into the UK have increased sharply since 2004 and reached a peak of 600,000 in 2007 but has fallen back a little since then. However it must also be noted that immigration into the UK is partially off-set by emigration out of the UK. However, Migration Watch has argued that immigration at current levels is a new phenomenon to the UK while government projections suggest that immigration will account for 39% of all new UK households in the next 20 years. Meanwhile, there are more than 300 primary schools in which over 70% have English as a second language; this is nearly a half million children.

There is a huge and contentious debate about the merits to UK society of immigration on such a scale. Some may argue that immigrants are a positive facet to society and generate significant economic growth and associated tax revenues while others may argue that immigrants are large users of public services and a drain on the public purse. Clearly, there is no simple answer to this question and it will depend on a range of factors concerning the skill base of immigrants and their personal and family circumstances.

It is not simply the overall level of immigration that is at issue here. The need for immigrant communities to have suitable community support arrangements means that there is inevitably a degree of concentration in particular areas. Whilst this creates intra-community cohesion, it can damage cohesion with neighbouring communities with the possibility of community conflict. The concentration of immigrant groups can also bring with it a concentration of particular social and economic issues and increase the level of demand for public services support.

The dysfunctional family/community

A dysfunctional family can be thought of as a family in which conflict, misbehaviour, and often abuse on the part of individual members occur continually and regularly, leading other members to accommodate such actions. Children sometimes grow up in such families with the understanding that such arrangements are normal. Such families can exhibit such behaviours as poor parenting, poor health, low educational outcomes and lack of employment over several generations. Dysfunctional families are primarily a result of co-dependent adults, and may also be affected by addictions, such as substance abuse (alcohol, drugs and so on). Other causes include untreated mental illness, and parents emulating or over-correcting their own dysfunctional parents. A common misperception of dysfunctional families is that the mother and father are on the verge of separation and divorce. While this may be true in some cases, often the marriage bond is very strong as the parents' faults actually complement each other. However, this does not necessarily mean the family's situation is stable. Moreover, the behaviours which are found in dysfunctional families can often spill over into other families such that such behaviours may become accepted or tolerated within the broader community. Thus we have the related concept of the dysfunctional community.

It is a debatable point as to whether the prevalence of dysfunctional families/communities has increased in recent years since there are issues of better reporting and changing cultural norms which cloud the picture. However, what is clear is that dysfunctional families and communities have substantial needs for public services such as health, social care, and education. Thus any increase in their prevalence can have significant implications for public services. Furthermore external factors such as unemployment, illness, natural disaster, debt and inflation can exacerbate the situation. The level of public sympathy with such families and communities is often low and coupled with the tight constraints on resources that this may have severe implications for relevant services.

Employment trends

The UK has seen a number of trends in employment which have implications for public services. These include:

- *Female Employment* – worldwide, the labour market has seen dramatic changes particularly in relation to female employment. For example, between 1959 and 2001, female employment in the UK rose from 48% to more than 70% (ONS 2002). More specifically, there have also been large-scale increases in the involvement of mothers in the UK labour market with more than two-thirds of working-age women with dependent children now being in employment. Of working-age women with children aged under five, 57% were in employment (ONS 2008b).
- *Occupational Mix* – the long-term trends in occupational mix are well known with a shift from unskilled manual work towards more skilled and cerebral occupations. However, significant changes are still taking place over relatively short time periods. This is illustrated in Table 2.10 below

It can be seen that over an eight-year period there were increases in all the professional and managerial occupational classes and reductions in the more manually oriented occupations. Such trends seem likely to continue.

- *Part-time working* – we have recently seen a substantial shift from full-time to part-time working which has, arguably, disguised the true impact of economic recession in terms of employment levels. In recent months, the ONS has reported *that while full-time employment* fell, part-time employment rose but not sufficiently fast enough to compensate the loss of full-time jobs. As has been the pattern for several months previously, the figures are being driven by women finding part-time jobs while men,

Table 2.10   Changes in occupational class

	2001 (%)	2009 (%)	Change (%)
Managers and senior officials	14	16	2
Professional occupations	12	14	2
Associate professional and technical	13	15	1
Administrative and secretarial	14	11	–2
Skilled trades	12	11	–1
Personal service occupations	7	9	1
Sales and customer services	8	7	–1
Process plant and machine operatives	8	7	–2
Elementary occupations	12	11	–1
Total	100	100	

Source: ONS

predominantly, are losing full-time ones. It is a debatable point as to the extent to which this trend will be reversed in the post-recessionary period.

There seems little to suggest that all of socio-cultural trends will do anything other than continue into the future, and evidence suggests that all are likely to have implications for public services demand.

Environmental factors

In this, the last of our classification of key public sector factors, we move perhaps towards the coldest end of the issues spectrum. These are typically the kind of issues that often get pushed down the priority for public policy by the imperative of having to sort out the hot issues. However, as it is sometimes said of the sea, it is unwise to turn your back on it for too long. The key issues here concern:

- physical environment
- energy
- natural resource depletion
- science and technological development

Physical environment

There are several issues here to be considered.

Climate change

What is plain is that it is not the future of the Earth that is at stake here. The Earth's continued existence is assured and it is the future of us as a species that is potentially at risk from the impact of climate change which is already under way. The International Panel on Climate Change (United Nations 2007) has carefully, but conservatively, evaluated what some of those changes might be by the end of the current century. The key impacts are:

- A temperature rise of some 4 to 6°C, compared with a maximum sustainable rise that could be tolerated of around 2°C.
- Sea levels, which are already rising by 3 mm a year, could peak at some 3 to 7 m higher than they currently are with the loss of whole countries and impacts on many of the major cities of the world.
- Rainfall and flooding, particularly in western areas are likely to increase, though the complexities of weather impacts are particularly difficult to forecast. Nevertheless they estimate that some 80 million people might be affected by significant seasonal flooding annually, of which 80% will be in Asia.
- While some will suffer significant flooding, drought and desertification may be the lot of others. Since the 1930s the Sahara has already moved 200 km south and it has been estimated that the impact on agricultural output in Africa as a result of drought may result in a reduction of 50% in the coming century.
- The movement of pests and diseases, particularly towards more northern and southern temperate areas can be expected. Already in the UK we are seeing the spread of 'bluetongue' amongst animals as the insects carrying the disease have a much greater northern range.
- The rising sea temperatures will not only give a source of more violent weather conditions as they, and the atmosphere, store more energy, but the rise in surface temperature will create a greater layered effect with the result that the colder, nutrient-rich lower layers will not mix with surface waters and as a result a major collapse of fish stocks is likely.

The economic impact of all this can only begin to be imagined. In the UK the Stern Report (Stern 2006) tried to assess the impact of the current expected changes in climate as a result of past activity as around a permanent reduction of 5% in global GDP, and if the predictions of the International Panel are correct the permanent reduction could be as much as 20%.

The key international environmental issue concerns carbon emissions and in the UK, the 2009 Budget set a target of a 34% reduction in carbon emissions (on 1990 levels) by 2020. Such a policy aim has wide ranging impacts for companies and individuals and also will have a number of impacts for public services:

- Public services will have to make their own contribution towards the achievement of carbon reductions.
- The large-scale public investment needed to achieve the carbon reduction targets may squeeze out alternative public services investment.
- Achievement of the carbon reduction targets may inhibit economic growth.

Pollution

Historically pollution was a major social and environmental problem in many countries. However, the full effect of modern pollution of the environment is yet to be fully understood, let alone addressed but it is a huge issue in many countries. As with the major polluting activities of the Industrial Revolution the impact is long-term and even if major and drastic changes were made immediately it would be many years before the impact on the environment became noticeable.

Inevitably there is an international dimension here. As major economies come to economic development so the extent of their pollution activities extends beyond their borders to create major international problems – particularly around climate change and environmental impact. Recently geologists have begun to recognise the impact of human activity on the long-term ecological, environmental, and geological cycles of the Earth. Some have even suggested that we have moved into a new geological era that they have called the Anthropocene in recognition of this fact.

Energy

Energy is important to public services for two main reasons. Firstly, public services are big users of energy and secondly, energy supply and cost affects economic performance which in turn has knock on effects for public services.

Put crudely, current key fossil energy sources are finite and are running out. In 2007, a report (BP 2007) appeared to show that the world had enough 'proven' oil reserves to provide 40 years of consumption at current rates. However, scientists led by the London-based Oil Depletion Analysis Centre suggested that global production would peak before entering a steepening decline which will have massive consequences for the world economy and the way we live our lives. According to the 'peak oil' theory our consumption of oil will catch, then outstrip our discovery of new reserves and we will begin to deplete known reserves. In 2009, the Chief Economist of the International Energy Agency suggested that the public and many governments appeared to be oblivious to the fact that the oil on which modern civilisation depends is running out far faster than previously predicted and that global production is likely to peak in about 10 years – at least a decade earlier than most governments had estimated. While new fields may be discovered the marginal cost of production and thus the price of the oil is certain to be higher. Furthermore, the recent huge oil spill at the Deepwater Horizon rig is likely to lead to much greater controls over drilling for oil under the sea bed.

At the same time the alternative nuclear capacity is reaching the end of its physical life, and there are considerable public objections to its replacement, with the likelihood that there will be a gap as the old supply ceases, before a new one can be built and commissioned. Furthermore, even if we see nuclear energy as an alternative to oil it must be noted that deposits of uranium will also probably be exhausted this century depending on the growth in the use of nuclear power. Furthermore, it seems that controlled nuclear fusion is far away as ever.

As yet the use of alternative energy sources from renewables is only operating at the margin, and has also been the subject of local land use objections. There is not a significant capacity to expand energy from these sources in the immediate future. As a consequence, it seems likely that energy costs will continue to rise and there are also some concerns that shortfall in supply may lead to disruptions sometime in the period 2012–2015.

There are several issues which have implications for public services:

- Energy costs of public services may rise disproportionately compared to other costs.
- Public investment in new energy sources (e.g. the Severn Barrage at £23bn) may squeeze out other public services investment.
- Rising energy costs and insecurity of supply may inhibit economic growth and growth in public spending.

Resource depletion

Since the Industrial Revolution there have been concerns about the exhaustion of non-renewable mineral resources. The concerns are serious because modern society and technology depends on a variety of metals, including ones such as copper, lead, zinc, platinum, silver and gold which are widely used but geochemically scarce. Such concerns are growing stronger today because some of these minerals which are being depleted are core to certain 'green' technologies (e.g. the use of palladium in catalytic converters of cars). As developing economies grow so the competition for key resources will increase. The vast bulk of these scarce minerals are to be found in China which will probably wish to utilise much of the availability for its own economy.

Some will argue that new reserves of such minerals will be found but these reserves are likely to prove much more expensive to access and therefore the costs will be high. Also there is no guarantee that we will be able to develop the technologies to access them.

Science and technological development

As with most parts of society the continued pace of science and technological development has huge and divergent implications for public services in all countries. Science and technology can drive up costs of public services provision; can improve the quality of services and can enable more efficient service delivery. Two examples will illustrate this.

Medical science and technology

In 1967 the first human heart transplant took place in South Africa and the patient survived 11 days. Today there are numerous transplant centres throughout the world and patients are living for decades after their operation. Sixty years ago in the UK there were no artificial joint replacements because there was no surgical capability to do them. Today thousands of patients have such operations each year. The basic point is that the supply of a new medical or surgical service fuels demand for that service where none previously existed. Such developments start in the research phase and soon become broad scale provision and this has substantial costs associated with it.

There are of course many other examples of where developments in medical science and technology have, or will, fuel demands for health (and social care) services. Some of these include:

- diagnostic techniques (e.g. CT, MRI)
- pharmaceuticals (e.g. cancer, eye diseases)
- other organ transplants (e.g. kidney, liver)
- gene therapies

Moreover, behind these headline-grabbing developments there are many smaller-scale developments taking place which will have similar effects, but only if there is a direct cost effect of more expensive health technologies. But there is also the implied demographic effect of increased longevity as a result.

Information and communications technology

The scope and scale of ICT means that it has enormous impacts on and implications for public services in many different ways. Just a few examples are listed below:

- Impact on methods of service delivery (e.g. e-government, telemedicine)
- Improved communications and coordination (email, video conferencing, web sites)
- Better analysis of issues (data analysis, relational databases)

In some cases these developments can drive up the costs of service provision as they enable us to do a wider range of more expensive things, yet in other cases they can facilitate more efficient working. It seems likely that science and technology will continue to influence public service provision for the foreseeable future.

Conclusion

This chapter has provided a comprehensive overview of the challenges and pressures facing public services both in the UK and most other countries. The financial and economic challenges in many countries, including the

UK, will take many years to resolve to a satisfactory position, but vigorous action is clearly needed. Hence, we see this as the 'hot water frog' issue which will radically impact public services in the medium-term.

However, it is important to realise that the other 'cold water frog' issues will also have serious and *long-term* implications for public services:

- The ageing population has enormous long-term implications for public services.
- Energy and environmental issues will place fresh and significant challenges on public services.
- The lack of trust in politicians may further inhibit support for policy actions.
- The lack of community cohesion and social problems will tend to militate against family and community-based solutions.
- Long-standing inequalities at both economic and community levels may inhibit the social acceptability of essential economic solutions with dangers of outbreaks of social violence and public disorder.

Thus the long-term future of public services needs to be considered from this standpoint. Although the immediate concern for the future public services is dominated by the economic and public finance context, the ability of public services to cope with these wider ranging issues cannot be overlooked. In the next few chapters we will look at how the current reform programmes have tried to address both the economic and wider issues, and how these may need to be replaced with more substantial transformational changes to be successful.

3
We Are Not Alone – How Others Have Coped

Countries generating large public budget deficits with increasing levels of public debt implement policies which are described as 'fiscal consolidations'. There are international examples worth looking at for help in achieving fiscal consolidation. However, one has to be focussed. Over history there are lots of examples of such consolidations but many occurred so long ago as to have little relevance to the current situation. Also many will have taken place in developing countries which again will have little or no relevance to the UK and developed countries.

Earlier we suggested that it was the collapse of the post-war economic consensus in the 1970s that set the stage for the current pattern of public service issues. Hence we have focussed on recent fiscal consolidations in OECD and EU member countries from that period onwards. There is much evidence (OECD 2007) available about the success or otherwise of the many fiscal consolidations that have taken place since the 1970s and the factors that are likely to produce success. These are summarised in Table 3.1. It is worth noting, though, of the 85 fiscal consolidations across the 24 OECD countries that were considered, the average consolidation was around 2% of GDP over a two-year period. The current consolidations of 8% or more of GDP and the longer timescale are at the very top end of previous experience, and in some cases, such as Ireland, currently go well beyond anything seen since the mid-1970s.

Other Countries' experiences

In our search for relevant comparative examples that most closely fit current experience, it seems most sensible to start by looking for an example within the Western economies that most closely parallels the four peculiar characteristics of the UK:

- an initial structural economic problem,
- a financial sector of disproportionate size to the economy,
- a largely unregulated and loosely controlled financial environment,
- a significant level of public and private sector debt.

Table 3.1 Patterns of past fiscal consolidations

Issue	Summary of findings
Size of fiscal consolidation needed	Where countries are facing large deficit/GDP ratios and/or debt/GDP ratios the tougher initial budgetary conditions required for fiscal consolidations are more likely to be successful than for smaller consolidations. This is probably partly a function of necessity combined with greater public awareness of the problem and acceptance of the need for action.
Role of economic growth	Fiscal consolidation will be assisted if the economy can grow its way out of trouble since increased economic growth will generate additional tax revenues. Thus it will be of great assistance if such consolidations are taken during a period of steady growth in regional or world economies.
Financial system	Fiscal consolidations may be required following major shocks to the banking and financial systems of a country. The success of the fiscal consolidation is more likely to be effective if the problems of the financial system have been clearly identified and remedial actions taken.
Tax increases versus expenditure cuts	A controversial issue is the balance to be struck between tax increases and public expenditure reductions. Evidence suggests that consolidation efforts that emphasise reducing expenditure (especially current expenditure) tend to result in larger and more durable consolidations than those which rely wholly or primarily on increasing revenues.
Pace of consolidation	In practice most episodes of fiscal consolidation were of the 'cold shower' variety in which the structural budget balance is abruptly tightened by between 1 and 4% of GDP in a single year. However, in practice, 'slow but steady wins the race'. Gradual consolidations that spread the fiscal pain over a longer period tend to be both larger and more successful than 'cold shower' consolidations which try to get it all over with in one or two years.
Fiscal rules	The existence of well-specified and comprehensive fiscal rules is important for effective consolidations. Fiscal rules can support a government's medium-term consolidation plans by providing a clear guide for the budget balance over time. Transparent rules can also help to sustain that consolidation by raising the political cost of deviating from those plans when the initial pro-austerity consensus begins to dissipate.
Budgeting systems	Having strong budget frameworks can keep the consolidation process on track. Slippage on the expenditure side is the main reason for the failure of fiscal consolidations. Countries whose budget systems were characterised by a multi-annual planning horizon and a prudent approach to budget preparation were more likely to deliver the tough budget cuts they committed to.
Consensus	The likely success of the fiscal consolidation will be enhanced if there is broad based support across the political spectrum and among the population for the actions being proposed.

Iceland

Such an example exists, but is hardly an encouraging one – Iceland (House of Commons 2009). Fuller details are given in Box 3.1. The experience of the Iceland economy in the autumn of 2008 perhaps gives some negative indicators to the UK Government in looking at how to handle the future public sector changes and UK economy. There are four salient lessons.

Box 3.1   The Icelandic banking crisis and its aftermath 2008–2010

Iceland is relatively small country, with only 320,000 inhabitants – less than the population of major UK cities. Traditionally its principal industries have been in fishing, aluminium smelting, and tourism. Strategically Iceland has been of great importance in the Cold War period to NATO with a major airbase at Keflavík which was used for long-range bombers. The importance of Iceland strategically has meant that Iceland traditionally has not operated his own independent defence forces, but these have been provided on a rotation basis by other NATO allies.

In 2008, following the international financial crisis, there was a catastrophic collapse of the three principal banks of Iceland – Landesbanki, Glitnir, and Kaupthing. Between them, these three banks had 85% of the total business of Icelandic banking. When all three went into financial administration forced by the Icelandic Government it created a major overseas crisis which had lasting effects on the Icelandic economy. In part this was exacerbated by the action of the UK Government in particular in protection of the significant number of overseas depositors who had accounts with Icelandic banks.

The causes of the crisis go back to 2001 when the banks in Iceland were deregulated. The banks expanded rapidly, but the domestic deposit base was very small so that there were insufficient funds to expand the banks to the level which was desired. As a result Icelandic banks increasingly depended upon overseas deposits and short-term funding from other banks internationally. The three banks held foreign debt in excess of €50 billion, compared to Iceland's GDP of €8.5 billion. Prior to the 2008 collapse the rapid expansion of financial services in Iceland contributed significantly to the growth of GDP in the economy, and the wealth of the Icelanders. The Icelandic government operated a relatively benign economic policy, part funding the liquidity of banks by the issue of currency in exchange for bank bonds. One of the inevitable consequences of this was an increase in the level of inflation, which had risen to 14% in the 12 months prior to the collapse in September/October 2008. This compared to the national target of 2.5% and as a consequence the Central Bank kept interest rates very high at 15.5% for the same period. This high level of rates compared with 4 or 5% earned elsewhere encouraged foreign depositors to place money with Icelandic banks which, until this relatively late stage, were still obtaining triple-A ratings from credit rating agencies.

Coupled with this significant level of overseas deposits, largely re-invested in overseas companies, Icelandic GDP growth in the period up to September 2008 was around 5.5% per annum. This encouraged Icelanders to increase their standard of living and take on the significant amount of household debt – on average 213% of disposable income.

In September 2008 the Lehman Bros banking conglomerate collapsed in the United States after filing for bankruptcy and with the US Government no longer willing to support it. The immediate effect of this was to severely curtail the amount of interbank lending internationally. One of the consequences was that the Icelandic banks were unable to roll over their significant amount of interbank loans and, unable to fund this, they resorted to asking the Central Bank of Iceland to cover their immediate liquidity. However, the significant amount of international debt held by banks considerably exceeded the GDP of Iceland and completely overwhelmed the amount of reserves held by the Icelandic Central Bank. As a consequence, it was announced that receivers would be appointed by the Financial Supervisory Authority (FME). This had immediate and serious consequences for the Icelandic economy. The national currency – the kronor – fell precipitously and the market capitalisation of the Icelandic stock exchange fell by 90%. This impacted immediately on the real economy with a GDP decrease of 5.5% in the first six months of 2009. Outside of the Icelandic economy the Governments of countries who had nationals with significant deposits in Icelandic banks took preventative action to stabilise the impact of the Icelandic banking crisis on their own financial systems. They did so as a matter of urgency, partly because the statements by the Icelandic Government were ambiguous as to whether or not foreign depositors would receive equal protection compared to Icelandic nationals. This preventative action created a further crisis in Icelandic banking and may, in part, been responsible for putting the third Icelandic bank (Kaupthing) into administration.

Following the immediate impact of the Icelandic banking crisis, loans and support arrangements were agreed with other Nordic countries – Denmark and Norway – and through the European Central bank (ECB). Other offers of loans from countries such as Russia were also considered, but eventually an IMF loan package of $4.6 billion was agreed using IMF central funding and loans and swaps from other Nordic countries. Other countries such as Poland, Russia, Faroe Islands, Germany, Netherlands, and the United Kingdom also agreed loan arrangements relating to the protection of depositors in their own countries.

The result of the crisis was a significant future liability on the Icelandic population. It is estimated that the total amount of debt outstanding to other countries represented 75% of the Icelandic GDP for 2007. Iceland's GDP is expected to shrink by as much as 10% as a result of the crisis, creating an economic depression in the country. Unemployment rates have increased dramatically to 9%, compared to less than 1% pre-the Icelandic banking crisis. A number of other companies within Iceland have cut jobs or declared bankruptcy. Importers have been particularly hard-hit with the Government's need to restrict foreign currency to essential products only. Icelandic pension funds are expected to shrink by some 15 to 25%, and as a result, the Icelandic Pension Funds Association believes that benefits will have to be cut. Inflation rates continue to be high and may top out at 75%. For the remainder of those remaining in employment, some 14% have experienced reductions in pay and 7% have had their working hours reduced. These figures are actually lower than expected.

Politically, the impact of the Icelandic banking crisis was considerable. Many of the senior politicians involved in the period up to and including the crisis had been removed from office or have resigned, often for health reasons. The Icelandic population has expressed severe dissatisfaction and continuing resentment of the situation and in particular have been critical of the actions of overseas Governments who, it is perceived, have made the problem worse. The Icelandic Parliament has decided that is necessary to join the EU in order to access support funds for the future, even though this has been an unpopular policy in the past. In April 2009 Iceland's state prosecutor brought in independent investigators to look into the question of practices in Icelandic banks in the period up to and including the crisis with a view to bringing criminal charges. A number of civil actions have been started by other Governments and agencies against the individuals involved in the banking crisis.

Firstly, the rapidity with which economic good fortune can turn into economic disaster. Although clear signs of weakness were flagged by some commentators as early as April 2008, it was only during September and particularly over the week of 6th–12th October 2008 that the Icelandic economy rapidly turned from desirable location for investment to international pariah. On 29 September 2008, all of the credit rating agencies were still evaluating the sovereign debt of Iceland at various levels of the 'A' category. By 10 October, three of the four had reduced the ratings to 'junk' levels. The Icelandic economy moved in the course of the year from showing a public sector surplus and reasonable levels of growth, with low levels of unemployment, into one with a long-term economic deficit, with the rapid decline in GDP (5.5% in the first six months of 2009), and with unemployment at 9% – nine times the level of the previous year. Economic disasters like this are rather like wars – easy to get into, but it takes a long time to extract yourself. It's been estimated it will take a generation before Iceland recovers from the 2008 disaster, and the agreement to repay the UK and Dutch Governments will mean that the Icelandic economy will pay 6% of its GDP to those Governments in the period 2017–2023.

Secondly, the folly of ignoring the international dimension to dealing with economic change. The rapid growth of the Icelandic banks resulted in almost 50% of their deposits being held by overseas depositors. When the Icelandic banks ran into trouble and had to be placed into administration by the Icelandic Government through the financial regulator, the impact was felt not only in Iceland but also by many overseas depositors. As the Inquiry of the House of Commons Treasury Committee on the Icelandic Banking Crisis (House of Commons 2009) amply demonstrated this created serious problems. The first of these was who was actually undertaking the regulation of overseas branches and subsidiaries of Icelandic banks? Even if this issue of regulation could be sorted out there was difficulty of coordinating the pattern of regulation and the relative powers of the individual regulators. In the case of the UK it was clear that, even if the Financial

Services Authority (FSA) had a regulatory authority over UK subsidiaries of Icelandic banks, the extent of its powers was limited to informing the Icelandic regulator (the FME) and there were no powers to ensure that UK financial regulation was enforced upon the banking sector in Iceland. The second was the confusion that was created between the Icelandic and UK Governments when conversations between Chancellor of the Exchequer and Finance Minister of Iceland led Alistair Darling, the then Chancellor, to believe that the Icelandic Government would favour domestic depositors over foreign depositors. The consequential and immediate response of the UK Government was to move to use counterterrorism legislation to protect the UK national interest which not only exacerbated the problem with respect to the Kaupthing Bank, but also damaged future inter-government relationships when it came to negotiating an arrangement to repay funds guaranteed by the UK and Dutch Governments to their nationals.

Thirdly, the political fallout. So great was the fall of the Icelandic economy and so damaging was a long-term impact that it was inevitable that the Icelandic population, amongst others, would look to see who was to blame for the disaster. Almost all of the senior politicians who were in power at the time the crisis erupted are now out of office. Some have retired, usually for health reasons, and others have been replaced. The Icelandic populations through the 'pots and pans revolution' forced major changes in Government and the worries over public attitudes could be seen in the reluctance of the President to sign the repayment arrangements for overseas Governments without a referendum to back his final agreement to legislation passed by the Parliament (the Althing). That the referendum rejected the initial proposals is indicative of the simmering public discontent that may yet cause further political difficulties as the impact of the economic changes works through the Icelandic economy. Similarly, overseas governments and the Icelandic Government are pressing criminal charges against a number of those involved in Icelandic banks, and although the civil actions may yet get settled without coming to Court, the continuing investigations launched in April 2009 into the issues around the management of the Icelandic banks may yet result in criminal convictions. In dealing with the long-term economic consequences, the Icelandic Government is already showing a more aggressive attitude towards the exploitation of its natural resources in fishing and other minerals which will have international repercussions and relationships between Iceland and some of its former allies and may yet create further environmental, defence, and economic issues.

Lastly, the dangers of quantitative easing (QE). QE is a financial and economic policy whereby the central bank of a country creates additional money which it uses to buy government bonds and other financial assets, in order to increase the overall money supply in the country. The creation of additional money eases issues of liquidity within the country. At the time of the Icelandic crisis some commentators felt that Iceland had almost reached a position where it might repudiate some of its international debt, but generally it was felt the consequences of this for its role in the European Economic Arrangement, and its subsequent application to the EU, although this was a most marginal decision based largely on the need to access European Central Bank funding to help shore up the economy, meant that the Government of Iceland would only do so as a last resort. Nevertheless, before the Icelandic crisis had come to a head, the Government was in the habit of issuing currency against bank bonds thus financing and encouraging the banks' activities. The consequences of this in terms of high inflation were obvious, but the impact that this had in maintaining high interest rates was material in continuing to attract foreign deposits to support Icelandic banking activity. This feedback arrangement exacerbated the situation, and although quantitative easing has been used in the UK, and elsewhere, as an alternative to the issuing of government debt, the Icelandic experience is a cautionary note on the overreliance on this traditional way of dealing with long-term debt problems – financing it with the issue of currency, and relying on the consequent inflation to reduce the real value of the outstanding debt.

So, while the Icelandic situation does not give particular encouragement about the successful handling of the economic crisis created by the collapse of the financial systems in 2008, it does give some indicators about the 'tightrope policy' that the Government treads in handling the UK situation. We return to this a little later, but before we do so it's worth looking at a couple of more successful examples of the way that other countries have addressed the problem of fiscal consolidations and public sector deficits and debt which give more encouraging picture.

Sweden and Canada

The two most frequently quoted examples are those of Canada and Sweden who addressed significant financial issues in the public sector in the 1990s with some apparent success (see Boxes 3.2 and 3.3). The popular mythology has it that both of these countries faced a similar problem in the 1990s. The public sector deficit had already risen to a level which was unsustainable as a proportion of GDP, and the overall level of public debt had reached proportions that approached 70–80% of annual GDP. Both countries addressed these issues by making drastic changes to the nature of public sector in their countries, but were able to do so within a relatively short period of time (3–4 years) and without there being a significant level of public dissent or loss of the integrity of public service delivery. In both cases it appeared that the political party that implemented these changes gained respect from the electorate for doing so and did not suffer the kind of consequences envisaged by Mervyn King, Governor of the Bank of England in a private letter (that was published shortly before the May 2010 election) in which he suggested that whichever party won would have to take such unpopular decisions that it would be 'out of office for a generation'. Such examples therefore appear encouraging to the new Coalition Government in implementing its pattern of changes.

Box 3.2 Canada's public sector reforms of the 1990s

In 1993 the Canadian administration of Prime Minister Jean Chrétien introduced a policy to deal with a budget deficit of around 9.1% of Canadian GDP – some C$39 billion. (This compares to the current UK deficit of around 11.5% of GDP). Canada also had an accumulated debt of C$487.5 billion and the cumulative service charges on this debt were absorbing some 26% of all federal expenditure. In the period of Programme Review between 1994 and 1999 Canada took steps to introduce policy changes to reduce this deficit and at the end of the period had achieved a small budget surplus. In the so-called bloodbath budget of 1995 the Minister of Finance announced a Programme Review aimed at reducing the deficit by C$17 billion expenditure over three years involving the loss of 45,000 jobs. This was followed in 1996 by a second budget Programme Review Phase 2, which was required to find a further C$2 billion reduction by 1999 and loss of a further 10,000 jobs.

These changes were implemented as the result of a zero-based budget review process. All nonstatutory expenditure was subjected to a 'Star Chamber' process where Cabinet members scrutinised all departmental budgets. Key questions were asked about what the outcomes of a particular policy were, whether it could be provided elsewhere, and, most explicitly, whether it could be afforded by Canadians. The Government, it was claimed, had received considerable public support for the changes that it implemented. In part this was recognition of the fact that the Canadians resented the way in which their economy had been represented to the world as the equivalent of 'third rate banana republic' because of the current level of public deficit. The outcome of the public consultation was interesting. Variations proposed by the public as being acceptable were not what had been expected. It was deemed necessary to increase welfare payments generally, whilst other programmes were cut by 50% and sometimes eliminated altogether. There was no attempt to make an across-the-board 'salami slicing' approach to budget reductions.

The consequences, however, were not painless – hospital waiting lists shot up, some hospitals closed, and thousands of medical staff lost their jobs. The remaining hospitals were often overcrowded and infection rates rose. In education, average class sizes rose from 25 to 35 children and separate special-needs classes were abolished. Science and transport budgets were halved and national railway, airports, and air traffic control were privatised. Overseas aid and fisheries subsidies were also reduced. Defence was cut by 15%, mostly achieved by merging the Central Commands of the Armed Forces. Many of the heaviest cuts were passed on into the provinces, which ran the key front-line health and education services.

The significant reduction in the public sector workforce was achieved by implementing two policies. The first was a pension's arrangement whereby anybody close to pensionable age could retire with no actuarial reduction of their pension. The second was an early departure initiative for employees who were declared surplus. These employees received a cash payment based on salary, age, years of service, and pension eligibility if they decided to resign. As a result of these two initiatives large staff reductions were accomplished without the need for significant compulsory redundancies. However, the impact on the morale of the public service was considerable, as was the impact on the age distribution of public employees. With a further hiring freeze announced in December 2003, the remaining public services staff show very uneven distribution with significantly older workers and significantly younger workers missing from the age profile which may create a future problem as the current cohort of people in their 40s and 50s comes to retirement. There's also been some suggestion that the total wage bill has not decreased as much as expected because of the hiring of consultants and temporary staff. The impact on public sector delivery was also adversely affected as the workload on individual public servants increased and caseloads in some cases became unmanageable.

Nevertheless, the reductions in the Canadian public sector deficit and the programme review have been deemed to be a success. The Liberal party was re-elected in 1997 with a reduced but nevertheless significant majority. However, after the disastrous failure in the Canadian conservatives in 1993 – they were reduced to just two MPs – the opposition was neither substantial nor well organised.

Although the Programme Review was successful in the period 1993–1999, the long-term issues with regard to the Canadian public service delivery had not been remedied by the cuts programme. By 2009/10 the Canadian federal government was already back into deficit and the workforce had begun to grow again to the level of the 1990s. A further round of public sector cuts was announced on the across-the-board basis with all departments operating budgets to the period up to 2013 frozen at the 2010 cash level. Further reductions were proposed in public sector workforces as part of the programme. As in the 1990s the proposal to deal with this issue by reduction in public services rather than increases in taxation appears to have the widest support of Canadians. However it is clear that on this round the level of support of Canadians for significant service reductions is considerably less than it was in the mid-1990s and the effect on public servants is such that there is an increased level of opposition from them to the bearing the brunt of a further round of reductions. The Canadian reform of public services remains unfinished business.

Box 3.3   Sweden balances its budget

In line with many European countries Sweden, after experiencing a period of sustained growth during the 1950s and 1960s, went into financial difficulties during the crisis of the 1970s. Like a number of other countries, including the UK and Sweden, chose to subsidise some of its basic industries such as steel and shipbuilding to maintain employment during this period. Nevertheless, the basic uncompetitiveness of much of Swedish industry continued into the 1980s. Government policy during this period was devalue the krona thus creating a temporary short-term competitiveness which benefited industries such as chemicals, plastics, electronics, and car but created long-term inflation pressures within the Swedish economy.

During the 1980s the Swedish economy was also significantly deregulated in an attempt to improve the internal market. Monopolies in transport and public utilities were deregulated, including a major deregulation of the financial services industry. This contributed to a rapid rise in lending, particularly on the property market by the end of the decade. Because of the devaluations, industries which had significant export markets accumulated significant surpluses which they resolved by investing in the stock market and property. This further encouraged the growth of asset prices. This created the conditions for speculative asset price led bubble in the early 1990s. The banks and financial sector nearly collapsed and this, combined with an international economic slowdown, caused the Government to abandon the attempt to maintain the exchange rate and promoted a severe economic crisis. As a result of the downturn in the economy GDP fell by approximately 5% and the unemployment rate rose from 1.5% to 8.2%. The traditional centre left Social Democratic Party lost power to the conservative right wing.

The incoming Government made attempts to introduce a more modern form of public sector management to correct the long-term issues in the increasingly large public sector welfare states that had arisen since the Second World War. These were in line with the reforms of the public sector adopted widely across Europe generally known as 'New Public Management', including the introduction of explicit measures of performance; decentralisation; and the introduction of private-sector styles of management with contracting out, privatisation, and a stronger focus on the citizen as a consumer of public services. The uptake of these reforms was somewhat patchy, with significant changes being seen in the care of the elderly but with less significant changes in education and health.

By 1994 these reforms had failed to address effectively the significant loss in taxation income and rise in public expenditure which accompanied the economic downturn. By that time the public sector debt exceeded 50% of GDP and was rising rapidly (it would reach 80% of GDP by 1998). Yet by the end of the decade the public finances had seen a significant turnaround creating a small surplus. Although the incoming Social Democratic Government made minor adjustments to the new public management reforms of its predecessor, it did not seek to dismantle these completely and go back to the old system. Changes in the audit arrangements, for example, were intended to improve the performance management reporting, and to some extent were successful. Similarly attempts to downgrade the amount of public support given to private schooling were later reversed into a more even playing field between public and private provision.

The greatest single improvement, however, was in the approach taken to balancing the budget. The previous fairly highly decentralised solution was amended to give a greater sense of overall control and direction. The earlier, traditional, public finance management arrangements have an inherent tendency, particularly in coalition situations, to ratchet up the budget requirement of Government, as a result of compromises and negotiating a position between the parties. The new budget arrangements which were introduced set global maxima for a smaller number of budget heads which included all costs, including pensions, but excluding the cost of debt interest. Any proposals to spend within these totals had to be a 'zero-sum' proposal. Proposals to increase expenditure had been matched by cuts elsewhere. This meant that unless there was significant majority support for an alternative, the balanced-budget proposals of the Executive were likely to gain overall support in the budget-setting process. As a consequence the net increases to the budget from original to final proposal completely disappeared after the new initiatives were introduced, with the one exception of 2003 when incoming Government had to renegotiate its priorities and the budget rose for that one year only. The new budget discipline was material in ensuring that the long-term position of the Swedish public sector was more secure.

After the turmoil of the 1990s the first decade of the 21st century showed a more even growth rate for Sweden. The economy and public finances were stabilised. Sweden was not immune from downturn as a result of the 'dot.com' bubble, but the net effect was significantly reduced and the crisis of the 1990s was not revisited.

In undertaking fiscal consolidations, there are three things that have been drawn from the experience of Canada and Sweden that seem to be carried forward in UK public policy:

- *Do it quick*. Both Sweden and Canada sought to make changes to their public sectors shortly after the election of a new Government on the assumption that it would be necessary to implement the serious changes early so that the benefits could be seen by the time the next national election came round. Certainly this was the very clear advice of Goran Persson, the then Swedish Prime Minister who implemented the changes, in speeches that he gave on the Swedish experience during 2009/10. Although he described himself as being 'the most unpopular man in Sweden', shortly after the changes were implemented he suggested that once the public were aware of the necessity of making the changes they would tend to back the honesty and transparency of a political party that was committed to the need to make the changes and showed a clear willingness and commitment to carry through. Certainly, in comments made about the reputation of the Canadian Prime Minister Jean Chrétien (who was known as 'Mr No' in the popular press) it seems that short-term political unpopularity had long-term benefits.
- *Do it all at once*. Both the Canadian 'bloodbath budget' and the actions of the Swedish Government were committed to make a single major change which would address all the deficit issues at once. Again the clear advice of the former Swedish Prime Minister was that the whole of the issue had to be addressed in a single package of measures and an approach to dealing with the issue in stages was unlikely to prove acceptable. It was inevitable that the changes would provoke significant opposition and special pleading and if an extended period of time was taken to come at the issue time and time again, then it was inevitable that opposition would

build to the stage where it would become politically impossible to achieve the change. The Canadian experience was based on the back of previous attempts to deal with the public sector deficit through a range of 22 individual initiatives that had proved unsuccessful in the past. The approach that was adopted was a single rigorous zero-based budgeting arrangement which challenged every non-statutory expenditure head and not only asked questions about the outcomes resulting from the expenditure, but also asked what agency was best placed to deliver it – national, local, or voluntary – and finally whether it could be afforded in any case. The Coalition Government appears to have taken this message to heart. The last Budget of the outgoing Labour Government proposed arrangements which would have dealt with around 70% of the deficit over the period of the next Parliament, the Coalition Government is now proposing measures which will deal with 105% of the deficit over the same period.

- *Build public support by consultation.* Canada in particular undertook a significant level of public consultation in making the changes needed to deal with public sector deficit. The outcomes of this consultation were not what had generally been expected. On the whole people did not attempt to defend every single item of current expenditure. When asked to decide upon priorities there was a general agreement that the level of welfare payments actually should be increased, whilst the number of other programmes were cut by 50% or eliminated altogether. The apparent success of this consultation exercise encourage the Coalition Government to embark on a wider discussion exercise through its 'Big Society' initiatives, and a number of local government bodies have similarly undertaken exercises to ask the public for their views on where the cuts to budgets should be made. However it's important not to overplay the importance of consultation in the Canadian exercise. The zero-based budgeting exercise was based on 'Star Chamber' type of analysis which was informed by the consultation; but the decision was not handed over to the public to make.

There were two further lessons from the Swedish and Canadian experiences which do not appear to have been carried forward in the thinking of the UK Government:

- *No protections.* Goran Persson, the former Swedish Prime Minister, and Jean Chrétien, the former Canadian Prime Minister, have both made it abundantly clear that in carrying out the policy of reducing the public sector deficit in their countries nothing was ruled out. Indeed Chrétien made explicit that nothing was 'off the table', and Persson has suggested that it is a very dangerous precedent to suggest that any part of the budget should receive protection. Perhaps the most cogent explanation of the reasoning behind this approach was given by Sammy Wilson, the Northern Ireland Assembly Finance Minister, in a presentation to the

CIPFA Northern Ireland Conference in 2010. He made it clear that, not-withstanding the UK Government's wish to protect the National Health Service and not to have any real terms cuts, he was not prepared to carry this forward in the Northern Ireland Devolved Administration for two reasons. First, the impact of protecting any significant level of service has a consequent impact on the services which may make the achievement of the overall objective practically impossible. The Institute for Fiscal Studies has estimated that the cost of protecting the NHS budget in real terms, together with the proposal to protect the overseas aid budget raises the impact from an average 14% reduction for all government departments to 25%. The need to have some differential between priority spending areas and non-priority spending areas lay behind the requirement of each Government department to prepare initiative reductions of 25% and 40% prior to the Comprehensive Spending Review. The second reason was that within the protected budgets there would be a tendency for people to ignore the need to find efficiency savings and this distorted priorities. To some extent the need to find efficiency savings, even within the protected budgets, is there because it has become clear that in the National Health Service the impact of demographic change, inflation above the average level, and increases in demand as a result of improved medical care means that reductions of the order of 5–8% are being looked for in the budgets of health service organisations in any case. Nevertheless the point is well made that areas outside the protected budgets may have a higher priority than areas of inefficiency within the protected budgets which are given insufficient scrutiny because of protection.

- *Making the fix permanent.* In looking to the future, the changes in the Swedish public sector sought to address areas where there would be future budget problems if issues were not addressed. Significant changes were made in the areas of education, and pensions, for example, which were aimed at ensuring that once the adjustment had been made the deficit did not creep up again over a period of time requiring subsequent changes. This contrasts, in part, with Canada where the impact of the current recession has created a demand for further reductions in the Canadian public sector. Notwithstanding the 'do it all at once' approach these further reductions are proving to be more difficult than were the first. Nevertheless, the fact that Canada retained a relatively tight regulatory regime on its banks, and therefore did not have to bail them out in the 2008/9 crisis, has meant that the changes it now needs to make to the public sector are less than in other countries. Sweden, on the other hand, is now running a balanced budget as a result of its long-term changes. Although the UK Government has started to address some of the longer-term issues around pensions, a number of the significant issues that we introduced in Chapter 2, and which would have long-term implications for the public sector deficit, do not appear to be currently on the radar.

Economic contexts

The relative success of the public sector finance reforms in Sweden and Canada in the mid-1990s have to be set in the context of the economic environment of those two countries during that period. Both countries began their reforms at a time when their economies were not doing well, but by the time the reforms were being implemented the economy, both international and domestic, had improved considerably. In some part, the improvements in the public finances of these two countries were addressed by a growing economy, increasing taxation receipts, and reduced level public welfare expenditure. Therefore, in looking at the UK situation into the future is important to set the likelihood of success in any readjustment of the public sector finances in the context of the likely economic growth rate of the economy. Indeed it is this factor, and the associated risk, which is central to the debate. It is the point where opinion diverges dramatically between political parties and commentators. So it is therefore worth looking at the current state of some other economies that are ahead of the UK in dealing with a crisis in their public finances but are doing so against a backdrop of poor international economic conditions.

Box 3.4 outlines the case of the Republic of Ireland. Having made the decision to support the economy by taking on the deficits of the failing Irish banking sector the Irish Government was forced to implement serious cuts in 2009/10 to address the consequential debt and deficit problem. The Irish economy, having moved into recession, exacerbated the public sector deficit position. A major readjustment (up to 40%) in property asset prices is still working its way through the economy. The Irish Government has subsequently faced the problem of not being clear what the total liabilities of the banks were, because of the complexity of interbank dealings, derivatives, and the securitisation of assets. The Irish Government has found it particularly difficult to devise an exit strategy from its unconditional guarantee position which does not reverse the 'hot money' that flowed into the Irish banks when the guarantee was given. In September 2010, the Irish Government finally determined, through its arm's-length agency NAMA, to crystallise the liabilities of the banks. The Anglo Irish Bank, the most aggressive and reckless of the lenders into the property market during the boom, alone has an estimated debt of £30 billion. This debt, taken by the Government, increased its borrowing requirement for 2010/11 from 12% of GDP (compared to the UK's 10%) to nearer 32%. The nervousness of financial markets to such a deficit position has resulted in increasingly wide funding rates for Irish sovereign debt, thus worsening the deficit position. A further round of significant reductions had to be proposed, and the public reaction to these is both resentful of the Government and expresses considerable anger against the banks. The Irish economy appears to be heading for a 'double dip' recession as a result of these changes, notwithstanding the Government exhortation to consumers to maintain and increase the expenditure into the economy. Ireland therefore continues to be one of the more difficult economies as part of the so-called PIIGS grouping – Portugal, Ireland, Italy, Greece, and Spain.

Box 3.4   Ireland – the fall of the Celtic Tiger

During the period of the late 1990s and the first decade of the 21st century the Irish economy experienced a period of considerable growth. Significantly, financial subsidies from the EU to its farming community, and enormous infrastructure investments, helped to develop the economy and build new industries. These changes also included a major property boom, which at one stage contributed around 30% of the economic growth of the country. There was in the same time a significant increase in asset prices, thus setting the conditions for a property-based speculative boom similar to that experienced in a number of other countries. This boom was financed by aggressive lending on behalf of Irish banks that were substantially deregulated. One bank in particular – the Anglo Irish Bank – grew rapidly as a result of aggressive lending into the property market.

With the downturn in the international economy leading subsequently to the collapse of the financial system, culminating in the bankruptcy of Lehman Bros, interbank lending, which had been used extensively by Irish banks to support their lending, as the domestic deposit base was too small, created a financial crisis within the country. Wishing to avoid a serious effect on the Irish economy, and wishing to protect domestic depositors, the Irish Government chose to issue an unconditional guarantee of all Irish bank lending deposits in October 2008. This move, which was taken unilaterally, came as a surprise to many of the countries who were also in the Eurozone. A number, including the UK, were forced to match the Irish guarantee in part by increasing the deposit protection of their own bank depositors.

The unconditional nature of the Irish bank guarantee meant that it became particularly an attractive place to deposit spare bank funds, with the result that the Irish banks continue to attract significant overseas deposits and deposit from other banks. However, the impact on public finances was considerable. From a reasonable deficit of around 25% of GDP the total indebtedness of the Irish government rose rapidly, and continues to rise to levels which are predicted to be more than 100% of GDP. In part the 'blank cheque' that the Irish Government offered to sign adopted the losses of banks and made them part of the public debt. One of the great difficulties that the Irish Government has had is that it is unable to quantify the total amount of that debt, partly as a result of the use of derivatives and the securitisation of assets currently held by Irish banks which have an uncertain pattern for future repayment.

In December 2009 the Irish Government was forced to take steps to reduce its budget deficit to around 3% of GDP over a five-year period. To meet that target it cut public expenditure in 2010 by €4 billion, around 2.5% of GDP, and committed itself to a further €6.5 billion reduction before 2014. If successful, it was hoped that these reductions would reduce the maximum amount of public debt to GDP to 86%. These reductions were achieved by making significant reductions in public expenditure, reducing public sector workers pay, introducing a 'pension tax' to pay for future pension liabilities of the public sector, by introducing a slew of charges for the use of public services, including health.

However, by the second half of 2010, it became clear that these measures would be insufficient. The increasing uncertainty about the total amount of liability being taken on by the Irish Government as result of its bank bailout made bond-holders unsure and uncertain the Irish Government would continue to reduce its deficit sufficiently. Interest rates for sovereign debt rose further increasing the interest rate burden that the Irish Government had to bear. The Irish Government had taken steps through the National Asset Management Agency to take on the worst performing property loans from Ireland's banks in exchange for bonds. This attempt to take the cost of the banks 'off-balance-sheet' was not successful and as a result the cost of these bonds is subsumed in the total amount of debt owed by the Irish Government.

The Irish Government has now undertaken a further series of expenditure reductions in the attempt to bring its finances under control, and prevent a 'sovereign debt crisis' similar to, but not as bad as, that of Greece, in return for financial support from the EU. The long-term solution to this problem is the growth of the Irish economy to restore, through taxation, the public finances to a more stable state. However, the further withdrawal of public funding now seems likely to create the conditions in Ireland for 'double dip' recession, to the extent that the then Taoiseach, Brian Cowen, encouraged Irish consumers to spend rather than save in an attempt to encourage economic growth. The unpopularity of the Government increased following these measures and led to a period of political instability resolved only by further elections.

Unemployment rates in Spain have already risen considerably as the economy moved into recession and the Government has made unpopular decisions to address its deficit. Notwithstanding the actions already taken, in September 2010 credit rating agencies have begun to down rate Spanish sovereign debt thus increasing the costs of borrowing, and worsening the situation. The situation in Greece came to a head in May 2010 when the fragility of the Greek economy within the euro was exposed, and it became apparent that at its accession to the Eurozone the true state of the Greek economy had been concealed, in part, by the actions of some merchant banks through financial instruments that presented an apparently more favourable position of the Greek economy. The cultural issues with regard to taxation and public sector expenditure within the country (it has been said that the level of evasion and avoidance of tax in Greece is such that the payment of tax is virtually a voluntary activity) has led to considerable public disorder on a number of occasions. The political commentator Andrew Neil has remarked that it was the civil unrest in Greece and the problems that it faced with regard to its sovereign debt and downgrading of its credit rating that encouraged the Liberal Democrats, who were then in negotiation with the Conservatives over the Coalition

Government arrangements, to modify their pre-election position with regard to the speed of adjustment of public finances to a point closer to the Conservatives namely that of a more rapid adjustment with the aim of eliminating the deficit of the period of a single Parliament and thus allowed the Coalition to reach an agreement.

So the recent history of countries attempting to make a public sector financial adjustment against the backdrop of a national and international recession is not encouraging. There remains a real possibility of repeating the circumstances of the 1930s when repeated reductions in public expenditure rebounded through the economy reducing the level of aggregate demand, driving the economy lower, and reducing even further the level of tax receipts while stubbornly maintaining pressure on public expenditure, thus failing to remedy the underlying deficit situation. The possibility of this continuing for a substantial period of time has to be borne in mind, as the experience of Japan in the 1990s shows (see Box 3.5). Although the Japanese economy has some peculiar characteristics which relate to the unique culture of the Japanese people, careful analysis of the so-called lost decade illustrates the impact of not addressing the under capitalisation of banks following the collapse of an asset price bubble; the ineffectiveness of low interest rates in promoting economic activity (Keynes called it 'pushing on a string') and the significant impact as reforms are worked through before they show any sign of improvement in the domestic economy. The experience of Japan also indicates the political and social consequences of undermining the essential sense of equity within the society, which is currently being worked through in the context of the further downturn in the Japanese economy which came as a result of the international recession in 2008/9.

Box 3.5   Stagnation in Japan

In the period following the Second World War a number of countries, including Japan, Germany, and France, adopted a set of policies that might broadly described as a Coordinated Market Economy approach, in contrast, the US and UK who adopted much more 'liberal' open capitalist free market economy arrangements. The Coordinated Market Economies were characterised by close interrelationships between Government, trade unions, and businesses and was seen, in part, to be responsible for the 'economic miracles' that constituted a revival of major economies from the Second World War.

Coordinated arrangements within the Japanese economy were particularly strong. These included the close relationship between manufacturers and their suppliers; the lifetime employment guarantee for the significant minority of workers who were employed in major industries; a symbiotic relationship between the Japanese state and industry – a single party remained in power the whole of the period from the Second World War to 2009; close working relationships between trade unions and industry; and the implicit guarantee by central government against a substantive bankruptcy of any major part of Japanese industry. With rigid controls on currency and overseas lending the Japanese consumer was encouraged to save significant amounts of income. In part this reflected the fact that there was a cultural expectation that children would look after parents in old age, with a correspondingly weak and underdeveloped pension and elderly care systems. Savings for retirement were therefore high. In Japan these arrangements were solidly backed by strong corporate control society, which valued the group above the individual. In part, they carry forward the basic principles of the Meiji restoration from 1868, in which Japan chose specifically to adopt a western style economy in contradistinction to its Asian neighbours, and a strong internal culture relying on domestic reinvestment to grow the economy. This strong focus on the cultural integrity and unity of Japan, when influenced by the taint of militarism, was partly responsible for aggressive colonialist behaviour of Japan in the interwar period, leading ultimately to its entry into the Second World War. Post War as Japan continued to have significant financial internal surpluses, together with a significant trade surplus, the yen appreciated against overseas currencies. Japanese companies invested heavily in innovation and capital investment, which further reduced the unit cost of Japanese goods and increase the trade surplus further.

By the early 1980s, the strength of the Japanese economy and the relatively defensive nature of its trade surplus created significant international pressure on Japan to comply with deregulatory regimes being implemented in many major OECD countries. As a result, Japan deregulated its financial institutions and banks in the early 1980s, but the continuance of the Coordinated Market Economy approach meant there was considerable reluctance towards the establishment of a financial supervisory regime. With significant amounts of financial surplus, Japanese companies invested heavily in each other using the so-called tokkin money, to the extent that the earnings of some Japanese industries came largely from investments in other companies, and in property, which resulted in significant increases in the value of property assets. This created the conditions in the late 1980s for a major speculative bubble. When in the early 1990s there was a downturn in the international economy the speculative bubble burst, and the Japanese economy was plunged into recession, with a dramatic fall in asset prices, and the stock market. Financial institutions, and banks in particular, found themselves with significant amounts of non-performing loans on their balance sheets and facing the kind of international crisis on a domestic level that was later to be experienced in 2008/9.

The response of the Japanese Government was to dither in a period of significant delay in response to the crisis. Although interest rates were slashed to near zero in order to stimulate the economy, the Japanese Government was tied into a complex system of interrelated relationships to support the economy, and was unwilling to recapitalise the banks in order to encourage the flow of lending. As a result, many of the banks were left to restructure their balance sheets over a period of time, and became virtual 'zombie banks'. These banks recovered their balance sheets but during the process of doing so stopped their lending into the real economy. Indeed, it proved difficult for many banks to find homes for their loans funds which attracted even a reasonable rate of return. A number of banks resorted to placing deposits with other banks in default of doing anything else.

Gradually during the late 1990s it was realised that there needed to be a significant number of reforms to liberalise the Japanese economy and place it on a more liberal market-based footing. This involved Japan finally dismantling the arrangements of the Coordinated Market Economy, which had been the mainstay of its economic growth during the years of the economic miracle following the Second World War. The abandonment of the links between major manufacturers and their suppliers, and the abandonment of the lifelong employment guarantees, together with the implicit bankruptcy guarantee from central government, all proved difficult to achieve. They brought a sharp increase in the unemployment rate from an historical average of around 2% to 5.5% by 2001. Despite these changes it proved difficult to break the high level of interrelationship between industry, trade unions, and the government, and the inherent cultural underpinnings of traditional Japanese society attitudes. Nevertheless, by the latter part of the next decade Japanese economy was more open, and there was a significantly increased level of foreign investment in Japanese industry. The speed of change, however, had been very slow and the period of stagnating growth has been referred to as 'the lost decade'. As the process of liberalisation continued, the return on assets of Japanese companies fell from its high of 8% in 1990 to a low of 2.5% in 2001 before recovering to 6% by 2005.

As a major manufacturing and exporting country Japan was hit hard by the global crisis of 2008/9. Japanese GDP dropped 3.3% in the last quarter of 2008 and continued throughout 2009. Unemployment went up from 3.8% in October 2008 to a post-war peak of 5.6% in July 2009. Yet, notwithstanding this, the impact of the financial crisis and property market speculative bubble did not affect Japan as greatly as other Western economies. In part this was the result of Japanese banks, having been in 'zombie' status for such a long period of time, not investing heavily in the sub-prime mortgage securities, derivatives, and securitised products. The impact of the collapse was therefore not transmitted through the Japanese financial system. During this period, Japanese savings were looking for significant return within the country but failing this they built up their holdings of US Treasury stock, like China, to significantly higher levels than had been historically the case. The wish not to see the value of these assets depreciated acted as a significant break on the Japanese economy so that it proved more acceptable to take the losses through manufacturing them to see the value of these assets diminished. Nevertheless, in 2009 there was a major change of government – the first time since the Second World War. The result of the liberalisation of the Japanese economy had been to increase the level of inequality from well below average of OECD countries to an above average position. In cultural terms, this proved unacceptable to many Japanese, and the new Government elected in 2009 did so on an implicit undertaking that it would readopt some of the key characteristics of the Coordinated Market Economy.

The impact of economic theories

In his introduction to the 'General Theory', John Maynard Keynes said:

> The power of economic theory is greater than is generally imagined. Practical men of affairs, who believe themselves quite immune from its

influence, are usually the slaves of some defunct economist, and madmen in authority, who hear voices in the air, are distilling their frenzy from some academic scribbler of a few years back. (Keynes 1935)

The current debate about the speed of adjustment for the UK public sector deficit is very largely bound up by the different views of economic reality that are a result of economic theorising. Essentially there are two contrasting views: that of economic orthodoxy, for which 'sound money' is shorthand and that of the economic radicals which might be broadly described as Keynesian. Neither of these two shorthand descriptions does full justice to the range of economic thinking that lies behind them, but it does influence the way that governments think and act.

There is not scope within this book to rehearse in detail the characteristics of 'sound money' and Keynesianism in all its variants. We will return to this issue briefly when we look at the radical alternatives later. However, it is worth drawing out three key points because these tend to underpin basic economic thinking. That tends to influence the way that the political establishment, in its widest sense, views public policy, which in turn influences the degree to which it is felt that a more or less rapid adjustment to deal with the public sector financial deficit is felt desirable.

The orthodox economic theory assumes that, provided there is free flow of information; transparency within markets; no overt monopolies or monopsonies; and flexibility of prices, then the overall market equilibrium that will emerge is one which will ensure that there are no productive resources unused, and one which maximises the collective welfare of the community. There are a lot of assumptions that lie behind this bald statement, and the impact of variations in them has been the stuff of economic analysis over many years, but it remains the basic prediction of economic orthodoxy, and of the Anglo-American liberal economic tradition. Whilst there is a legitimate role for the public sector within the economy, the general assumption is that it should be at a minimal level. From the earliest, works of people such as Adolph Wagner, in his book *An der Theorie des Finanzwissenschafts* (Musgrove and Peacock 1958), aimed at showing that there was an optimal size for the public sector. If the public sector became too large its effect was to 'crowd out' private sector initiative, enterprise, and economic activity, and overall, this reduced the level of growth, and welfare within the equilibrium economy. The monetarist critique suggested that the public sector should not attempt to manage economies, and instead should adopt simple monetarist rules to avoid inflation and minimise the level of its interference. This thinking underpinned the deregulation and resurgence of the Anglo-American liberal economic tradition during the 1980s, and was material in the development of the New Public Management ideas of the 1990s and first decade of the 21st century.

One of the key outcomes of the orthodox theory is the pattern of distribution of income. It is an output of markets, and not an input to them.

However, left to its own devices an unregulated capitalist market economy produces a pattern of income distribution that is widely felt to be socially unacceptable in both Western-style democracies, and even in more authoritarian far eastern regimes. It was typified by Will Hutton who described it as the '40:30:30' society in his writings (Hutton 1995). In a capitalist economy 40% of people did well in terms of distribution of income, a further 30% did well when the economy was growing, but tended to be losers when the economy was in recession, whilst 30% found that the market economy left them with inadequate income levels that placed them at or below the relative poverty line for their society. In order to achieve electoral success political parties need to maximise their votes from the majority of the 40%, and a significant part of the middle 30% – especially in the 'first past the post' electoral system. Generally it is felt to be politically, socially, ethically, and morally unacceptable to have such a high percentage of people within a free-market economy below the poverty line. Countries therefore generally have some form of welfare system aimed at reducing the bottom 30% to a more acceptable level. The more acceptable level depends on the nature and culture of the society, and it is welfare payments in and around achieving what is felt to be equitable for society that broadly determines the overall level of public sector expenditure in relationship to GDP. In most European nations, and particularly in Scandinavian economies, reducing the overall level of poverty has a high priority and welfare arrangements are consequently high with public sector to GDP ratios in the order of 50%. In the US the belief in enterprise and personal advancement based on a meritocracy, however ill-founded in practice, tended to reduce the acceptability of welfare payments, with the consequence that overall the percentage of Americans in poverty is at a higher level than would be tolerated in Europe. The public sector to GDP ratio is therefore of the order of 30%. The consequence is that the UK public sector to GDP ratio averages out at about 40%, with minor variations up or down being the foundation of the individual manifestoes of political parties to right or left.

These three predictions of outcomes from orthodox economic theory have tended to underpin much of the discussion around the size of the public sector – both long-term and in the context of the current public sector deficit. Contrasted with these is the work of a number of radicals who have tended to provide a critique of the neoclassical orthodox 'sound money' pattern of economic thinking. One of the earliest of these was Karl Marx, whose analysis of the capitalist free-market system suggested that it had 'inherent contradictions' and would collapse internally, thus giving the opportunity of the establishment of a worker-led Communist system. While the revolutionary aspects of this were taken forward by Lenin and Trotsky and underpinned the development of the Communist systems in Russia, China, and a number of other states, the collapse of European communism after 1989 was seen to be the final vindication of the truth of economic orthodoxy, and the defeat of the Marxian critique. The subsequent events of the economic crisis in 2008/9 have been referred to by some as representing 'Marx's revenge'!

Other critiques of the orthodox economic thinking come from economists such as Veblen and Galbraith. Indeed, the best overall description of the pattern of behaviour behind economic bubbles and their collapse is to be found in J.K. Galbraith's book on 'The Great Crash' (Galbraith 1954), which was widely being circulated by concerned commentators in advance of the current financial crisis, and has proved such a classic exposition that it has never been out of print. Some commentators have suggested that the kind of experience described in the book is not the result of peculiar circumstances, but is an inherent feature of the capitalist market system operating under orthodox principles, pointing to the stock market crash of 1987; the dot-com bubble of the late 1990s; the bank crises of Victorian times; the railway boom; and pitching back as far as the pre–Industrial Revolution South Sea bubble and the 'tulip bubble'! For them, what has happened with the collapse of the finance and banking system and the property-based asset price bubble is the norm to be expected, not the exception, and public policy around regulation and management of the economy is needed to avoid such disasters in future.

However, perhaps the most salient critique of the 20th century of the orthodox economic theory came from John Maynard Keynes's writings during the 1930s culminating in his 1935 book *The General Theory of Employment, Interest and Money* (Keynes 1935). What Keynes wished to demonstrate was that the first prediction of the orthodox economic theory – that in a free market clearing arrangement resources would always be fully employed – was fundamentally untrue. He tried to establish that it was possible for the economy to move from one level of activity to a lower level of activity and both to be in stable equilibrium positions from which the economy would not move unless compelled to by external change. The economy therefore needed to be managed, and the key to do this was around the distribution of income which represented an input in the Keynesian system and not an output. In order to do this the markets could not be left in an unregulated arrangement, but the public sector would have to intervene to fund by deficits and surpluses putting money into the economy or taking money out of the economy through aggregate demand. The use of the 'multiplier' would ensure that the money, through circulation, generated a greater level of activity than the initial value of the input. In respect of public sector interventions, financed by taxation, he suggested that the generated level of economic activity would be greater than the tax removed and that the 'balanced budget multiplier' was therefore positive. This argued that it was desirable that there should be a significant public sector, and not a minimal one. This radical critique of the most fundamental outcomes of orthodox theory was the subject of detailed analysis and thinking during the 1950s.

The acceptance of this general principle that the economy needed to be managed in order to maintain a high level of employment underlay the thinking behind the Co-ordinated Market Economy policies of the 1950s and 1960s. It was Keynes's work through the Bretton Woods agreement of 1944 that provided the international infrastructure that underpinned these policies. But the synthesis of traditional economic thinking, and Keynes's work, that provided the 'macroeconomics/microeconomics' dissonance of economic thinking during the 1950s and 1960s, was always unsatisfactory. The collapse of the fixed exchange rate mechanisms and the Smithsonian Agreement of 1971 ushered in a new orthodoxy in Monetarism which has underpinned political economic thinking since. The development of economics during this period, which has tended to look back at the orthodox economic theory assumptions and provide theoretical 'tweaks', has been widely attacked as being both unrealistic and unhelpful. So for example the idea that the interests of the managers of financial institutions might not coincide with the interests of their owners has been analysed as the 'principal/agent' theory; the idea that actors in an economic market might be influenced by market-based trends, instead of their own analysis, has become part of 'behavioural economics', and the idea that people might use information in the market and the difference between producer and consumer in terms of information availability has been regarded as the issue of 'asymmetry of information'. Whilst these have provided some useful insights, they have not challenged the basic underlying economic theory, which is what Keynes intended to do. One of the severest critiques of orthodox economic theory is that it failed, quite impressively, to predict the collapse of the financial system under the international recession of 2008/9. Indeed, carefully constructed mathematical models, suggested that the risk of the 2008/9 circumstances occurring was in the order of one in eight billion – notwithstanding the commentary of Galbraith and his followers about the repeated nature of economic bubbles.

We will return to the issues of economic thinking as we examine alternatives to the current pattern of thinking in Part III of this book. However, at this point its worth briefly considering how the alternative approaches implied in economic orthodoxy and Keynesianism are applied to the thinking about how fast the UK needs to address its public sector deficit.

'Sound money' thinking emphasises the need to address the deficit quickly. Failure to do so will be perceived by the markets, who are in any case operating along 'sound money' principles, as placing a risk on the sovereign debt of the UK, reducing its credit rating below the current 'Triple-A' status, and thus ensuring that the significant level of debt that may have to be carried for some time would have to be funded of higher interest rates. It has been suggested that each 1% increase in average interest rate would add a further 1% to the structural element of GDP that would need to be addressed by the Government. The general assumption is that reducing the level of the public sector deficit by introducing a combination of expenditure and taxation changes would remove aggregate demand from the economy which would be replaced by a more rapid growth in the private sector which would tend to reduce the employment effects, with consequent lower welfare payments, and which would, by improving taxation receipts, mitigate the damage on public sector dependent areas and individuals. It would be preferable to make the majority of reductions through expenditure cuts rather than through taxation increases, as the latter would impinge directly upon private sector growth and enterprise capacity, and therefore a taxation-based policy would extend the timescale for adjustment. In any case, the more orthodox economic theory might suggest that a smaller size public sector was beneficial in the long-term.

A more Keynesian approach would point out that too speedy a reduction in the public sector deficit would reduce the overall level of aggregate demand and that consequent upon this, the multiplier effect would ensure that the economy had only low growth potential, or possibly entered a 'double dip' recession. Keynesians would also point out that it will be the natural tendency of individuals facing an uncertain economic future to increase their level of savings under the precautionary motive, which would further reduce the level of private consumption and exacerbate the situation. In answer to the criticism that recent Government refinancing of the banks by debt had failed to stimulate the economy, the more fundamental Keynesian comment would be that the recapitalisation of banks represented the poorest way of placing money into the economy in order to gain the maximum multiplier, since this was simply used by the banks to readjust their balance sheet, which, in any case, are going to take a considerable amount of time before they are re-stabilised, with consequent loss of lending capacity. Thus, without having a thorough going public sector funded input into the economy and alternative lending arrangements, the economy is likely to underperform for an indefinite period. However, taking a longer period to adjust the deficit will increase the overall total of debt paid, and extend the economic adjustment for up to 2 to 3 years, and run the risk of a sovereign debt crisis with down rating from credit rating agencies adding to the problems.

Any Government will be currently walking a tightrope of policy between the dangers of going too fast, or of going too slow. In part the pattern appears to resemble the 'Harrod–Domar' growth model in which the path to virtuous growth proceeded along a knife edge. If there is deviation to one side or the other the economy would crash into an uncontrollable position – either recession tending to depression or a sovereign debt crisis leading to practical community bankruptcy (such as the case of Iceland, Greece, or potentially Ireland) requiring long-term external bailout by supranational institutions who would demand, for their support, a more orthodox financial policy.

It is this dilemma which lies at the root of the policy differences between the US and most other European countries in their handling of the economy during the current economic crisis. The United States has adopted a much more 'Keynesian' policy with significant investments into infrastructure by the Federal Government. However, the overall effect of this is somewhat offset by the impact of state governments who are adopting a more 'sound money' approach and are busily cutting their budgets at the same time that the Federal Government is increasing theirs, and the federal deficit to boot. European countries, by contrast, are adopting a much more 'sound money' approach and despite attempts at the G8 summit in New York to align their interventions and policies, this fundamental difference prevented an effective coordination between Governments. The difference between these two approaches is difficult to explain in terms of the underlying assumptions of Governments about economic reality. It is more likely they are the result of the relative openness of the economies internationally. The United States with a very large stronger domestic economy, and a relatively small reliance on international trade, is much more able to adopt domestically determined policies without fear of reaction from the global financial markets. Europe, on the other hand, has very open internationally traded economies, and no doubt fears that if they adopt a more deficit financing approach then the result will be that the financial markets will take fright and the hot money flows will worsen interest rates and create further difficulties.

The debate on this issue is ongoing. When the UK economy posted poor results for the last quarter of 2010, Anatole Kaletsky writing in the *Times* commented on the difference between the performance of the UK economy with a contraction of 0.5% and its austerity measures, compared to the US economy, with its more Keynesian counter cyclical investment policy, which showed a growth of 1% for the same period. However, when subsequent UK economic information was more favourable, commentators suggested that the more monetarist UK approach will ultimately prove successful, and the more Keynesian US approach would be shown to be a 'busted flush'.

Conclusions: lessons for the UK

So, to what extent does the experience of other countries in undertaking fiscal consolidation give us guidance towards effective future policies, or reassurance that current policies are correct? In the UK, there were a number of other factors, peculiar to this country, which exacerbated the situation. In analysing the transferability of policy initiatives from any other country these special factors need to be borne in mind. There are four peculiar factors:

• First, as the UK public sector entered the international recession it did so from a poor starting point, as it already had a significant structural deficit which has been estimated by the Institute of Fiscal Studies at around £2 billion annually. In part this was the result of over ambitious spending programmes which failed to be matched by appropriate levels of taxation. Tony Travers of the London School of Economics has estimated that prior to the recession the UK was spending at around 42% of GDP in the public sector, whilst it was only taxing at 38%. This cumulative deficit had been running for a number of years, and, whatever the outcome of the international recession would, at some stage, have had to be addressed.

- Second, the UK has, partly as a result of its colonial past and Empire, always had a high level of openness to the international economy and London has always been a key centre of international trade financing. At present the UK financial sector based in the City of London accounts around 18 % of the UK's GDP – a significantly higher level that is necessary to fund the requirements of the UK economy. The size of this financial sector grew over the 1980s and 1990s as the UK moved increasingly away from manufacturing-based economy to a service-based economy. The reforms of the early 1980s and the Governments of Mrs Thatcher saw a significant rundown in industries producing primary products and manufacturing. Many of these industries had grown to be internationally uncompetitive and the incoming Conservative Government was unwilling, as a matter of principle and commitment to the prevalent monetarist economic theory, to continue the policy of earlier Labour Governments in the 1970s of artificially subsidising them. However as industries were run down, they were not replaced with equivalent manufacturing capacity, and it was widely accepted (perhaps unwisely) that service-based industries were the way that the UK economy should develop, rather than relying on a strong manufacturing base. So, when the international recession came, the financial nature of that recession and the way it was transmitted through the financial sectors meant that the UK was particularly vulnerable to its impacts, and particularly to its impact on the real economy. This vulnerability remains, for with the recovery in the financial sector, any Government would be reluctant to limit that sector's growth and contribution to tax and employment, even though it represents a continuing risk factor.

- Third, and related to this second point, was the enthusiasm with which the UK embraced the deregulatory environment of the mid-1980s through to the early years of the 21st century. During this period banks and financial services were significantly freed from regulatory activity, to the extent that when questions were raised in New York about the now defunct Lehman Bros financial accounting using the so-called Repo 105 arrangements – which effectively hid from the market the true impact of risky borrowing on the cash reserves of that organisation – the company simply undertook the transactions in London where the regulatory environment was less questioning of the validity of them. In a speech to Trade Union Congress Conference in 2010 the Governor of the Bank of

England, Mervyn King, accepted that during this period politicians and regulators had 'taken their eye off the ball' and had failed to manage the risk effectively that was being created by the banking sector. He contrasted this with the attractive character of the low inflation, high-growth and low interest rates economy that characterised the increasingly speculative market in the second half of the first decade of this century. It was the attractiveness of this growth, which boosted tax revenues, which allowed the then Chancellor Gordon Brown to realise his ambition of becoming Prime Minister in a long-running dispute with his predecessor Tony Blair. This ambition and the longevity of the feud that developed has been documented by Andrew Rawnsley in his book *The End of the Party* (Rawnsley 2010), and in Tony Blair's own autobiography published in 2010. The then Chancellor was encouraged to use taxation policy in order to develop a significant alternative welfare policy to that of the Prime Minister – who was anyway preoccupied with foreign affairs. The exercise of regulatory supervision of the risks being run by the banks, particular with regard to housing loans, was neglected.

- Fourth, within the UK there had been a significant growth in the level of overall indebtedness in the economy from the mid-1990s, which had been widely encouraged. After the impact of the recession in the early 1990s during the John Major Government, recovery had already started when the Labour Party assumed power in 1997 but it was largely fuelled through consumption, funded by consumer credit. This led to changing attitudes to indebtedness and savings ratios fell to historic lows. Much of the debt was taken out on the basis of the 'real income effect' in the housing market. House price escalation grew at a rapid rate generating the possibility of people taking out a mortgage up to, or in some cases greater, than the value of the property and still being able to repay the debt as house prices rose and people moved from property to property. Banks and other financial institutions chased this burgeoning level of mortgage debt, which increased not only in scale – to borrowers who might normally be expected to repay – but also in scope to include borrowers who were much more marginal. As a result, mortgages were either too large to be safe or had been lent to people who were vulnerable to non-repayment. This attitude to debt spilled out into the public sector. Governments who wished to make significant capital improvements were unable, or unwilling, to finance them through conventional debt relying instead on PFI and PPP financing packages effectively mortgaging the future taxation incomes of public sector organisations to the provision of services in increasingly large and complex contractual arrangements. At one stage it was reported that the Woolwich Health Authority had up to 60% of its annual income committed to debt and service repayments under this kind of arrangement as a result of a major reorganisation and expansion of facilities. This changing attitude to debt meant that as the recession bit, so individuals found themselves with debts that they could not repay, and therefore will need to significantly scale back their consumption in order to discharge, as far as possible, their indebtedness. The unwinding of these historically high levels of debt will add to the transition period to any recovery in public and private finances.

Figure 3.1 shows the significant hike in public sector debt in the UK as a result of the current recession and an estimate by the Institute of Fiscal Studies of the achievable rate of reduction.

The key point it shows is that recovering this debt is a long haul task. Whilst the individual political parties have debated, and continue to debate, the speed of the adjustments in the public sector finances that they are proposing as policy, in truth the different policies have only a very marginal impact on the slope of the line necessary to bring debt back to a long-term historic average of around 40% of GDP – which was the basis of Gordon Brown's 'golden rule' as Chancellor.

We conclude that although the international nature of the recession, and the way it was transmitted through a highly integrated financial sector to a globalised economy was perhaps inevitable, the UK was particularly vulnerable both in terms of the poor starting position and a higher–than-average vulnerability to its impact, and it will take a considerable amount of time before the public finances are restored to a level of normality. When we look at how other countries have dealt with this kind of situation in the past, we need to bear in mind that it is simply not possible to transfer one country's experience to another, yet undoubtedly there will have been lessons learnt elsewhere which might inform the current and future strategy to deal with the UK public sector financial crisis.

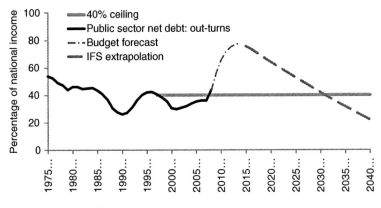

Figure 3.1   UK Public debt
Source: CIPFA/SOLACE/IFS

The comparative experience of other countries is instructive in examining some of the economic implications of policies aimed at addressing public sector financial deficits. However, no country provides a blueprint that, if followed in detail, will result in success. To a very large extent the changes currently being proposed in the UK public sector are being addressed in a relatively unique set of circumstances. The UK has a large financial services sector which makes it vulnerable, like Iceland and Ireland, but not so large in relation to its economy that is completely destabilising. The UK has already adopted many of the New Public Management ideas that underpinned the Swedish approach, but might usefully take on board some of the issues about addressing long-term structural stability through more formal balanced-budget approach than simply to rely on Governments keeping to a 'golden rule' as a matter of virtue. The zero-based approach of examining individual budgets used by Canada might better address the issue of public priorities than the more broad a brush 'salami slicing' approach of cutting all budgets equally, but only if the level of reductions being sought lies at a reasonable level and is not hiked by extensive protections of some budgets. The dangers of a prolonged economic recession lengthening the adjustment period, and undermining policies to address the deficit, are a feature of the Japanese experience (see Box 3.5), but the need for policies to avoid unacceptable equitable outcomes are also part of the Japanese experience, with the danger of social unrest and protest now beginning to emerge across a number of European countries.

Chapter 4 will look at the current set of Government proposals against a background of strategic options and outcomes to try and determine the underlying, but often unrevealed, thinking. The second part of the book will then look at the organisational and structural underpinnings that support and maintain that thinking, before the third part challenges it by looking at more radical alternatives and asking whether they might provide a better set of policies for going forward.

4
Strategic Background

In Chapter 3 we concluded that although the economic circumstances faced by the United Kingdom public sector have very strong similarities with those previously, or currently, being experienced across a wide range of Western economies the experience of other countries provides a guide, but does not provide a blueprint, for the way the UK public sector should be reformed in an age of austerity. In facing the future, with its particular pattern of characteristics, UK Governments will need to chart their own paths, learning from others as appropriate, but not slavishly following them.

Looking at the current government programme (HM Government 2010), it's clear that dealing with the public sector deficit and debt has the highest priority and the other social, governance and political ambitions set out in the document are dependent on achieving stability in public finances. Andrew Neill, the political commentator, has suggested that this is the 'glue' that holds together the Coalition Government. Having come to the view collectively that the deficit needed to be addressed more speedily than the Labour Government's plans on leaving office, almost all Government activity since, though it may have been addressing different issues, has had the deficit as a backdrop and conditioning factor. The focus has been on three key statements:

- the initial review of the outgoing Government's plans and the immediate £6 billion cuts package;
- the establishment of the Office of Budget Responsibility, it's review and forecasts of the strength of the economy, and the Emergency Budget;
- the discussion of options and initiatives leading up to the Spending Review of October 2010.

We will look at the content of each of the statements in due course, but in order to interpret them and look forward to the pattern of the public sector for the future two significant elements need to be addressed:

- *Vision* – what will we be aiming for? What should the public sector look like after the changes to deal with the financial deficit have been implemented?
- *Strategy* – how will we get there? How will we determine that we have been successful? What policies are an integral part of the strategy, and what is simply expedient and tactical?

Filling in these details, and answering the questions, is not immediately apparent. There are some generalised statements and aspirations within the Coalition document, and Ministers and commentators have implied, in what they have said, some thinking which might help to answer these questions. But nothing is explicit, and therefore this chapter will look at the framework for the future of the public sector in terms of vision or objectives and strategy to give a framework in which the current plans may be interpreted and some of the basic assumptions revealed.

What are the aims?

Interpreting the current pattern of statements made by Ministers and commentators suggests that there might be one of four possible patterns which sets the 'big' objectives for the future of the public service. These are:

- *No change* – which might seem a contradiction in terms but in fact is looking at the current pattern of changes as being largely temporary to get the public sector finances back on to a stable footing before continuing with an historical pattern of growth and development.
- *Reformed public sector* – this looks to address the deficit in the context of a major change in which public services and welfare is delivered, with the understanding that when stability has been reached the future trajectory of the public sector will be different from what it has been.
- *Small state* – the objective here is to deal with the public sector deficit by materially altering the boundary of the State's activities, and in particular making it a much smaller intervention than historically.
- *Reformed capitalism* – this looks to address the public sector deficit by changing the way in which the economy is managed so as to provide a long-term stable solution and prevent the re-occurrence of the circumstances which gave rise to the deficit in the first place.

These four patterns do not represent four distinct alternatives. Rather they are points on a continuum from 'no change' to the more radical alterations of 'reformed capitalism'. Nor does 'reformed capitalism' represent the end of the continuum, for there are a number of possible more radical alternatives.

However, at the present time these are not being espoused, and so, in looking at the government's proposals they provide something of an 'empty box'. More radical options will be discussed in Part III.

No change

It might seem bizarre to consider 'no change' as an objective, given the current state of public sector finances. However, the thinking behind this is that the public sector has grown in extent and pattern in such a way that it commands general public support. Whilst it might be understood that the current circumstances mean that there have to be temporary reductions in service, as soon as finances can be stabilised it would be back to 'business as usual', and services which have had to be curtailed, or investment which has had to be suspended, would be reinstated. This particular thinking fits in with some elements of the Labour Party, and the left of the Coalition partners, who fear that substantive change constitutes an 'attack on the welfare state' which they would resist. It also fits into the pattern of the managerialist conception of current politics that we introduced in Chapter 2. Politics, under managerialist thinking, is not about the achievement of significant visions, but about the effective and efficient delivery of public services on the more consumerist 'New Public Management' model. Politicians are not called upon to change the world, but to manage external circumstances in the best way possible. Changes therefore are likely to be small scale and organic, and if there are temporary setbacks, as the current circumstances might be presented, then they can be managed through, given enough time. This kind of thinking will therefore tend to make adjustments more carefully and slowly to avoid undue disruption and unplanned outcomes.

Reformed public sector

The underlying thinking here would say 'why waste a good crisis', so using the imperative to make significant changes in public sector finances to also make changes in the way that the public sector is both organised and services delivered differently with the aim in ending up with a more effective, more efficient, and possibly radically changed sector in the future. This kind of thinking seems to lie behind much of the Government's position. The foreword to the Coalition Government Programme makes it clear that both partners are expected to bring together their proposals for the reform of public service delivery, not on a 'lowest common denominator' basis, but by providing the basis for completely new Coalition policies, which are nevertheless aimed at achieving significant reform. Much of the discussion appears to be around the existing 'New Public Management' model of improved service delivery with its introduction of private sector reforms;

decentralisation and the creation of independent delivery units; and the development of community and co-operative organisations to deliver public services.

This approach means that Government will probably have to make choices in many areas but in some areas it seems reluctant to elucidate the nature of such choices or their implications. As an example, let us take the current UK budgetary position on defence. The reality is that a large proportion of UK armed forces (mainly the Army) is tied up in a protracted war in Afghanistan and seems likely to be there for some years to come. At the same time the defence budget is subject to significant cuts which will result in large reductions in armed forces manpower and also will have implications for equipment procurement. The application of cuts in the defence budget is understandable and fits in with the requirement outlined in the previous chapter that in making such cuts there should be no 'no go' areas.

However, the highly centralised Strategic Defence Review (SDR) which preceded the budget cuts was a hasty process (in comparison with what has been done in other countries), which has been heavily criticised in many quarters as being finance-led and not defence-led. Put another way, it seems more of a 'slash and burn' exercise rather than a true process of defence prioritisation which takes time to assess. The reduction in the defence budget coupled with the commitment in Afghanistan suggests that the UK needs to consider carefully its position in the world diplomatically and militarily. We are not a Great Power any more and we cannot resource the range of military activities that have been undertaken even in the recent past. However, Ministers will just not face up to this and, at the time of writing, have been talking up military intervention in the Middle East when we do not have the defence capability to do so. We must face up to the fact that the military choices we have made mean that the UK is taking a different position in world affairs than it has done in the past.

Small state

Matthew Parris, writing in the *Times* in early October 2010 (Parris 2010), criticised the article of a previous commentator who suggested that the Coalition Government was fixed on the managerialist solution to the current financial problems of the public sector (which might have placed it into the 'no change' part of the spectrum). He suggested that the Conservative part of the Coalition Government at least have a strong underlying ideology which was about minimising the size of the state, believing that this impinged on private initiative and freedoms, and that excessive public intervention created welfare dependency that is both costly and undesirable. Certainly, some of the thinking around welfare reform, which was such a central part of the Spending Review outcomes, could be seen in this light. Whilst this is not inherently part of the Liberal Democrat element of the Coalition partnership, it has long been a tradition of the more right-wing elements of the Conservative Party, although it has rarely been as clearly articulated as it was by Matthew Parris. However, it should also be remembered that in Chapter 2 we pointed out that while the 'small state' idea was traditionally part of Republican ideology in the USA, in practice the Bush administrations presided over huge growth in public spending, a situation which is now strongly challenged by the Tea Party movement. The importance of public services is not necessarily undermined by this concept, but the feeling is that such services should be part of the 'Big Society' thinking – that is provided by voluntary, charitable, and localised organisations run by individuals, and not the State. We will see later that this might considerably understate the importance of the 'Big Society' idea.

Reformed capitalism

The thinking behind this vision for the public services was perhaps best articulated by Vince Cable, the Business Secretary, in his presentation to the Liberal Democrat Conference in 2010. A long-standing critic of the activities of banks, institutional investors, and some elements of business practice, he suggested that part of the Coalition Government activities would be to look into these activities and provide significant regulatory reforms aimed at preventing the re-occurrence of the speculative bubbles that he had warned about whilst in opposition in the previous Parliament. Addressing these issues involves elements of the Co-ordinated Market Economy that introduce a specific regulatory and management role for the public services, and also is in line with the kind of budget reforms introduced in Sweden which set the pattern for public sector service changes for the future. This approach aims to make reforms to the public sector not by changing the priorities, structure, or objectives of individual services, but by changing the underlying regulatory and control frameworks and are seeking, by changing the system, to change behaviour and outcomes. These proposals were well received by the Liberal Democrat Conference, but with howls of protest by business leaders, the financial services sector, and a number of other economic commentators. More recently, the Prime Minister David Cameron was also criticised by business leaders for proposing greater and more real competition among private sector businesses. It does appear that business leaders who argue for greater competition in the public sector do not see such competition as a priority in their own backyards.

These four points that we've picked out on the spectrum, setting out the visions and objectives for the public services in the future, all found expression within the Coalition Government's Programme for Government and by subsequent speeches by Ministers, and in articles from political commentators. It is therefore difficult to pick out from this content which, if any, of the four 'visions' is the dominant one within the Government's thinking. Indeed, some commentators have suggested that whilst the Government might be held together by a common understanding of what needs to be done, it is being pulled apart by an unresolved tension as to what the final outcome should be. The tensions between them might yet prove to be some of the most difficult areas for the Coalition Government's policies, and it has been suggested that it is over this area alone that the Coalition Government might yet fall apart. It seems likely that the central focus will lie around the reformed public sector and small state visions for the future, with the status quo and more radical options being marginalised and/or watered-down.

More cynically, it might be argued that the public have no real interest in what the future shape of the public sector would look like, and are only interested in the immediate effect of any change upon them individually. Politicians have tended to be wedded to the idea of the 'March of Progress', believing that change is improvement; and that what is new is always superior to that which went before. But this idea, born of the Enlightenment, and strongly espoused during the rapid growth of industry and commerce in Victorian times, under the influence of scientific method and the expansion of knowledge, has been substantially undermined in the UK by the experiences of two world wars, a major Depression, and the loss of Great Power status in the 20th century. There is a much more pessimistic view that collective progress benefiting all is a chimera, and that any change is to the benefit of one faction at a cost to others, and that the swing of the political pendulum ensures that there is a broadly equitable balance between the factions over time. This fits in closely with the 'managerialist' revolution that has overwhelmed politics in the past 20 years – that people do not asked to see progress, only efficiency and personal choice which allows them to improve their personal circumstances. Politics, under these circumstances, is almost reduced the level of entertainment and informed discussion is replaced by scepticism and sarcasm. We do not hold entirely with the cynical view, the purposes and outcomes of public services are too important to the communities and individuals, and in Part III we will seek to propose radical solutions which, in part, are aimed at restoring the importance of political debate. Nevertheless, we have to recognise that in looking at the shape of the public services for the future a strong element of cynicism exists which undermines the ability of politicians to articulate a vision that gains public support and in many ways that cynicism is derived from the actions of those same politicians.

How will we get there? – strategy

We will look at the strategy implied in the Coalition Government's policy proposals for dealing with the deficit against a simple framework that was first proposed by Paul Jansen of McKinsey and Co (Jansen 2009). He proposed an approach described as 'Three Horizons' (H1, H2, and H3 for short) based on three strategic approaches:

- *H1 – Bridging*. These essentially are coping strategies. A coping strategy is one that is adopted to get an organisation through a particularly difficult patch, which is likely to be temporary. The classic example is that of a restaurant that will have a normal complement of staff to deal with taking orders, preparing food, serving, and washing-up. If the restaurant gets a sudden influx of diners then it will tend to adopt a coping strategy which emphasises taking orders, preparing and serving the food, but the washing-up can go hang until the restaurant is quieter. Coping strategies are essentially a 'get us through' approach. Within the context of adapting to the recession such strategies would be about trimming any obvious unnecessary costs; having a number of contingency plans to get the public sector through the worst of it; and using quick, rough justice, equality of pain, 'salami slicing' approaches to the reduction of budgets and costs.
- *H2 – Don't Waste a Good Crisis*. If significant changes have to be made, as they have to be in current circumstances, then this kind of strategic approach seeks to make changes which are of the longer-term outcomes and change the pattern of service delivery. Such proposals would seek to reset the costs of the organisation at a lower level. They would suggest taking on some of the 'sacred cows' of policy priorities. The approach would often be particularly aggressive, nominating and setting higher priorities for protection, and slashing at the lowest priorities completely. Where there are some provisions which are valued, but still subsidised, then the service provider may challenge users to make the services self-sufficient, or make proposals to withdraw support steadily and if the service does not attract alternative funding or significant political support, then it will be allowed to 'wither on the vine'. Where services are available, and valued, but essentially underused with excess capacity then users may be challenged to 'use it or lose it' and change their behaviours to take up the spare capacity, failing which it will be withdrawn.
- *H3 – 'Through Cycle' Structural Change*. This approach recognises the fact that the economy and public service finances may be going through a cyclical process, which will, in the course of time recover the basic financial position. However, the strategic approach here is to use the cycle in order to shift resources to strategic priorities and to make significant changes to the pattern of service delivery. This can include action to shift the public/private boundary so that individuals, communities, and private organisations are more responsible for delivery of community services. It can include identifying a number of legacy services which have been provided, often a statutory basis, for which the original justification is no longer valid or can be significantly challenged. Such services can be rapidly downscaled or removed altogether, or shifted across the public/private

boundary to have provision made elsewhere. Part of the changes working through the cycle might be to shift organisations through reorganisation to lower cost restructured service providers. This can address inter-organisational boundary situations which can create significant inefficiencies in service provision. Finally, the opportunity can be taken to invest heavily in new and developing technologies across the cycle to allow the final outcome to be delivered from a completely new technology platform that significantly reduces the cost base.

These three strategic approaches are applicable to different timescales. H1 – Bridging is typically something that happens in the short-term, and can deal with short-term crisis. H2 – Don't Waste a Good Crisis is something that will typically be dealt with by a number of specific projects or programmes which will operate in the medium-term to deliver change. H3 – Through Cycles Structural Change is typically aimed at a final endpoint which is some distance away and therefore likely to be a long-term strategy.

This threefold approach – short-, medium-, and long-term – was developed further by the International Futures Forum which looked at the interrelations between the three approaches and the way in which they complemented each other and could be used as a practical tool for designing a future strategy. In their view the H1 strategy worked well in the very short-term but will suffer from rapidly diminishing returns if prolonged. If the environment turned out to be one where there was not a rapid return to the pre-crisis position, then the value of the H1 approach would be lost. The H2 arrangement took time to gain the benefits, and to some extent the value of the immediate change tended to be lost, but the final outcome was an improved level of service delivery compared to the pre-crisis level, contrasted with the H1 solution in which the final outcome was, at best, only at the same level as previously. The H3 approach took a long time to show any significant improvements, requiring, as it did a major long-term view and restructuring. Initially its improvements will be marginal and often seemed to be ineffective, and therefore unattractive when faced with a significant immediate crisis.

The three approaches, however, could be seen as complementary to each other in two ways. Firstly, a combination of say H1 and H3 could ensure an immediate response to the crisis which met some of the need, but with the longer-term restructuring delivered towards the end of the crisis cycle. H1 represented an approach which 'got you through', until H3 delivered the final improvements. The H1 changes were therefore strictly temporary and were to be abandoned as soon as the structural changes started to deliver. Little or no effort therefore needs to be placed in maintaining the H1 arrangements. Secondly, the H1 and H2 arrangements can often complement one another in that changes that were developed using an H2 approach could be used in a 'pilot' sense by H1 changes and that therefore the value of the existing service delivery pattern could be maintained for a longer period, or even enhanced, compared to original pre-crisis point. However, it was almost inevitable that after a period of time the effectiveness of the new working arrangements, operating under a crisis management approach, would give diminishing returns. For example, a manufacturing industry which received a sudden large increase in orders might adopt an H1 strategy of working overtime to deliver the product. If the demand was sustained, then new improved ways of gaining efficiencies by the better use of existing equipment might enable the organisation to cope for a bit longer; but, if the situation was sustained for a significant period of time the new efficiencies, even if backed up with overtime, would start to show diminishing returns to meeting the crisis. In such circumstances a completely new technology might prove to be the only way in which the shift in demand could be met in the long-term. But, because of the long lead-in time to implementing and training on the new technology, a feasible approach might be to work the additional overtime, until the new technology could deliver. A lot depends on the degree to which the H1 strategy can be maintained, the speed of delivery of H2 and H3 approaches, the depth of the crisis, and the length of time within which the crisis stage is to be endured. The linkage of these three approaches – H1, H2, and H3 – to public services delivery in the current circumstances is clear.

The strategic approaches of H1, H2, and H3 can be further refined:

- The H1 approach which is short-term, expedient, and temporary is based on the assumption that it is 'business as usual', and that any crisis is temporary and the normal pattern of organisational behaviour and outcomes will be reasserted once the underlying environment is restored, and that the system has the power to be self-rectifying. The concept is that of a natural equilibrium to which the organisation, within its environment, will return once the disturbance, which moved it away from equilibrium, has been dealt with. The basic situation remains unchanged and unchallenged, as do its constituent supporting elements. It is most suited to an approach that believes that the economic environment is best explained by orthodox economic theory and that it will return to equilibrium quite quickly if permitted to do so, implying a relatively passive approach towards economic management, with no real requirement to make significant changes to the structure of the market economy. It is an approach based on status quo or stasis.
- The H2 approach is one which is based on the medium-term and does not imply 'business as usual'. A volatile environment has permanently changed the circumstances within which the service organisation must operate, and the changes which are called for to make the organisation more coherent and consistent with that changed environment. The basic situation however remains unchanged, but some of the supporting elements may themselves need to change which will adjust the final shape of the organisation. Again, the assumptions of orthodox economic theory

could be seen as generally supporting this approach, whilst recognising that the economy may need to be managed, and in some cases regulated, in order to produce a satisfactory outcome. However, this should be seen as an adjustment, rather than the whole scale managed approach. It is an evolutionary approach.

- The H3 approach is far more radical. It is long-term and proposes significant revolutionary change. Not only are individual elements of a situation challenged, but also is the whole situation. It is now considered to be an unsatisfactory description of reality which must be replaced with something completely different, supported by the same basic groups of elements, but which has been radically reinterpreted in the light of environment which is no longer just changed, but is totally different. To quote Dr McCoy from 'Star Trek': 'its life, Jim, but not as we know it!' Such an approach implies a radically different view from orthodox economic theory. It goes even beyond an approach of the Co-ordinated Market Economy to the economy, to one that proposes a completely different way of looking at the way the economy actually works, and thus demands a completely different way in which organisations should operate and public sector services should be delivered.

What do current policies indicate?

John Morris in his book *The Age of Arthur* (Morris 2001) refers to the difficulties that historians have in interpreting the post-Roman period of British history where there are few, if any, contemporary written documents to give us an insight into the threats and concerns that affected those in authority at a chaotic time. In the absence of any clear statements about objectives he looked to the disposition of defensive forces to assess what threats must have been uppermost in the minds of the warlords. In the absence of any clear understanding about the long-term vision, or strategic pattern adopted by the incoming Coalition Government towards dealing with the public sector financial crisis it is to the pattern of individual policy initiatives that we need to look in order to understand the thinking that might lie behind them.

Since coming to office the Coalition Government has introduced three significant policy initiatives – an immediate change in spending priorities of around £6 billion (Box 4.1), the Emergency Budget of June 2010 (Box 4.2), and the Spending Review of October 2010 (Box 4.3).

Box 4.1   The initial UK £6 billion cuts programme

During the election period the Conservative Party announced that it would make a reduction of at least £6 billion in public expenditure immediately following the election if it were elected. On 24th of May the incoming Chancellor, George

Osborne, announced a package of reductions with the headline figure of £6.2 billion, although £500 million was reinvested in further education, apprenticeships, and social housing leaving a net reduction of £5.7 billion.

The major cash contributors to the reductions came from saving £1.15 billion in discretionary areas of spend – largely on consultancy and travel costs; and £1.7 billion from delaying or stopping contracts and projects already planned. Other contributions came from reduced property costs (£170 million); a recruitment freeze within the civil service (estimated £120 million); £95 billion from savings in IT spending; £600 million from the abolition of QUANGOs; and £520 million from other 'low value' spending.

The distribution of these reductions by Department was £780 million from Communities and Local Government (7.2% of departmental spending); Transport £683 million (4.6%); Business, £836 million (3.8%); Education, £670 million (1.1%); and the Department of Justice. Devolved administrations in Scotland Wales Northern Ireland were expected to find £704 million for the reduction though they were given the option, which they all exercised, of delaying these reductions for a year.

There was a considerable amount of expediency in the area selected for reductions. The reduction in QUANGOs was largely chosen because the organisations did not have a basis in primary legislation and therefore could be abolished at Ministerial discretion. Much of the reduction in spending came from withdrawing support for schemes such as the Child Trust Scheme which had not got underway significantly. Simple measures such as a recruitment freeze, and requiring ministers and senior civil servants to travel by second class, public transport, or by using car sharing have a similar 'housekeeping' air about them.

The immediate effect of the reductions Programme was to reduce the deficit in 2009/10, however almost all of the savings were offset by the decision not to bring in a rise in National Insurance was included in the outgoing Labour Government's Budgets for 2011. Across the five-year period, therefore, the effect of this change was negligible, representing 1% of government spending and contributing only modestly to the overall deficit requirement estimated at £156 billion.

The real intention of the announcement was symbolic. It was intended to show that a pre-election promise had been kept very early on, and to indicate that the incoming Coalition Government would prioritise reductions in spending as a major element of its policy. The announcement had no particular strategic significance, nor did the elements of it constitute a consistent and coherent programme.

Box 4.2   The UK emergency budget

On 22 June 2010 the Chancellor introduced an Emergency Budget proposing some changes to the Budget of the outgoing Labour Government. The changes were aimed at reducing the structural deficit to a balanced budget position by the end of the term of the Parliament; taking some steps to improve the business environment to help boost growth in the economy; and by using elements of tax and benefits reform to achieve a fair distribution of the burden of reducing the public sector deficit.

The changes to the structural deficit implied an additional £40 billion annual reduction by 2014/5. Of these £32 billion was to come from spending reductions, £11 billion from well for savings, and £8 billion from tax increases. The key points were:

- Of the total reduction in current and capital spending, approximately 12% was a reduction in capital expenditure, however almost all of this was frontloaded, compared to the changes in current expenditure most of which were planned to be introduced towards the end of the Parliamentary period.
- The reduction in capital expenditure amounted to 26% or more of the total capital budget, a very significant reduction that the Government hoped would be filled by private sector expenditure.
- Of the £11 billion welfare reductions almost half were expected to come from the change of indexation from the higher RPI calculation (which includes housing and debt costs) to the CPI measure which is largely day-to-day household expenditure based.
- The freezing of Child Benefit, which was proposed to offset increases in Child Tax Credit, constitutes the largest other reduction, amounting to nearly a quarter of the total. The remaining elements came from capping Housing Benefit, and expected changes to Disability Benefit as a result of a process of re-examining eligibility.
- The largest contribution to the additional tax increase came from increasing Value Added Tax to 20% and changes to the Insurance Premium Tax from January 2011.

The Emergency Budget noted the uneven pattern of regional economic performance in the UK, with its heavy emphasis on London and the South-East as a focus for growth, and its sectoral imbalance with an undue reliance on services, particularly financial services. Some modest proposals were introduced to improve the business environment with the hope of generating growth in the economy, which was material to addressing the public sector deficit long-term. The principal changes were:

- A reduction in corporation tax during the period of the Parliament from 28% to 24%, with corresponding adjustments in Small Profit Rate and the arrangements for capital allowances.
- An increase in the Enterprise Finance Guarantee that supports the borrowing of small enterprises, and the creation of a new Growth Capital Fund.
- Reversing the previous Government's National Insurance contributions increases for employers.
- Developing a Regional Growth Fund to generate growth together with further reductions in National Insurance contributions for employers in low growth areas.
- The elements of the fairer distribution of the burden package were:
- An increase in personal allowance for basic rate taxpayers, aimed at removing significant number from the tax system.
- Rebalancing of the Capital Gains Tax rate to a higher level of 28% aimed at reducing the anomaly between the taxation of earned income and capital gains.

- A levy on Banks balance sheets and Bank bonuses taxation aimed at reducing the risky borrowing practices of banks.
- A policy aimed at freezing Council Tax in local authorities in the next tax year.

In line with the Coalition Government's Programme for Government document this pattern of changes amalgamated some of the thinking of the Conservative party without of the Liberal Democrat party. It was set within the context of the overall agreement to accelerate the financial recovery of the public sector. The Emergency Budget package was clearly aimed at achieving a faster reduction in the public sector deficit that set out in the last budget of the Labour Government in March 2010. As a result the Office of Budget Responsibility estimated that public sector net borrowing would decline to 1.1% of GDP by the end of the period; the structural deficit will be eliminated and a the small surplus of 0.8% of GDP created by the end of the period; and having hit a peak of 70% of GDP in 2013/4 debt would decline to 67% of GDP by the end of the period.

However there was more criticism of some of the detail of the Emergency Budget and its impact on the two other objectives of economic growth and enterprise, and fairness. The economic growth initiatives were not specifically targeted at areas of low growth, and has the most significant tax changes affected all businesses within the economy, it seems unlikely that the initiatives will be sufficient to hold or reverse the existing pattern of unequal growth between regions. Similarly, although the changes to bank levies and taxation would gain significant new receipts for the public sector, they did not seem likely to significantly change the behaviour of banks, who would continue to operate within the current relatively unregulated arrangements.

Equally, although the Budget Report claimed that the impact of changes will be to ensure that those who were wealthier would pay a larger proportional share, the work of bodies such as the Institute of Fiscal Studies identified that the net effect of welfare cuts and tax changes will impinge most heavily upon the poorest and most vulnerable. Other commentators suggested that some of the proposed changes to Housing Benefit and Disability Benefit would prove difficult to implement and might have serious consequences for the individuals involved.

Box 4.3 The Spending Review, October 2010

The Spending Review which was announced on 20 October 2010 resolved some of the key issues about the pattern of expenditure over the five-year period of the Parliament to 2015. It represents an incremental set of changes to those which began with the Labour Government's March Budget, the £6 billion package, and the Emergency Budget. It detailed the Government's budgetary priorities to achieve an overall reduction of £81 billion in public expenditure and had a number of key features:

- It confirmed the decisions to protect the health budget, and to expand in real terms the relatively small overseas development budget. In addition the budget in education for schools also received protection. However, these protections were at little more than an inflation level, and represented zero growth in real terms. The only exception was the overseas development budget which grows in real terms. However, when the distribution of the additional funding is taken into account, and the increase in demand particularly in health and education is considered, most public sector organisations in the sectors, even though protected, will still need to find efficiency savings of up to 5 to 8% in their budgets overall.

- In normal circumstances the impact of these kinds of protections would have been to push the average reduction for all other departmental budgets well above 25%, however, in practice the average reduction was reduced to 19%. This was because the Government decided on the trade-off between welfare benefit payments (AME) and departmental budgets (DEL). In addition to the £11 billion of reductions already announced in the Emergency Budget in June, a further £7 billion worth of reductions was announced in the Comprehensive Spending Review. Of this £7 billion addition £2.5 billion was to be gained from reduced child benefit payments, and a further £2 billion from changes to disability and employment benefit payments. The remainder came as a result of a 'salami slicing' approach across a wide range of other benefits reducing eligibility criteria and in some cases reducing benefit payment amounts.

- Within government departments there was a differential effect, the outcomes of a traditional bilateral bidding process between departments. Because of overseas commitments, and pre-existing contractual commitments which were more expensive to exit than complete, Defence received proportionately smaller reduction of around 6%. On the other hand the DCMS budget (covering cultural services) was cut by 40% and the DCLG budget (covering communities and local government) by around 28%. Police and justice budgets also took a larger-than-proportionate reduction.

- The overall impact on GDP of the reductions in the Government's policy package was estimated at 2%, about the equivalent of next year's growth estimate by the OBR. Approximately 500,000 public sector jobs were estimated to be lost, with an assumption that these would be replaced by equivalent private sector employment growth over the same period. Public sector employees remaining in employment were subject to a wages freeze, and significantly increased pension contribution reductions, particularly affecting those earning more than £20,000 per annum.

- The impact of the changes was 'end loaded' towards the end of the Parliamentary period, with a number of major changes being deferred in terms of being introduced, and with some taking time to work through the economy.

- Universal benefits aimed at existing pensioners were reduced slightly in value, but were not otherwise significantly altered. However, the move to increase the age at which the statutory pension was payable was accelerated and the 'pension credit' arrangements frozen in order to reduce the overall pensions liability.

- The capital/revenue expenditure trade-off was not significantly amended in the announcement, reflecting the fact that capital expenditure was already reduced to 50% of planned levels. However, there were minor reductions to capital expenditure plans for flood defence schemes, and reductions to transport schemes. Part of the Defence budget arrangements included a significant sale of

Government assets. One of the most significant changes was the virtual removal of subsidy arrangements for social housing, with a consequent expected impact on the number of new houses to be built being offset on the assumption that there could be a more efficient use of the existing social housing stock.

- A number of budgets were 'adjusted' so that the funding was directed at new objectives. The overseas development budget was, in future, to be seen as part of the overall security strategy, being directed at alleviating poverty and reducing risks from political hotspots and unstable states. The Climate Change Levy was to become part of general taxation, instead of being applied as an incentive to companies to reduce carbon emissions.

The Spending Review was supported by a number of strategic review documents that were published shortly before the Review was announced. The proposals in the consultation document '21st Century Welfare' were to be taken forward, but the cost reduced and the project for significant change re-phased. The Government's Strategic Defence Review re-evaluated the principal risks against which the changes in the Defence budget were to be set. The review by John Hutton on public sector pension costs saw the publication of an interim document, though more work remained to be done. On the whole, however, there was a perceived mismatch between the strategic conclusions and direction set out in these review documents and the final detail of the Spending Review.

The final details of the changes implied in the Review will only emerge some months after its announcement. Major reductions in grant levels to local government were reflected in individual local authority decision-making during their budget cycles, and the reductions of subsidies for transport were only be seen in terms of changes to income and fare structures at the January review dates. Organisations that are supported by grant money in cultural areas will react to reductions in grant distribution by increased charges or reduced activity at some future point. The changes to flood defence capital expenditure may result, in the future, in increased insurance premiums for areas deemed to be at risk. Similarly, the impact of reductions in central and local government expenditure will be seen in changes in private sector levels of activity, particularly in construction, IT, services, and supplies, and it has been estimated that private sector job losses may be equal to those directly lost in the public sector.

The initial proposals in the £6 billion package do not, on their own, give us some very clear pointers as to the detail approach of the Government. However, they do tell us two things. Firstly, they represent variations to the previous Government spending plans that were inherited by the Coalition Government when it assumed office. A substantial number of the proposals represent the cancelling of previous Government's spending proposals. They, therefore, represent a clear statement that the Coalition Government was serious about the overall targets set out in its Programme for Government of achieving a balanced budget within the lifetime of the Parliament, and its commitment to be in office for a five-year period in order to achieve this. The proposals would therefore be very largely symbolic of its intentions. Secondly, they represent a variation from the outgoing Labour Government's proposals as set out in its last Budget in March 2010. The Budget proposals were based around a structural deficit of around 5.8% of GDP, and those proposals would have dealt with 70% of that deficit by 2016/17. The proposed tax increases and spending reductions were broadly split 30:70. What subsequently emerged from the Coalition Government proposals did not overthrow these proposals, but increased them in scope and shortened the timescale. The Coalition Government proposals therefore aimed to eliminate the deficit both actually and structurally by proposing changes equivalent to 105% of the deficit by 2014/15. Borrowing, as a result of these changes, was reduced by around 17% overall, and the tax and spending split was 20:80 for the new measures, giving a net overall split of approximately 25:75.

These changes are consistent with a greater adherence to a 'sound money' approach rather than any element of deficit financing, and show a greater concern for the dangers of additional interest costs following adverse interest rate variations. The lack of a radical change in policy is also suggested of a more managerialist vision which believes that the proposed approach is more efficient and effective once it has been 'tweaked' than was the previous package of proposals. The change is therefore one which is more evolutionary than revolutionary, indeed so small was the initial change (barely 1% of the reduction that was needed) that almost represented a modified status quo. In terms of the strategic analysis these changes were distinctly of the H1 category.

It is not entirely fair to assess the Government's overall pattern of proposals on the basis of their initial actions. As has been said, it represented an earnest of what was intended, rather than the complete policy package. The shape of that package began to emerge with the Emergency Budget in June. That Budget was accompanied by a major economic commentary from the newly created Office of Budget Responsibility (OBR 2010a). The proposal to create this Office, whose task was to comment on the efficiency of Government Budget proposals in achieving their fiscal and economic objectives, was seen as a counterweight to the largely voluntary nature of the 'balanced budget over the cycle' and 'golden rule' that had underpinned the previous Government's financial proposals. The fact that these had effectively to be abandoned as the financial crisis took hold, and immediate and strong action was called for, was seen as a fundamental weakness in the credibility of Government and the trust that can be placed in politicians by the electorate. Immediately before the election the outgoing Labour Government passed the Fiscal Responsibility Act which sought to bind an incoming government to a defined policy of achieving deficit reductions. The OBR proposal was seen as a means of going beyond that, as it was felt that some of the guidelines set out in the Act were insufficiently strong to achieve international fiscal credibility.

The detailed proposals set out in the Emergency Budget were largely around increases in direct taxation – largely VAT, but the most significant element was the weight that was being placed on reductions in government expenditure. So a total reduction requirement in the annual budget of £40 billion was proposed to be achieved by 2014/15. This consisted of a reduction of £32 billion per annum from spending reductions, £11 billion per annum from welfare savings with the balance coming from tax increases. The outline proposals indicated three trade-offs to be resolved by the Spending Review:

1. *Protected and unprotected budgets.* The decision to protect NHS spending in real terms (this means nil growth in effect) and the Overseas Aid GDP target increases the pressure on unprotected budgets from average reduction of 14% to 25%. This set the floor for reductions in the departmental expenditure limits which represent the overall financial targets for Government Departments, and therefore their constituent agencies.

2. *Departmental expenditure and welfare expenditure.* There is a trade-off between reducing the level of overall welfare pavements and departmental direct expenditure. The Emergency Budget proposed £11 billion annual reductions in welfare pavements (26% of the total reduction required), compared to departmental spending which would take 55% of the required reduction. If this pattern of reductions had remained unchanged at the Spending Review then it would imply that departmental budgets on average had to take a 25% reduction. Decisions to increase the level of welfare payment reductions by, say, an additional £4 billion, which was widely being canvassed in advance of the Review, would have implied a reduction in the average departmental savings target to around 20%.

3. *Capital and revenue expenditure.* Although the Emergency Budget proposed only modest changes to the level of capital expenditure beyond those already proposed in the £6 billion package, the net effect on the overall level of capital spending remains significant over the consolidation period. The assumption that the Government was making is that this balance will be taken up by private sector investment in public facilities.

The Spending Review resolved these trade-offs. Government departments were asked to prepare proposals for a 25% and 40% reduction in their budgets in advance of the Review in order to allow for prioritisation, but the scope of the changes required at the high end of this review total was significant. The outcomes of the Comprehensive Spending Review suggested that, despite the OBR's view that its proposals were consistent with the achievement of the Government's overall public finance objectives; there were two significant risks that could derail the policy.

Firstly, consistent with the Government's 'sound money' orthodox economic thinking the immediate direct impacts of the proposals on the public sector were shown to be offset by a steady growth in the overall economy, resulting in a shift of employment from public to private sector. However, a number of commentators suggested that these assumptions could be wildly optimistic, with the result that if the economy did not show the strong growth that was being predicted the total number of welfare claimants would rise and, even at the low unit cost resulting from the Government's proposals, the total welfare bill could increase while at the same time taxation receipts fell. The Government could therefore find itself falling short of its target particularly towards the end of the Parliamentary period – at the very time when the impact of some of its initial proposals were being felt, and when it was looking to re-election – requiring a further round of expenditure reductions or taxation increases. Even if the economy did show a reasonable level of buoyant growth there would be a differential impact between different parts of the country depending on the dependence of local economies on the public sector, with the possibility that strong growth might show an employment market overheating in London and the South-East, whilst other areas retained significant levels of unemployment. Secondly, the impact of the changes in terms of individual groups of people and the perception of fairness was much in dispute. Although the Government announcement suggested that care had been taken to ensure that those with higher incomes pay proportionately more of the overall cost, the decision to make bigger reductions in the welfare budget, and the relative impact of loss of income between lower-income groups and upper-income groups imply that the actual change in living standards will fall disproportionately heavily on those in relative poverty. The impact of that in terms of public perception, social unrest, and clamour to amend initial policy decisions may yet derail the overall shape of the package.

Doubts had also been raised about the achievability of some of the changes that are being proposed. Assumptions which are made about the reduction of overheads, and 'bureaucracy', are not necessarily based on a good understanding of the relationship between these costs and front-line service delivery, as we shall see later. Further, the relative rate of change is such that it has been suggested that the Government may only achieve around 60% of its planned level of changes, even without resistance or obstruction by public sector organisations. If this were the case, then even if the economy was buoyant, the overall package of proposals set out in the Comprehensive Spending Review might not be met.

The pattern of the Coalition Government spending proposals across the three policy initiatives suggests that its overall view of the future the public sector tends towards the reformed public service element. Some of the proposals remain aimed at the 'small state' spectrum, but these are not clearly articulated. On the whole the proposals appear to be using the ideas around

'New Public Management' to push private sector techniques further into the public sector and to adjust the public/private sector balance. However, they fall well short of a radical dismantling of the State, nor do they envisage proposals that would radically alter the economic principles under which the Government is acting. This appears therefore to be an issue of greater continuity of a traditional approach to public sector finances, rather than any radical change. In strategic terms the proposals are dominated by H1/H2 thinking. The linkage between the individual proposals and the strategic analysis that preceded them is weak. In some cases work commissioned to support the overall shape of the approach is either incomplete or has not reported at all. Some of the long-term changes which are of more strategic nature already show signs of drift, particularly in the key area of reform of welfare payments. As a result the coordination of individual proposals into coherent programmes represents one of the principal managerial and administrative challenges to the Government. There is a danger that individual initiatives will fragment, and that there may be unforeseen consequences as the proposals are worked through a departmental basis. There is no real suggestion that independent agencies will be asked to operate differently, and indeed, the only external independent agency from central government – that of local authorities – will be expected to conform to the overall pattern of central government policy. Even the one area of independent taxation from central government, Council Tax, will remain tightly regulated with only minor variations from permitted limits.

In respect of the longer-term 'cold water frog' issues that we discussed in Chapter 2, the proposals of the Spending Review did not generally address them positively. The change in pensionable age accelerated existing proposals to deal with the issues of future pension liabilities, but the long-term issues around social and health care for an ageing population were swept up in the decision to protect the health service and not directly considered. The decision to take into general taxation the Climate Change Levy, and some of the individual investment decisions around alternative energy, seemed expedient rather than strategic, and commentators suggested that the Government 'green agenda' had been significantly undermined. Issues associated with the regional disparity, and income distribution were, at best, not specifically addressed, and in some senses might even have been made worse.

Conclusion

Sifting through the clues provided to us by current Government policies as they have emerged leads to three conclusions.

Firstly, the Coalition Government has simply failed to communicate its vision of what the public sector will look like after the fiscal consolidation policy, that is its essential raison d'être, is concluded. In part this may represent not a failure to articulate a vision, but a lack of agreement as to what that vision should be or even a fear of putting that vision before an electorate who might not like the vision. There is clearly little belief that this is a temporary matter and that the 'no change' approach is credible. On the other hand the 'reformed capitalism' end of the spectrum attracts few supporters, and those that it has, even in Government, exhibit a considerable frustration. The balance seems to be struck between those members of the Government who look for a reformed public sector and those who are looking for a smaller state. The fault line between these two visions may become more critical in the future. Secondly, the kind of initiative that has been produced so far falls well short of the radical H3 end of the strategic spectrum. Some may be presented as such, but the more pragmatic nature of some of the policy decisions, and the ease with which they are subsequently reversed or significantly amended following public criticism, suggests that most of them are strictly of the H1/H2 category. The strategic approach is more adaptive than revolutionary. Lastly, the dominance of policies in and around fiscal consolidation is so great as to drown out the influence of some of the significant longer-term issues. Even if the current policies prove totally successful, they may leave a future legacy of unresolved issues that undermine what has been achieved. It may well be that we are 'out of the frying pan, and into the fire'.

So, in moving forward, we can see that the traditional approach of the UK public sector towards financial crises is little changed by the current circumstances. It is to the analysis of this traditional paradigm that we now turn. Part II will look at the historical development of the current pattern of public service provision that underpins the paradigm and provides much of its supporting stories and legends. We will look at attempts that have been made to improve efficiencies in public services delivery in the past and try and assess the degree to which they have been successful. It will then go on to look at the way the public sector is organised and structured for service delivery in a traditional pattern and what insights this shows on the relative efficiencies that can be expected from current policies based on this approach, before concluding Part II with an assessment of the key risk areas faced by the Coalition Government in addressing the future shape of public services, and the likelihood that the current approach will prove successful.

Part II

The Traditional Model of Public Service and Its Prospects for Success

5
The Development of Modern Public Services

In our consideration of the issues facing UK public services we have, so far looked at a range of issues which, although dominated by thinking about the current economic situation, also include a number of major structural changes in the nature of society and our economic future that are in danger of being ignored. Considering how to face up to these issues the experience from other countries who are in a broadly similar situation (or have been in such a situation in the past and have addressed the issues) does not give us any firm guidance as to the strategy and policies which will deliver satisfactory outcomes. We, thus, find ourselves in a situation where the UK is about to embark on an economic experiment and readjustment of its economy, and the pattern of public service delivery, long-term, which is pretty well unique. No doubt other countries in Europe, and the United States, will look with interest at how the UK copes over the next few years with the social, political, and economic adjustments that will be called for.

The first steps in making those changes have already been sketched out in terms of the policy initiatives that have been undertaken by the UK Coalition Government since its election. These appear to be based on a particular strategic pattern which falls short of the radical paradigm change that we will argue is essential to a successful outcome. In this second part of the book we look at the underlying organisational, managerial, and political structures that appear to dominate the current approach to public service delivery. The American philosopher George Santayana (Santayana 1951) once said: 'Those who cannot remember the past are condemned to repeat it.' It is not particularly easy to look into the 'seeds of time' and decide what key drivers of change have emerged and controlled the responses and policies of reform, but it is important that some attempt should be made. Thus while later chapters will provide a critique of the current UK public services model, in this chapter we undertake a brief historical review of the development of the UK public sector, in terms of growth and functions, because we believe that these show that the current approach is part of a traditional pattern of response that has firm historical roots and which will be difficult to dislodge.

However we do not approach this historical analysis in chronological fashion since we do not believe that would be constructive. Instead we approach the topic from the standpoint of four distinct themes and we consider the impact of historical events of those themes. While we consider these themes from a UK standpoint, many of the same themes will also be found in other countries to a lesser or greater degree. The four themes are:

Theme 1: The increasing scale and complexity of the public sector over time.

Theme 2: A persistent tendency to look solely for centralised solutions when critical issues have to be faced.

Theme 3: A reluctance to adopt radical changes, and a marked tendency towards an evolutionary change process that builds on existing structures.

Theme 4: An inability to resolve the inherent public sector tension between the deserving and undeserving poor in welfare provision.

Theme 1: Size and complexity of public services

Prior to the start of the 20th century, and for many centuries previously, the involvement of government and the state, in the UK and most other developed countries, was largely limited to three areas of activity, namely:

- *Defence of the realm* – expenditure on armed forces
- *Maintenance of law and order* – police, courts, prisons etc
- *Trade* – regulation and promotion of trade matters

For example, examination of the 18th-century UK Prime Minister, William Pitt the Younger shows that his working life was dominated by issues of trade, war, and the raising of tax revenues to finance those activities (Hague 2005). This is very different from today where Prime Ministers will also have to regard to health, education, and pensions as being key political and social issues. Given this limited range of activity described above, not surprisingly public services, in the UK and other developed countries, were much smaller and restricted in range than is the case today.

Figure 5.1 illustrates the growth in public expenditure in the UK in the 20th century, and across the millennium.

It will be seen that over the past hundred years or so UK public expenditure as a percentage of GDP has grown substantially with strong peaks during the times of the two world wars. However, one of the problems that should be noted with this kind of analysis is relatively porous boundary between the provision of services directly by government agencies, funded

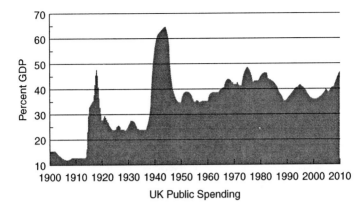

Figure 5.1 UK public spending as % of GDP

from taxation, and the provision of those services through the private sector. In many cases what we would now consider to be public services have historically been provided by other agencies.

Similar growth trends can also be observed internationally as shown in Table 5.1.

Overall we suggest several phases of development (excluding world wars) can be identified in most countries which contributed to the significant upward trend in public expenditure in the 20th century leading to public services being much larger and complex and having a greater direct impact on the life of the average citizen.

Citizen welfare

During the twentieth century, the state became increasingly involved in improving the social welfare of its citizens. Partly this was for altruistic reasons but partly also for the achievement of other aspects of government policy. For example, in the early part of the century, poor nutrition and poor housing were impacting negatively on the health of poorer people in society. In turn this was impacting on the productivity of employees in industry and on the fighting effectiveness of conscripts in the Army. During the First World War, recruiters had uncovered a dismaying fact that almost two in every five volunteers for the British Army were entirely unsuitable for military service on the grounds of health. Not surprisingly in the light of these facts, Government came under pressure from industrialists and generals to do something about this situation (Wikipedia a). Major welfare reforms took place in the early part of the century, which resulted in an increase in the size, and scope, of Government involvement in social welfare issues. The main aspects of this were two key pieces of legislation. These were the Old

Table 5.1   International public expenditure trends

It can't go on
Government* spending, % of GDP

	1870	1913	1920	1937	1960	1980	1990	2000	2005	2009
Austria	10.5	17.0	14.7	20.6	35.7	48.1	38.6	52.1	50.2	52.3
Belgium	na	13.8	22.1	21.8	30.3	58.6	54.8	49.1	52.0	54.0
Britain	9.4	12.7	26.2	30.0	32.2	43.0	39.9	36.6	40.6	47.2
Canada	na	na	16.7	25.0	28.6	38.8	46.0	40.6	39.2	43.8
France	12.6	17.0	27.6	29.0	34.6	46.1	49.8	51.6	53.4	56.0
Germany	10.0	14.8	25.0	34.1	32.4	47.9	45.1	45.1	46.8	47.6
Italy	13.7	17.1	30.1	31.1	30.1	42.1	53.4	46.2	48.2	51.9
Japan	8.8	8.3	14.8	25.4	17.5	32.0	31.3	37.3	34.2	39.7
Netherlands	9.1	9.0	13.5	19.0	33.7	55.8	54.1	44.2	44.8	50.0
Spain	na	11.0	8.3	13.2	18.8	32.2	42.0	39.1	38.4	45.8
Sweden	5.7	10.4	10.9	16.5	31.01	60.1	59.1	52.7	51.8	52.7
Switzerland	16.5	14.0	17.0	24.1	17.2	32.8	33.5	33.7	37.3	36.7
United States	7.3	7.5	12.1	19.7	27.0	31.4	33.3	32.8	36.1	42.2
Avearge	10.4	12.7	18.4	23.8	28.4	43.8	44.7	43.2	44.1	47.7

Sources: Vito Tanzi and Ludger Schuknecht; IMF; OECD

* 1870–1937 central government, 1960–2000 general government

Age Pensions Act of 1908 which provided for a non-contributory but means tested pension and the National Insurance Act of 1911 which provided a contributory but non-means tested cover against sickness and employment for some classes of worker.

In the interwar period the provision of services by the public sector and public sector administration arrangements came under significant financial pressure, and largely the result of poor economic decisions and implementation of 'sound money' orthodox economic policies. Significant periods of industrial unrest led to the General Strike of 1926, but when the recessionary impact of the inflationary speculative bubble of the US stock market rebounded in 1929, and orthodox policies continued to drive down the level of economic activity, the recessionary impact became long-term and persistent. Ultimately economic recovery came with rearmament in advance of the Second World War, but in the interim the pressure on public finances and on delivery of public services became acute. In many local areas the continuing Poor Law system and the system of local authority administration became unable to cope. As the Second World War drew to a conclusion the public mood to address some of these critical issues with more radical reform was clear.

The Beveridge report in 1947 proposed significant changes to the delivery of public services. Following the end of the Second World War the new Labour Government embarked on a huge programme of improvements in social welfare, which basically involved the implementation of the Beveridge recommendations (Beveridge 1942). Beveridge made recommendations for the development of comprehensive systems of social security and the development of a national structure of health services. The social security developments were underpinned by the passing of the National Insurance Act of 1946 and the National Assistance Act of 1948. The National Assistance Act 1948 replaced the Poor Law. However, perhaps the flagship policy of this period was the creation of the National Health Service (NHS) in 1948, which brought into public ownership large numbers of what were previously private or voluntary hospitals. Yet the provision of what are now termed family health services (general practitioners, dentists, community pharmacists, and opticians) all remained in the hands of private practitioners. However, even though the services were provided by these private practitioners the funding for the services was public and the practitioners obtained most of their income through the means of contractual arrangements with the NHS. This somewhat strange arrangement was basically the political compromise that had to be made by the Government to get the NHS formed. The 1944 Education Act brought together, in a national set up but locally administered system, the existing dispersed arrangements for education through church, charitable, and local authority responsibilities. This provided for the provision of universal, free, state secondary education and provided the framework for the education services we have today.

Once Governments had become involved in various aspects of social welfare they had virtually committed themselves to responding, to a lesser or greater extent, to increases in the need for services. Unfortunately, at the time of initial involvement, it was not always perceived that the needs and hence demands for services would grow substantially. Take, for example, the NHS. At the time the NHS was formed, there was a strong belief that the pool of sickness, and hence the need for health services, was finite and the provision of a certain level of resources to the NHS would meet all the health needs of the population. With the benefit of hindsight, that view now seems naive and current conventional wisdom is that the demands for health services are virtually unlimited.

There is now a general recognition that in a modern state, governments needs to be actively involved in many aspects of social welfare (e.g. education, health, pensions, etc). Politicians of the left and right may argue and debate the extent of that involvement but few politicians of the right would suggest that the welfare state be contracted back to pre–First World War levels.

Economic management

During the period 1935–1945 there was an increasing international acceptance that Governments needed to have a much larger involvement in the management of their economies. This was the period of Keynes, the development of macro-economics and the use of large-scale public spending in the USA and Germany to boost flagging economies. In the period immediately following the end of the Second World War, large parts of the UK economy passed into public ownership through the large-scale nationalisation of industries such as coal, steel, electricity, and gas. These policies reflected the view of the then Labour Government that public ownership of such strategically important industries was essential for economic management purposes.

In some senses the post–Second World War settlement represented the high point of public services provision in the UK. Since that time it has been generally accepted that Government should have a strong role in economic management. However, the extent and nature of that involvement is open to political and ideological disagreement as the debate between the merits of monetarism and Keynesianism in the 1980s illustrated. This debate polarised opinion between supporters of the 'big state' pattern of post-war public services, and those who felt that attempts to public sector management of the economy were doomed to failure and that 'small state' levels of intervention were necessary in order to maximise the prospects of economic growth and public welfare improvements.

In the modern world, Governments are involved in economic management in a number of ways and the following are current examples of how public service organisations in the UK are involved in and have a role in economic management:

- *Government Departments* – several departments are concerned with aspects of economic management and economic development.
- *Regional Development Agencies* – these have responsibilities concerning social and economic development within UK regions, but are being wound up.
- *Office for National Statistics* – ONS collects and collates a wide range of economic information
- Intellectual Property Office – concerned with the issue of patents and trademarks to foster business innovation.
- *Local Authority Economic Development Departments* – these have substantial roles concerning the economic development of their areas.

Onward and upward

The post-war expansion in public services delivery, and the continuing pattern of historic and administrative and organisational arrangements, created significant tensions from the mid-1970s onwards which changing economic circumstances only exacerbated. Almost immediately for the new local authorities that had been established in 1974, the pressure of economic change undid many of their ambitious plans for improvement in their areas. Looking more recently, the 1970s, 1980s, 1990s and the past decade have therefore seen increasing struggles in the shape of public service delivery. One of the struggles has been the dilemma of efficient service delivery and local control. The size of the UK post–Second World War public sector as a percentage of GDP rose to the point where it significantly exceeded the United States but was significantly less than that of some European counterparts. In part this created a sense of dissatisfaction on behalf of the public who would like to see European level public services but are only prepared to pay North American tax rates. The pressure has therefore been on the delivery of more efficient solutions for public service delivery and administration. Believing that existing public service organisations are substantially unresponsive, Government in the 1970s and 1980s extensively promoted the use of market and quasi-market solutions to drive up efficiency and output. Significant areas of existing public service provision, such as water, public transport, and public utilities, were taken out of direct public control and handed to new private sector organisations through privatisation. The initial benefits of this in terms of increased inflows to the Exchequer as public assets were sold off, and the immediate improvements in customer choice and presentation, were later offset by a widespread criticism of the lack of public control over what were deemed to be public essentials and the failure of the newly established regulatory bodies to exercise effective control over the newly privatised industries. Similarly, the use of internal market structures was widely criticised as creating significant additional overheads for public sector organisations without delivering significant improvements in service levels.

Regulatory functions

During the 20th century, the State became increasingly involved in a series of regulatory functions.

The introduction of the Town and Country Planning Act extended the scope of public sector regulation into new areas of land use. In part these recognised not only a different mood in the general public, but also an acknowledgement that the impact of the economic depression of the 1930s had created a seriously unhealthy, poor, and inequitable society, which conscription had revealed and which the Army and rationing had to address.

Other regulatory developments during this period have concerned such matters as consumer protection, environmental health, and health and safety at work regulation.

The 21st century

In 1997 a Labour Government came to power after 18 years in opposition. Initially the new Government abided by the public expenditure targets set by its predecessor but in subsequent years it presided over the most substantial post-war growth in the percentage of national income devoted to public services. To some extent, much of this growth in public spending might be regarded as 'more of the same'. For example, in the period from 1999–1900 to 2007–2008 spending on the NHS in England grew on average by 6.4% a year in real terms well in excess of the rate of NHS growth in previous decades and well in excess of the average growth in public spending (4%) for the same period (IFS 2008). However, some available evidence (Appleby 2007) suggests that a significant part of this growth in funding was not used wisely and led to a substantial reduction in the overall productivity of the NHS. However, much of the growth in funding clearly went in improving the range of health services and the ease of access to those services although we now see, with the benefit of hindsight, that much of growth money was obtained by excessive borrowing.

A considerable proportion of the recent growth in public expenditure has also been devoted to what might be regarded as 'new' areas of government activity. These are often controversial areas and may people would argue that the state is now getting too involved in areas of activity that have traditionally been private matters or that the state is involved in forms of social engineering. Some examples of these controversial activities include:

- *Parenting* – concerns about the health status, educational outcomes, and behaviour of many children and young people have led government and local authorities to become heavily involved in the parenting agenda since effective parenting is seen as a key means of improvement. This can involve the provision of information, parenting training courses, and so on. Whatever the merits of these parenting programmes the reality is that traditionally this has not been an area of state involvement and parenting has been regarded as a private issue.
- *Promotion of equality of outcomes* – today most political commentators from any political party would probably accept that equality of access and opportunity (by different geographic areas, different groups in society, etc) to services such as education, health, employment, and more is an essential pre-requisite for a fair and just society. However, it seems that in the past few years matters have gone beyond the equality of access and opportunity to promoting equality of outcomes via state involvement or

intervention. One example of this would be higher education where a regulatory regime to monitor access to HE has been introduced and large financial incentives have been offered to certain disadvantaged groups in society to encourage them to enter higher education.

- *Dilution of mission* – several examples can be quoted of situations where, arguably, the key activities or mission of a public service organisation have been diluted or diverted as a consequence of a requirement to promote another aspect of public policy. One example of this might be schools who as well as promoting educational achievement, are now also asked to pursue a range of objectives concerned with, for example, healthy eating, citizenship, anti-bullying, racial awareness, and so on.

Clearly such a large-scale involvement of the state in non-traditional areas has had significant financial implications, and it is against this background that the current crisis in public finances is set.

Theme 2: The predominance of centralisation

The late Robin Cook was quoted as saying that the UK was the most centralised country in the EU (*Guardian* 2002) and others (*The Economist* 2010a) have suggested it is the second most centralised country in the developed world after New Zealand which is a very small country. This is a tendency that goes back a long time. Most other countries have either got constitutional arrangements whereby within the country there is both a federal structure and a state structure with clearly delineated powers and duties at both levels (e.g. USA, Brazil) or some form of regional structure whereby responsibilities are devolved from central government to regions in the country (e.g. Spain, Turkey).

The growth of UK public services in the post-war period has presented UK Governments with the dilemma of uniformity and local variation. The development of significant national policies in welfare, pensions, education, and health has led central government to wish to have a uniform level of provision meeting its policy objectives and manifesto commitments. As a major provider of funds, this has resulted in the direct use of 'agent and principal' organisational structures aimed at ensuring compliance with national policies. However, this approach has sometimes rebounded. In 1945, Aneurin Bevan, later to become Minister of Health argued for a national NHS rather than an NHS run by local authorities. His argument for such centralisation (Cabinet Office 1945) was that 'We have got to achieve, as nearly as possible, a uniform standard of service for all.' However, in reality, throughout its life, the NHS has been plagued by major inequalities in service standards and service outcomes and some have argued (Klein and Buxton 1978) that the inequalities in the NHS were greater than those in the education sector which is delivered by numerous local councils.

The dispersed and local nature of many of the service delivery elements through local government, and local boards has created pressure for inspection and control mechanisms and these have particularly become a feature of most government arrangements in the 1990s and first decade of this century. The orthodox, traditional, hierarchical type of organisation, and inspection and regulatory regimes has created a significant overhead, and whilst being initially effective in drawing up to a minimum standard in key underperforming areas, has failed to create a significant breakthrough into genuine transformational change.

Into this pattern of local change came the decision to move towards a more devolved arrangement for parts of the UK namely Scotland, Wales, and Northern Ireland. The changes which have been implemented all reflect the different historical and constitutional base of the entities. Scotland has achieved a Scottish Parliament, with substantial economic powers and control of public service delivery. Proposals by the Calman Commission would extend that into areas of finance, and taxation independence. Wales, reflecting its historical linkages with England, has only an Assembly, with substantially less powers than the Scottish Parliament. Nevertheless, it has control over local service delivery, and, like Scotland, is increasingly developing patterns of public sector services that differ significantly from the English model. Moreover at the time of writing, Wales has voted yes to referendum proposals to transfer law making powers from Westminster to Cardiff. Northern Ireland, reflecting its history of community conflict, has a much less open arrangement, yet, nevertheless, is increasingly developing public sector service delivery models that separate it from England. It is not clear, as yet, where this process will finally lead to. After years in which the changes in the devolved administration areas were substantially modelled on an English centric system, the drift in these arrangements may move more significantly towards a wider political, economic, and administrative independence. The substantial differential even within England between North and South, with the very much higher economic dependence of the North on public sector activity, may yet create pressures for a regional pattern of differential service delivery within England itself.

It remains to be seen whether the increasing independence of the newly devolved administrations acts as a countermeasure to what has been a long-standing pattern.

Theme 3: The tendency for evolutionary change over radical change

Although there have been major upheavals, rebellions, and civil wars, arguably there has never been a thorough going revolution in modern

British history for almost a thousand years. As a result the UK's constitutional arrangements are substantially unwritten, partial, and are part legal, part convention and practice, and part tradition. The history of the UK public sector is therefore largely dominated by evolutionary changes resulting in overlays which have added layers of complexity to older arrangements that, having no constitutional basis, did not have to be dissolved and fresh ones recreated.

Despite the economic difficulties of the interwar period and the clear inadequacy of some local bodies in economically deprived areas to meet their obligations as established by Royal Commissions, no attempt was made to substantively review administrative arrangements for the delivery of public services. The move to extend, centralise, and develop new levels of public services in the post-war period to meet the needs of a modern economy was also coupled with a wish to look again at how these services were to be delivered locally. The Local Government Boundary Commission was established in 1945 and rapidly come up with proposals to radically alter the existing historic arrangements towards largely unitary authorities. They were not followed through. Partial reform followed in the late 1950s and resulted in some amalgamations and consolidations in the 1960s, with the biggest single change being in London in 1965. However it was clear with the development and extension of public services into major areas of social care during the 1960s, as well as the extension of the 'welfare state' principles, that local administration would need to be looked at again.

The Redcliffe Maud Commission was established in the late 1960s and reported in 1969. It recommended an arrangement of single-tier unitary authorities throughout England apart from three significant conurbation areas. A minority report authored by Derek Senior proposed arrangements based on a city region principle. Yet even the more modest proposals of the main Commission report were not ultimately acted on. The historic two-tier arrangement, based on counties and boroughs persisted. The Local Government Act 1972 implemented from 1974 a major process of consolidation, but did not change the basic shape of public administration.

Post-War Governments of any party have faced two dilemmas in governance and efficient public service delivery organisation. Firstly, the dilemma of single purpose versus multifunction entities. The post–Second World War world saw the establishment of substantially fragmented public services. During the 1970s and 1980s public services continue to be fragmented with new statutory obligations being transferred to quasi-non-government organisations (QUANGOs); the establishment of arm's-length delivery agencies for many central government functions; and the stripping of existing powers from most function local authorities into separate bodies in key areas such as housing, transport, and water. With the creation of these multiple agencies comes an increasing problem of coordination. It was widely recognised that many organisations, funded through separate funding streams, with separate regulatory environments, and different organisational structures, nevertheless need to cooperate to deal with social and economic issues that impinged on all of them differentially. So, for example, in dealing with the misuse of drugs the police might bring together their public order and administration of justice functions to meet the social care and physical environmental issues being dealt with by the local authority, and match that with the health and preventative agenda that fell within the remit of the local health service. The complexity of these issues resulted in a plethora of partnership activities which were often significantly ineffective, as the independent organisations continue to operate within their individual control regimes. Subsequent attempts were made to combine these separate partnerships in a single all-embracing partnership arrangements when the overhead of running coordination activities and developing effective strategic planning became too great. Secondly, the dilemma of size and community representation. The abolition of many small administrative areas in 1974 recognised that they were too small to administer their areas effectively, or deliver efficient public services. Nevertheless the larger, claimed to be more efficient, units of public services administration were felt to be remote and distant from the public they intended to serve, and unresponsive to citizen and customer need. The differential economic and administrative clout of organisations in the multitier system, notwithstanding any political differences, did not lead to effective cooperation between the tiers. As a result there have been repeated proposals to establish, or disestablish, or amalgamate, various units of local governance and the piecemeal reform that has created as a result of this has resulted in a system of organisational churn which has led to a highly diverse and relatively incoherent pattern of local administration. The same large/small dilemma has also been seen in the health service with regional, area, district, primary care, and hospital arrangements subjected to a significant level of change as an attempt is sought to bridge the gap between the efficient delivery of service and the responsiveness of the operating unit.

These dilemmas and attempts to resolve them have resulted in a significant level of partial changes over the past 30 years which has failed to provide a coherent solution and has resulted in significant diversion of resources and attention towards structural rather than delivery issues.

Theme 4: The welfare dilemma

The inherent inequality in the market economy has driven the development of public services arrangements, and with it the key feature of public services namely the separation of payment and consumption. Exactly what services are provided has varied through time and the boundary between what community services are provided publicly and what privately has been a shifting boundary, but the key feature of public services has been the provision of low, or zero priced, services backed by taxation. The development of the distinctive public services delivery model has been justified by:

- The provision of pure public goods, where the 'exclusion principle' meant that once the service is provided, everyone else gains benefit, and thus such provision – street lighting is a modern example – would not be voluntarily provided by a market system unless for altruistic motives;
- Services where significant community externalities exist, that would not be provided for in a market system at a sufficiently high level – sewerage and public health prevention measures for example;
- Services that generate significant social and community cohesion advantages and that imply a 'trustee' relationship for those unable to exert direct market purchasing power – the most disadvantaged, the poor, and the young.

However, the separation of the private sector market economy where payment is made at the point goods or services are acquired, and the public sector where payment and delivery are separated, and payment is made through taxation, has given rise to the problem of 'freeloading'. The separation of payment and delivery means there is no incentive for the individual to ration the use of public services, and as a result, demand for public services appears almost endless. Equally much public service provision is intended for those who are unable to pay by reason of unemployment, infirmity, age, or personal circumstances; there is little to prevent someone who does not wish to contribute to the economic welfare of the community through employment and taxation, to utilise the public services on offer, and to live at public expense. As we shall see this problem has persisted as long as the development of public services to meet the demands the market economy has existed. Throughout time different measures have been used to try and ensure that welfare payments are only made to those who are deemed to be 'deserving', but without evident success.

Government after government over the past four decades has attempted to address the problem of a growing 'benefits culture' where people seem content to live, albeit in relative poverty, at public expense. Proposals to make people 'work for their benefit' and to introduce harsher criteria for support and more rigorous monitoring have failed to make significant inroads into the issue. As major reductions in the welfare bill are a key part of the current proposals to address the public sector deficit this whole issue is being looked at again but effective policy solutions remain elusive.

Conclusions

The above sections have summarised the recent historical development of UK public services according to four main themes and have highlighted the

driving forces for such developments. In looking to the future there are perhaps three key reminders from the past which should be borne in mind:

- The traditional pattern of UK public administration has been remark-
  ably persistent. There has seemingly been an unwillingness to alter radically existing administrative and public service delivery units to match
  the needs of a rapidly changing economy. Yet clinging to the historic
  and traditional pattern, whilst it might foster a sense of community, has
  not resolved key economic and social dilemmas. The increasing size of
  public services in the economy, and the current crisis in public finances,
  can either be an opportunity to make a radical change to meet this and
  future demands or provide the excuse for further partial, imposed, and
  ineffective changes which seek to consolidate the existing structural
  weaknesses.
- Historically things appear to have continued in stasis until the need
  to change became overwhelming, and unavoidable. Since the development of the market economy and the Industrial Revolution changes have
  tended to be generated because of economic necessity. Yet, over the past
  two decades there have been repeated attempts at change in the public
  sector organisation and service delivery arrangements. The increasing
  attempts at partial changes have created organisational turbulence not
  experienced hitherto. In some cases changes have been implemented
  only to be replaced by further changes before even the plans to implement the original proposals have been prepared. This may reflect a sense
  of desperation, and an increasingly critical and sceptical electorate. It may
  also reflect a sense of helplessness in politics and a lack of solutions.
- The challenge of poverty. From the first, public sector service delivery has
  been dominated by the persistence of poverty. This has required a level of
  social interaction within the public sector that goes well beyond private
  sector service delivery alternatives. The public services have always had to
  deal with those who are in need of service, but were unable to pay for it.
  The separation of payment and consumption has generally carried with
  it tensions which have been resolved differently at different times. The
  tensions between the taxpayer and consumer of public services are significant resulting in an apparent schizophrenia whereby taxpayers resent
  the imposition, yet as service users demand more, without apparently
  being able to connect the two. And critically the distinction between the
  deserving and undeserving poor has tended to dominate questions about
  how far the state should go to support its citizens, and what is to be done
  for those parts of the community whose choice of lifestyle, behaviours,
  and belief place them amongst the unwilling rather than the unable.

The historical development of UK public services to the present time demon-
strates the persistence of the four themes identified earlier, namely increased

size and complexity; tendency to centralisation; evolutionary change; and the dilemma of welfare. The current proposals for the future of UK public services have not moved away from this historical pattern of development. Changes made utilising these four themes in the past have been impermanent and increasingly unsatisfactory. As we have seen, in recent years the pace of reform attempting to deal with the long-standing issues in the public sector has rapidly accelerated to the point where the 'churn of reform' has itself almost become destabilising. We will now go on to argue that this is largely the result of the existing traditional hierarchical 'command and control' structures adopted in the UK, and it is only by addressing this key underlying pattern of service delivery that we are likely to get the 'step change' that the current crisis calls for.

6
The Characteristics of the Current UK Public Service Model

Ask for a diagrammatic representation of almost any UK public service organisation and almost invariably you will be presented with a chart (usually outdated) describing a hierarchical bureaucracy. The pattern will be that of a triangle rising to a senior management position – a chief executive role at the top and extending through numerous layers to teams and front-line staff at the bottom of the pyramid. Within the pyramidal structure you may find individual departments which will, in turn, be almost a fractal representation of the whole organisation – that is, they will be small hierarchical bureaucracies in their own right contained within the larger organisational entity. So common is this model that if you try and draw a new organisation using a standard software package the only option that you will be presented with is one that draws a hierarchical bureaucracy; and the only relationships you will be presented will draw a manager/subordinate relationship, and manager/assistant relationship, or a subordinate/co-worker relationship.

This chapter is not going to make the assumption that this organisational arrangement is so obvious that it needs no explanation. By looking at some of the detail which we might otherwise tend to miss we will be able to see whether this type of organisation, which is so dominant, is likely to be successful in meeting the challenges of change that we set out in Chapter 2, and the current Coalition Government's plans, which we set out in Chapter 4.

Features of a hierarchical bureaucracy

We draw out four principal features of hierarchical bureaucracies.

Organisational style

Hierarchical bureaucracies invariably operate a 'command and control' organisational pattern. The organisation assumes that instructions will pass from the senior management at the top of the organisation down to the operational front-line who will deliver the services and functions so planned and organised. There is an instinctive tendency to divide such organisations into 'thinkers' and 'doers'. The underlying pattern of the 'command and control' organisational style is based on McGregor's 'Theory X'; that is the assumption is that people will only do the very barest minimum that they can conceivably get away with, and need careful oversight and direction if they are to work efficiently. Command and control hierarchies are instruction laden. The higher up the organisation you get the more your work is that of thinking, planning, driving change, and communicating the messages to deliver the day-to-day service and function of your organisation. This can lead to a significant problem of communication. On the whole, communication up and down the organisation is subject to distortion both in volume and content. In our experience even small comments made at the most senior level tend to get amplified as they passed down the organisation, turning from comments on best practice to become virtual instructions at lower levels. In like manner comments and communication from the front line of the organisation is very often filtered and diminished in volume as they pass up so that a really serious issue, for which instruction or guidance is needed, becomes a whisper once it gets to the level of the senior management team. Most large hierarchical bureaucracies have complex internal communication networks, programmes, and plans to try and ensure that there is a consistency of message throughout the organisation. Big organisations will spend a significant amount of money in communicating corporate visions, objectives, and values from the top. In some respects the public sector is often better positioned, because the perceived moral value of the services to be delivered – 'the public sector ethic' – is a part of the individuals reason for entering the public service and value sets are often more closely aligned. There can be a tendency for public sector organisations to neglect communication as a result, and the development of more market-based delivery arrangements using private sector approaches has, to some degree, undermined this historical position. As a result public sector internal communication plans have seen a significant increase. Nevertheless much evidence suggests that these communication plans are often ineffective at delivering a common message.

Organisational relationship

Within a hierarchical bureaucracy the principal relationship is that of manager/subordinate, or, in more generic terms that of 'principal and agent'. The principal sets the objectives and tasks for the agent to carry out. The principal will be privy to certain knowledge which the agent does not have, and vice versa. The agent may not know what the overall objectives of the principal are, and the principal may not know the technical information to be able to do the job. Because of this 'information asymmetry' the principal will usually install an inspection and monitoring regime to make sure that the agent is carrying out their functions in a way that will achieve the principal's objectives. There is a certain cost to the principal in devising and implementing the inspection and monitoring regimes. Very often the principal will seek to avoid these additional costs by passing the responsibility for reporting on to the agent, who must give regular feedback reports on progress. Particularly within the public sector, where it is difficult to determine the outcomes of a particular policy that has been planned by the principal, there is excessive reliance on reporting workloads and throughput, rather than outputs and outcomes. And, because it is difficult to determine a single metric which will describe the range of activities being carried out by an agent there is a tendency to multiply performance measures. This burgeoning of performance targetry continues despite the observation of 'Goodhart's law' which suggests as soon as a performance measure is given the status of a target it ceases to be a measure of performance.

Roles and responsibilities

Within the typical pyramidal structure of the hierarchical bureaucracy each of the individual units within the organisation will tend to have a clear description of the job, and the specification of the skills the individual needs in order to fit that role within the organisation. The job description and person specification will often form an essential part of the person's contract of employment, giving great certainty, but a certain rigidity. The pattern of the organisation will typically have clear lines of accountability generally upwards to a managerial function, which in turn will have reporting responsibilities to high levels of the organisation, and so on. Such organisational types find it difficult to handle situations where reporting responsibilities are divided between individuals, or where the subordinate is responsible to more than one manager. This often indicated in organisational diagram by a 'dotted line' linkage, but there is a strong tendency to clarify such multiple reporting lines with one being clearly dominant over the other. Additionally, within an organisation there will be a whole series of organisational norms, rules, and regulations which will set out the scope of the individual to exercise their autonomy within the job. Certain tasks will fall within the delegated responsibilities of the individual, so that if the individual moves outside that specific delegation, or wishes to do so, then there will be a general need to ensure that clearances are obtained from a higher level. As such, hierarchical bureaucracies work well with repeated tasks of similar pattern or activity, but handle significant variance or uncertainty poorly. The constant need to refer up difficult decisions tends to overwhelm the higher levels of the organisation.

Objectives and targets

As the hierarchical bureaucracy cascades tasks, responsibilities, and functions down the organisation, so it tends to cascade objectives and targets. At the most senior level of the organisation there will be a number of broad objectives and consequently far more open and ambiguous targets. However, as you pass down the organisation so these targets tend to become much more specific and the objectives narrower in scope. The organisation creates a 'work breakdown structure' in which the responsibilities are divided up with increasing levels of specialism and narrowing of scope as you pass down the organisation. Targets will often be designed along 'SMART' principles – Specific, Measurable, Achievable, Relevant, Time limited – and the assumption would be that as these SMART targets are achieved at the bottom of the organisation so they are aggregated at the next level up and so on to the top of the organisation. Like the roles and responsibilities these suit organisations where functions are clearly divisible, and the service is uniform, repeatable, and the only thing that varies is the level of demand.

Organisations with these four characteristics are persistent. One of the key features of the development of UK public services has been his evolutionary rather than a revolutionary pattern of change. Previous models have been subsumed and developed, rather than replaced. This pattern indicates the persistence of the universal paradigm of hierarchical bureaucracy. The rise of the market economy and development of the Factory System imposed a greater level of uniformity than had been the case for the production of goods and services beforehand. A more flexible regime of natural time, governed by the time of day and seasons, was replaced by clock time where day and season became almost irrelevant. The Factory System involved the splitting up of complex tasks into smaller, more specialised, functions – the work breakdown structure with individual functions being uniform and repeated. It was therefore not surprising that as public services developed that they would adopt a similar 'mass production' approach to the delivery of uniform services, and therefore it was almost inevitable that the hierarchical bureaucracy would emerge as the key organisational form. These historical developments were often seen by writers and commentators as having an inhuman element about them. Individuals were treated as components within a greater machine. The metaphor of machines is very commonly used in respect of hierarchical bureaucracies in the delivery of public services. When proposing changes to the pattern of public services the UK Civil Service will refer to it as 'machinery of government' changes. Individuals will describe their insignificant function as being 'a small cog in the machine', and if you want to be disruptive within an organisation you may well describe it as 'throwing a spanner in the works'.

Although there were strong parallels with development of the Factory System, there were other important factors at work during the period of the rapid growth of public services following the Industrial Revolution that also favoured the development of hierarchical bureaucracies. The scientific approach to change, by altering single components in repeated scientific experiments, and the principles of the Enlightenment of using reason and logic to analyse complex problems both tended to favour the development of a machinelike approach to organisations. Such organisations could be taken apart, analysed, and single changes made to effect improvements. This has been the principal approach to change in hierarchical bureaucracies. Max Weber, identified in his writings three types of organisation – the personal, based on grouping around a charismatic leader; the traditional, which he subdivided into the feudal and patrimonial forms, which is essentially based upon precedent and usage; and the rational/legal based on an organisational bureaucracy – and was clear that the most efficient and effective was the latter (Pugh and Hickson 2007). Weber concluded that 'the decisive reason for the advance of bureaucratic organisation has always been its purely technical superiority over any other form of organisation'.

The value of the hierarchical bureaucracy as an organisational form for public services should not be underestimated. As an organisational type it has clarity, transparency, and is widely understood. In the complexity of the delivery of modern public services, the need to have full-time officials for whom the delivery of those services is a specialist lifetime function means that such organisations, with their clear career structure development and creation of niches for professional specialisation, have considerable advantages. As the social underpinning of representative democracy for public service delivery and developed in the late 19th and early 20th centuries, so the hierarchical bureaucracy with its tendency to uniformity, rationality, and ability to deliver the same repeated service gave a significant reinforcement to the process as a means of ensuring equality and equity in the treatment of individual citizens, as against the bias implied in the earlier patronage system.

And as the public sector grew so it became necessary to develop the hierarchical bureaucracy. There was a tendency as a new functional area was developed, and new specialisms created, to establish a separate bureaucracy to deliver it. As specialisms subdivided so it was also possible to hive off new organisations and for them to take with them the same basic hierarchical form. Very often these divisions were driven by function, but sometimes by geography with the development of local government. Yet, as these multiple hierarchies developed so there arose boundary issues between them. The tension that we observed historically between the multi-purpose, geographically based, organisations, and single purpose, more centralised, organisations has existed from the first, and remains an unresolved, and possibly irresolvable dilemma. One of the possible solutions has been the development of multitier organisational forms, with the 'upper tier' organisation being more functionally driven where perceived economies of scale in the delivery of functions were deemed more important, whilst 'lower tier' organisations had a much more geographical community focus. However the establishment of two hierarchical organisations with one being perceived to be dominant over the other creates continuous patterns of tension between them and 'turf wars' tend to dominate supposedly joint activity. Whilst these patterns exist within a function, they also exist within the whole structure of UK public services, which have now got to such a large and complex state that there are multiple competing hierarchies which themselves are part of hierarchical arrangements. However, when they are not part of the same organisational entity then there is considerable scope for confusion over authority and who is principal and who is agent.

Key issues in hierarchical organisational forms

The hierarchical bureaucracy is the principal pattern by which UK public services, and indeed public services in most developed countries, are delivered. It's now time to turn our attention to the current 'age of austerity' that UK public services face and to ask whether this prevalent organisational form is 'fit for purpose' in answering some of the demands of change in the coming years. There are three principal tests that need to be passed:

- *The size and speed of change.* After decades of uniform growth in the cost of public services, and in their scope, future decades are predicated on reversing these previous trends and reducing the overall level of public services, or at best stabilising them so as to bring the public sector as a percentage of GDP back to its long-term average of around 40%. Any organisational form is going to have to deal with a more significant level of change that has been experienced hitherto, and its adaptability both to the scope and speed of change will be essential.
- *The drive for efficiencies.* It is not clear whether it is a key objective of the changed public services that the state will be smaller, or simply reformed. However, what is clear is that there is a desire to ensure that whatever solution emerges the 'front line' is as far as possible protected. Interpreted, this implies that the organisational form must be a modern 'lean organisation' type and that inefficiencies will need to be driven out. A second key test therefore for any organisational form will be its ability to operate efficiently, and to identify and deal with any inefficiency that is inherent in service delivery.
- *Fairness.* In order to change to be acceptable it is clear that it will need to be supported by the public and electorate. The public have a keen sense of what is and what is not fair in delivering a changed pattern of public services. A sense of fairness between generations, and between parts of the country, and between individuals is an integral part of the objectives of the Coalition Government, and the Opposition, in proposing their policies for change. The degree to which the organisational pattern of UK public services can promote and deliver publicly acceptable equitable solutions will be a third key test.

The response to change

The traditional pattern of hierarchical bureaucracies is very well adapted to situations where the same service or function is discharged to meet multiple demands on a uniform basis. Indeed, within the public sector, one of the principal criticisms of public service organisations is that they adopt a 'one size fits all' mentality and that the citizen, customer, or client is offered very little choice and variation in services. As we've already seen, the development of private sector methodologies in the public sector during the past three decades has often been aimed at promoting the 'choice' agenda and providing a wider range of services to the public. One of the principal criticisms of this approach has been the implied redundancy in provision, which is a matter for commercial decision but which has public taxation effects in the public sector.

Within the public sector bureaucracy the traditional pattern of response to changes in demand has been to adopt monotonic linear thinking. The work breakdown structure that underpins the hierarchy breaks down the overall functions of the organisation into discrete units of service and task. The principal and agent arrangement produces metrics which allow the task to be measured. It becomes a relatively simple calculation to work out that if demand for the service is at a particular level, then a specific number of work units – and functions are often measured in at work units, numbers of cases, length of road to be repaired, volume of calls to be answered etc – can be calculated and thus the necessary resources to deliver that quantity provided. If more is demanded, then proportionally more resources are required. However, one of the principal issues for the public sector is that services are free at the point of delivery. The consequence of this is that demand can be virtually limitless, since there is no overall linkage between the cost of providing the service and the volume of service demanded by the user. Unlike private sector companies whose continuing existence is determined by the 'bottom line' – the profit they make when the final accounts are drawn up – public sector organisations are dominated by their budget – the key document of planning for a particular level of service which underpins the taxation decision.

Because of the dominance of the budget/taxation decision, and the use of linear monotonic thinking that underpins the bureaucratic delivery arrangement, the total quantum of service available to be delivered is broadly fixed. There is little scope for varying it in quantity. Consequently most public sector organisations are effectively operating a rationing system that limits the demand made on services. Means testing, eligibility criteria, the need to make specific applications, restrictions on opening times, and even the expedient of simply not responding to some requests are all means by which the public sector chooses to ration the services provided in the interests of 'fairness'. As budgets become limited, so these criteria become more stringent, and/or the quality of what is delivered is reduced in order to increase quantity.

When faced with a new demand, or a new function, the hierarchical bureaucracy will take an adaptive approach to change, based upon the 'learning cycle'. It will plan for a particular pattern of delivery, with or without a variation. It will then examine the outcomes and evidence from delivering that plan, before modifying and adapting the plan for the next budget cycle of service delivery. As a result the traditional pattern of budgeting tends to be incremental, making small changes on a regular basis across the organisation.

When significant changes need to be made within a traditional public sector bureaucracy then the small-scale, incremental, approach is often replaced, at least in theory, by a programme or project approach. These approaches tie in to the strategic framework of H1/H2/H3 thinking that we introduced in Chapter 4. The H1 approach, largely consisting of short-term, expedient, coping strategies generates a significant number of small-scale changes which, within a large hierarchical organisation present particular challenges. The individual changes can often be managed either within the functional unit that provides the service affected, or increasingly by the use of 'task groups' or 'taskforces'. This latter approach reflects a behavioural tendency, which we will comment on later, of organisations to be protective of service areas, and therefore unwilling to make significant changes where that might result in the loss of function or loss of employment. The difficulty with the H1 pattern of change is the coordination within a large organisation of the individual initiatives. The total resource take for the organisation of implementing the change is often uncalculated, and there may be specific resource areas – predominantly IT, property, or technical services – that are overwhelmed by demands, which individually achievable, but in aggregate become impossible if the timescale is restricted. Further, the implementation of a wide range of small changes can often be subject to 'the law of unintended consequences', where changes can be mutually contradictory; or the impact on a particular group can be disproportionate or inconsistent; or where the objectives of the organisation appear to be distorted without anyone ever giving sufficient attention to the overall impact of changes.

The H2 or H3 approach to strategic change management demands a higher level of coordination – generally that of a project or programme. Project management is generally well understood and there are a number of tools adopted by organisations to ensure that projects are properly specified. Programme management is much more intangible, consisting as it does of a significant number of interrelated projects which are grouped together in an overall programme of change. At times of very significant change it is likely that a number of big projects will be linked together by a significant change in an organisation's external environment, or the implementation

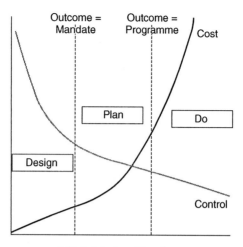

Figure 6.1   Stages of a programme/project approach to change

of a new technology, or simply by a major change in available resources. In a time of austerity it is likely that there will be particular demands to develop a programme management approach to change. If an organisation chooses to adopt the very radical, paradigm shifting, H3 type of change then it is almost inevitable that some form of programme management will be needed to deliver it.

Figure 6.1 shows a diagrammatic representation of the three stages of a programme/project approach to change.

During the period of the project/programme the level of control that can be exerted by the managerial cohort of a hierarchy diminishes as the project moves from the design of its objectives and outcomes, through project planning, to project implementation. Conversely the level of resources committed to the project rises during these three phases. To be effective project needs to recognise when each stage is reached and to 'sign off' the work done at that stage before proceeding to the next. So, typically, the senior management and/or Board of the organisation will determine the objectives to be achieved by the programme or project, the outcomes targets that will be set, and will set these out in a mandate for the programme or project manager to deliver. At this first level the project will be dominated by the work of the project sponsor who will have responsibility within the organisation for the overall project or programme to the main board. It will be their task to ensure that if there are difficulties in achieving the necessary resources within the organisation and/or commitment to achieving the mandate that these are dealt with effectively. Once the mandate has been agreed the project or programme manager will need to devise the details of the individual projects or the detail of the project itself that will deliver the mandate and set up the necessary functions, tasks, and resources to achieve that. At the end of the second stage the project arrangements need to be signed off at board level and the resources committed. At the third level the project moves into implementation – the project manager becomes responsible for delivery, and the role of the project sponsor becomes that of receiving assurance from the project assurance function that all is on target and the outcomes will be achieved. At each of the two key sign off decision stages the decision is 'adopt, adapt, or abandon'. Until one of those three decisions is reached the next stage should not be started.

This is a complex task for an organisation to achieve. Some of the difficulties that are experienced in project and programme work are well rehearsed in the works of Reiss (Reiss 2007), and interested readers might well look to the texts listed in the bibliography if they are further interested. In a great many cases hierarchical organisations are extremely bad at implementing projects or programmes. There are said to be five principal reasons (Reiss 2007) why 95% or more of projects failed to deliver the scope of the project, within budget, and to time:

1. A total failure of organisations to understand the Project Triangle. Three elements –scope, time, and cost – form the Project Triangle. Any two of them can be determined, but the third will emerge as the result of fixing the first two. If a project has a set scope and a set budget, then time will emerge as the project plan as the variable. If there is a set budget and a set time, and the project scope – that is, what it delivers – will emerge as a result. There is a tendency to try and fix all three points, and the consequence is that the project gets de-scoped, the timescale extends dramatically, or the cost soars. There are numerous examples in public sector project changes – very often involving major IT systems – which clearly demonstrate that untrained project sponsors, managers, or ignorance at Board level set an impossible task which is consequently not achieved.

2. The two decision points of determining the mandate, and signing off the project approach, are not adhered to. Too often projects in large organisations take a length of time to deliver which means that either technology changes, or there becomes a greater awareness of the possibility of technology change, or they're simply becomes a change in objectives as a result of a changing business environment late on in the project. Once costs are being heavily committed, going back to the drawing board and redesigning the mandate is an extremely costly exercise both in terms of work lost, work redone, and time taken.

3. Not recognising the problems of the unknown. Projects and programmes are often divided into runners, repeaters, and strangers. Runners refers to a process within an organisation where the delivery of a function or

service can be seen as a series of 'end to end' projects with each one having a start and finish point. So, for example, the maintenance of a road network might be seen as a number of discrete projects but there is such similarity between that the organisation of the delivery into individual tasks is a well trodden and well rehearsed path, and presents no real challenges. Repeaters refer to a project which is fairly commonplace and for which there exist a number of known techniques for handling the issue. A classic example is decisions to be made about prioritisation in the building up of a corporate budget. There will be a number of techniques that the organisation will adopt regularly – service reviews, identification of service units and outcomes, preparing options for change to meet budget targets, and so on – and whilst these can be considered overall as a project, the techniques are so well known that integration within the organisation is not that difficult, though it does have significant resource implications. Strangers are difficult projects or programmes because what is being attempted is completely unknown. Because 'nothing like this has ever been done before' is the key phrase, these projects or programmes are difficult to manage and their resource take can be significant. The project suffers 'scope creep' with new functionality being added at a later stage.

4. The nature of the project structure does not fit within the hierarchical work breakdown arrangement of roles, responsibilities, and tasks that the organisation is divided into in order to deliver function. Typically a project or programme management approach cuts across existing hierarchies. It confuses reporting responsibilities. It calls for resources to be made available from within existing functional budgets that are already managerially committed. It has implications that affect the tasks and employment within the organisation, but which are very often not properly reflected in the more technical work programme delivery. As a result many bureaucratic organisations try to 'bolt on' programme or project management responsibilities within the existing hierarchy and it simply does not work. As a result, Reiss (Reiss 2007) suggested that organisations that face repeated programme or project work, or are subject to a highly unstable environment, might better adopt a full-blown programme management structure, but this does not always prove unsatisfactory since such organisations necessarily have to 'handover' the completed and delivered project or programme on implementation to an operational arm. The programme managed organisation therefore tends to become entwined with an operational organisation creating the possibility of two contrasting and competing organisational forms – hierarchy and programme management – within the same organisational entity.

5. Organisational inertia and organisational culture that militate against significant change. In attempts to encourage a more project or programme approach to managing change in organisations the development of functions such as project sponsor or project manager have been writ-

ten into the hierarchy. Such individuals are often referred to as 'change agents' whose function, either on a temporary or permanent basis, is to effect change within the organisation. They can be backed up by specific resources in a specific change function, often located within an organisational development division. However, the seminal work by Georgiades and Phillimore in their influential article 'The Myth of the Hero-Innovator' (Georgiades and Phillimore 1975) assessed the effectiveness of such change agents drawing on examples from public sector organisations, particularly the health service. They concluded that the impact of such individuals often was subject to rapidly diminishing returns following any particular initiative – training or otherwise – as they were absorbed into an organisational culture which was aimed at producing standard repeated outcomes. Simply planting trained 'hero innovators' in 'an unprepared and hostile environment may do their cause more harm than good', since organisations will 'eat hero innovators for breakfast'. In their view in order to ensure that organisations receive hero innovators without 'gobbling them up' they suggested bringing them together in an organisational function, backing them up by a team, and by providing top management support for innovation. Nevertheless, and despite the development of such functions within hierarchical bureaucracies, it remains the case that very few organisations are capable of overcoming the inertia to change when major change is called for.

However, there is a final reason why hierarchical bureaucracies have difficulty in implementing change that transcends the approach, be that of an H1 task force orientated strategy, or an H2 project managed strategy, or an H3 paradigm shifting programme. Within an organisational hierarchy we've noted the difference between 'thinkers' and 'doers'. Typically the impetus for change and the approach to change comes from the 'thinkers'. Change tends to be a top–down approach. In part this is the result of information asymmetry. The senior management or Board of an organisation is aware of a changing business or budget environment and the need to plan for the organisation to deliver within that environment. Often working alone, or with a limited group of individuals, sometimes supported by external consultancy, a change programme will be devised. It will then be communicated and implemented within the organisation. Resistance from those who are not aware of the key information have not been consulted on the options for change, but who are directly impacted by the proposals are almost inevitable. The difficulties of communication up and down the organisation simply add to the problem.

The overhead costs of bureaucracy

In most organisations distinction is drawn between the fixed cost overheads arising from the organisation's existence and management style and the variable costs which are associated with the volume of service, product, or function delivered. In a significant cost-cutting exercise it is generally at the fixed costs or overheads that an organisation will look first to find efficiency savings. We've already seen how in the hierarchical arrangement and work breakdown structures of the bureaucracy there is a simple linear approach to calculate resource requirement, and how that overall resource require-ment is moderated by concerns, usually political, over the acceptable level of tax burden to calculate the volume of service to be provided. So it is not surprising when additional resources have been made available that they are intended to deliver increased functionality, new functions, or more of the same. There has been significant criticism, for example of the National Health Service, in recent years when the additional resources made available have resulted in a significant increase in the level of management overhead – in the National Health Service, for example, it's been noted that manage-ment costs have increased by some 67% in the past decade. We want to look now at some of the reasons why these fixed costs of organisations have risen so dramatically in recent years, and why, not surprisingly, they are treated as the first port of call for any efficiency savings. We will want to examine the extent to which the modern hierarchical public sector bureaucracy could be expected to find those savings.

There are three clear areas which help to explain the significant level of managerial overhead are borne by public sector organisations. They are not necessarily unique to the public sector, many private sector hierarchical bureaucracies will also exhibit these costs, but inevitably with an increasing volume of sales in the boom years from the mid-1990s to the onset of the recession in 2008 the private sector was more able to cover these costs with-out attracting adverse criticism. These areas are discussed below.

Command and control costs

The hierarchical bureaucracy is built around the relationship of manager/subordinate, or principal/agent. In order to exercise a level of control it is been common practice within hierarchies to look at the span of control man-ager to subordinates – that is the number of subordinates the manager can be expected to set performance targets, and have a sufficiently controlling relationship to identify whether targets are being met or not. Typically in hierarchical organisations the number of direct reports is relatively small – typically six or eight – and as a consequence organisations of a significant size can often have many intermediate layers of managers before the organi-sation gets down to the level where individuals are directly providing serv-ices to clients. As the reward structures of such organisations are usually based on the principle that the higher up the organisation the greater is the salary reward for expertise, risk, and management, large multilayered organisations have an inherently expensive structures. Over a period of time attempts had been made to 'de-layer' or 'flatten' the resulting organisational structures in an attempt to reduce costs. Very often these have been supported by IT systems in which the burden of reporting has lain with the subordinate or agent and where the use of benchmarking or exception reporting draws the attention of the manager only to those areas which are out with acceptable control limits. A number of business intelligence systems have been devised to report on a wide range of performance measures, often using a 'balanced scorecard' approach. Similarly, a number of innovative approaches to teamwork have been proposed for traditional hierarchical organisations in order to allow them to flatten management structures. Some of these use, for example, the principle of the 'self-managed team', where the team is responsible within itself for managerial activities that would have been carried out by someone high the managerial hierarchy. However, the concept of 'self-management teams' is virtually an oxymoron within a hierarchical bureaucracy given its basic underlying premise, and these approaches have not generally been successful. Indeed, within some organisations multiple layers of management have been seen to be a positive advantage, not only giving a long and sustained career path with appropriate salary uplifts in order to retain staff, but also giving the opportunity, by various manipulations of job descriptions and person specifications, to create posts and intermediate positions for favoured staff in an extension of a quasi-patronage system which tends to run counter to the underlying principles of the hierarchical bureaucracy that we have described earlier.

To these costs of managerial layers, needs to be added the inherent costs of undertaking the monitoring and inspection process which is an integral part of the principal and agent relationship. On the whole the performance targets and measures which are set by the principal are not necessarily those collected or used by the agent to control or monitor or manage their own functional delivery. Certainly, within the very extensive set of performance measures and controls set up under the Labour Government between 1997 and 2007 there were few measures under the inspection process which did not require specific collection and reporting to the plethora of inspection agencies that were set up in local government, education, and the health service in particular. In some cases these inspection agencies became an extension of the pre-existing financial audit function – such as the Audit Commission, or National Audit Office – but in a great many cases completely new QUANGO organisations were set up to discharge this responsibility on behalf of central government departments acting as principal. However it was noted from around 2007 onwards the great many of these measures were both expensive to collect, expensive to inspect and monitor and report, and did not necessarily add significantly to an understanding of the actual performance of an organisation as perceived by its customers, as opposed to its sponsoring Department. In part this was the predicted outcome of the work of W. Edwards Deeming (Deeming 2000). W. Edwards Deeming was a management consultant who was drafted into the US Administration in Japan following the end of the Second World War to try and ensure a reconstruction of Japanese industry on more efficient lines. He was partly responsible for the development of the modern manufacturing systems-based process which is generically become known as the 'Toyota model'. He was a significant critic of traditional forms of managerial organisation. Deeming's view was that establishing such performance targets usually resulted in a three-stage organisational response:

- *Stage one – distort the data.* As soon as a performance target is set it encourages clever thinking to ensure that the data which is collected against that target shows that the target has been achieved. At its worst this can simply be the omission or inclusion of data or making up information to show that the target has been met – a form of organisational lying. However more likely will be the use of definitional changes to make sure that data has been so manipulated as to seemingly achieve an outcome even though nothing has changed in managerial or functional or system terms. During the decade of performance targets there was ample evidence, for example, from health service organisations in the UK of this kind of data manipulation. As time went on it became necessary for monitoring and inspection agencies to increasingly define what data was to be collected, and how things were to be measured. Although this was used to try and ensure consistency and to avoid the more obvious manipulations on several occasions the definitions failed to deal with the diversity of environments that organisations faced and the data became increasingly meaningless – as Goodhart's law suggests it would.
- *Stage two – distort the system.* Short of complete falsehood there is generally only so much that can be done by data definition to ensure that reported outcomes match targets. A more general response is to make distortions in the system of service delivery to ensure that recorded data matches targets. Again, the National Health Service provided some fairly classic examples during the period of significant performance measures. When waiting-list reduction was a high Government priority the length of the waiting-list was manipulated by not recording somebody as an entrant to that waiting-list and instead placing them on a 'waiting list to go on the waiting-list' list! And notoriously the then Prime Minister, Tony Blair, was considerably embarrassed in public when he was told that his target of ensuring that, if you needed an appointment with a GP then you would be seen within 48 hours, had been manipulated by a number of practices so that it proved impossible to make an appointment request outwith the 48-hour window – so that people with long-term, but less urgent conditions who needed to see their doctor were unable to make an appointment for say 2 to 3 weeks hence, but were instead instructed to phone back within 48 hours of the required date. And inevitable consequence of these system and distortions was for tighter and tighter monitoring

and control definitions and inspections to try and eliminate them. The data distortions, however, rendered the reported information useless for decision-making.

- *Stage three – change the system.* In Deeming's view it was only when an organisation had gone through the first two stages that it would respond to the performance measure and target as it has been originally intended it should by altering the service delivery system in order to ensure that they complied with it. This was only likely to occur after a considerable period of time and thus the performance measures system provided, at best, a slow and uncertain response from public sector organisations.

The burgeoning of performance metrics and measures in the public sector did not necessarily add up to a proportionate increase in efficiency, whilst it definitely added to a significant increase in costs. There is some evidence to suggest that in some organisations that had no particular form of metric analysis some of the information that was generated in response to the demands of central government, though under a strongly centralising policy which was often greatly resented, was nevertheless useful at local level for addressing some performance inefficiencies. However, it was generally perceived that whilst this had a strong initial impact there was rapidly diminishing returns and that further performance measures, or tighter targets, did not generate an equal improvement in efficiency or outcomes. There was a tendency to 'plateau' in performance improvements. This is perhaps in line with the experience of the private sector. One study by the Hackett Group in 2006 noted that organisations that were world-class performers tended to use significantly fewer metrics than average performers. The information they used was less, but more critical. Nor is it clear that the metrics, even when collected, were generally used managerially to improve performers. A 2007 survey carried out by the Economist Intelligence Unit found that 90% of corporate executives said that they made decisions based on inadequate information, and that less than 10% felt that they received relevant information when they needed it and wanted to make a decision. Over half felt that they were deluged in data and thus lost the critical information, and nearly 60% felt that data was often faulty, inaccurate, or incomplete. Generally speaking senior management decision-making remains largely informal and instruction based on consultation with colleagues and most agreed with the statement that 'strategic decisions always require a strong element of intuition or judgement'. So, even within the private sector the overhead of performance metrics does not necessarily give competitive advantage.

Asymmetry of information also leads to a significant practice of 'games playing' within the organisation in which individuals use information as a means to garner status or power, and where decisions that are taken that are less than optimal because information is not properly shared. Decisions which are made separately in the absence of intercommunication and information, which is a feature of hierarchical organisations, will often result in suboptimal outcomes. However, the individuals in the organisation are capable of learning from previous outcomes and amending their decision-making accordingly. One of the conclusions from games theory is that repeated situations will tend to result in organisational inter-cooperation even when it acts to the disadvantage of one individual until there comes a point where one individual realises that they are constantly being disadvantaged in which case dysfunctional personally focused decision-making sets in. Thus, within many organisations there is a tendency to an overt level of cooperation, but inherent level of suspiciousness that the collective decisions may be personally disadvantageous which ultimately leads to suboptimal outcomes for the organisation, and delays in decision-making. Such outcomes, which result from the command and control management style, are inherently likely to be costly and increase overhead.

Organisational integrity costs

We've already noted that, with the rapid growth in public sector functions and scope, the tendency to create more and more hierarchical bureaucracies to deliver the increased public service activity. We commented on some of the difficulties that this creates and the dilemmas of functionality against geographical basis, and the complications of multitier arrangements between different organisations. Essentially when a new organisation is set up as a specific entity it generates boundary issues with other organisations who carry out similar, competing, or complementary functions. Maintaining organisational integrity becomes part of the organisation's implied objectives even if this is not explicitly stated. This can particularly be the case in the public sector where the organisation's objectives can have a clear moral or ethical value or status and where the damaging or dysfunctionai effects to the community from abolition or change are often the first point of protest when change is suggested. Maintaining organisational integrity can place limits on inefficiencies and result in defensive practices that increase costs.

Limits on efficiencies

Given the size and complexity of the UK public sector, cooperation between different public sector service deliverers is usually essential to an efficient public service. During the past three decades the 'balkanisation' of the public service with the many 'most function' geographical organisations being stripped of their functionality, and with the creation of new independent organisations to deliver services, has meant that the cooperation requirement is greater now than it is ever been. Dealing with what John Stewart called the 'wicked issues' – that is, long-standing chronic community issues that defy single organisation simple solutions – has required the

Figure 6.2 Content of financial plans

establishment of numerous formal partnerships, often established as a statutory requirement. Yet, despite statutory obligations to cooperate and provide information such partnerships have often been difficult to create, and have not always performed well. Budgeting within the public sector remains on the primary organisational level, rather than the partnership level, and the impact of the imperative of retaining organisational integrity has tended to limit the ability of partnerships to provide effective and efficient solutions.

Figure 6.2 shows the percentage of local government medium-term financial plans which do not include the key elements listed.

It is clear that amongst most significant failing of individual organisational plans is to take into account the plans of other partner organisations with whom they are expected to cooperate (Audit Commission 2010). We strongly suspect that a similar exercise carried out in other parts of the public sector will show a similar result. In the absence of this joint activity organisations that find themselves under financial stress have a tendency to 'shunt' costs onto partner organisations for functions where they have common or complementary responsibility. Such changes do not generate a more efficient system, they merely create antagonism, take managerial and organisational effort to sort out, and do nothing to improve service delivery.

At the current time much is being made of the possibilities of shared services between organisations. As budgets are squeezed, the significant overhead carried proportionately by small organisations in delivering common accounting, personnel, property, and technical services are obvious candidates for sharing with other organisations as a means of obtaining economies of scale. A number of smaller district councils, for example, have adopted this approach even taking it to the extent of sharing chief executives, finance directors, and management teams. Small organisations, who will be unable to justify hiring technical high cost staff, given the extent of their service delivery, will often be attracted to setting up common technical services – such as building control, specialist audit, or IT functions – which can attract staff with the appropriate level of reward. However, many such shared services proposals have promised much but delivered little. One of the principal problems is not that of the technical integration of systems, or the contractual complications of staff contracts of employment – significant though both of these can be – but the cultural issues that arise when these key symbols of organisational integrity – the ability to pay your own staff, suppliers, and badge your own services – are lost to a shared service arrangement.

Defensive practices

Once an organisation has been established and given a statutory or discretionary function to deliver public services there is a tendency of those employed in the organisation to assume that what they do is in the public's best interests and that therefore their interests as producers and the public interest coincide. This can result in a displaced objective that generates a 'producer culture'.

A producer culture is generally the result of two factors:

- First an information asymmetry between the service provider and the consumer. Particularly in cases where the service provider is using a particular level of professional expertise to assess and determine the appropriate service to be delivered there can be a strong tendency to adopt a 'parent/child' relationship with the public. The public is therefore not treated as being the ultimate user and funder of those services and the producer tends to believe that the services have integral value which is independent of the user's opinion.
- Second where the service provider finds itself in a virtual monopoly position with the public needing to consume the service, then there is a tendency for the organisation to believe that the delivery of that service and its own self-interest coincide. In such circumstances the organisation can become heedless of public criticism or comment. Traditionally this rather patronising approach has been the case in the public services where the public often have no option but to consume the public services offered, though it also extends to the public utilities, even though these are delivered by private sector companies – a particular dilemma that affects these organisations.

Once producer culture becomes endemic an organisation can justify its own continued existence on the grounds of self-interest, and is little interested in delivering efficiencies or a quality level of public services. However because the public are often dependent on the services, the delivery of these should be based on the principle of trust. We set out in Chapter 2 the interaction of the professional, managerial, and political worlds noting the rise of the managerialist approach to service delivery. The political and professional spheres of operation were largely based on trust; the managerial approach has a more contractual basis. If managerialism is tainted by a producer culture then trust in the delivery of the public service is often lost. Organisations such as hospitals, public utilities, and transport where there is high dependence, an imbalance of information and knowledge, and near monopoly provision can often find that they are very heavily criticised for their poor public service delivery and that their image with the public is poor. Such organisations will often spend considerable amounts of money trying to improve their standing and devote time and effort to reputation management – thus adding to overhead. However, such activities to improve corporate reputation in the absence of genuine improvements to service delivery are likely to be seen by the public as 'spin' and can often give rise to an increasing level of cynicism that means that such costs are unproductive.

Behavioural costs

Despite their machinelike qualities the traditional pattern of hierarchical bureaucracies in public services delivery are staffed and controlled by human beings, who will respond to the environment in which they are placed and will sometimes generate dysfunctional behaviour which can impede the organisation's function. Dysfunctional behaviour has cost implications. There are overheads which are often incurred by organisations in their HR functions in dealing with the impact of dysfunctional behaviour throughout the organisation. There are also costs in the management time and focus taken up with dealing with the consequences of dysfunctional behaviour, and organisations can lose focus and the capacity to deliver effectively where such behaviour exists or gets out of hand. There is not only the human cost, the financial implications can be significant.

Roy Lubit, an occupational psychologist (Lubit 2003), uses his experience from practice to indicate some of the personality disorders and mild or severe mental health conditions which can exhibit themselves as bad behaviour with an organisation. Whilst the book is intended to be a handbook for how to deal with people who exhibit such behaviours, it makes the point that in large bureaucratic organisations such behaviour can often be tolerated within the organisation, and can, indeed, be implicitly valued. So, for example, a manager who exhibits symptoms of attention deficit hyperactivity disorder (ADHD) might present in an organisation as a dynamic, innovative, middle or senior manager with lots of new ideas which are developed in order to make the organisation flexible, efficient, and responsive to customers and the changing environment. On the other hand, such managers often pump out new ideas and activities leaving disorientated and confused staff trying to implement the last idea whilst the next one is already being formulated and pushed out. The 'churn of change' that results can demoralise, dispirit, and derail effective functioning. At the other end of the scale, so to speak, large bureaucratic organisations can attract individuals who exhibit a mild autistic behaviour, or some elements of Asberger's syndrome. Such individuals can maintain, run, and deliver a routine, almost regimented pattern of service, but may exhibit no social awareness of the implications of their 'jobsworth' attitudes. Poor customer relations, and inflexibility in delivery, can result. The lack of understanding of some of the social and human consequences that can arise within the bureaucratic organisation was addressed by Goleman and others in developing the ideas of 'emotional intelligence' (Goleman 1996), which they saw as adding to the technical and business information management portfolio that managers, particularly senior managers, within an organisation needed to have. The interest in this might reflect the degree to which the tolerance of dysfunctional behaviour within bureaucratic organisations existed. For example an analysis of the top 100 CEOs of American companies suggested that upwards of 30% exhibited some form of socially pathological behaviour, that is, that in pursuing the organisation's objectives they showed an ignorance, or unawareness of the social and personal consequences of their policies.

Whilst large hierarchical bureaucracies can sometimes accommodate and tolerate such behaviour, a much more serious aspect is the degree to which the managerial 'command and control' approach, and the dominant manager/subordinate relationship can actually act together to promote dysfunctional behaviour. In his book 'Management and Machiavelli' Anthony Jay (Jay 1988) uses Machiavelli's method of analysing what actually happens within a particular organisational environment in order to provide a critique of modern business management across a wide range of large bureaucratic organisations. He is careful not to accuse them of Machiavellian tactics, but in some cases it is clear that the amoral, ruthless, power seeking, and unethical attitudes, not bound by the norms or rules of behaviour, that form the substance of Machiavelli's precepts in *The Prince* could be properly applied to organisational behaviour. Similarly Jonathan Powell uses the maxims from The Prince to give shape to a commentary on the Labour Government from 1997 onwards in his book *The New Machiavelli* (Powell 2010).

When Niccolo Machiavelli wrote *The Prince* (Machiavelli 1532), he was out of a job and looking for a new wealthy patron to give him employment. In the preface to his book he was seeking to influence one of the leading Renaissance rulers of his day, Lorenzo d 'Medici of Florence, to give him a job. He suggested that in order to retain power a prince needed to be utterly ruthless, particularly when that individual had come to power from within a group of people of similar status – a situation not dissimilar to the promotion of an individual to a position of authority from within an existing team in a large organisation. The ruthless behaviour extended to isolating and removing any rivals, and ensuring that the state, or the organisation, was ruled by fear, rather than any affection. Whilst commentators suggested that he was only describing many of the political practices of Renaissance Italy his exposure of those practices attracted the opprobrium of the Church, the embarrassment of rulers, and made him notorious – associating his name for ever with the ruthless acquisition of power for its own sake. However, if we take some of the relationships implied in *The Prince*, and look at large hierarchical bureaucracies, we can see situations in which such learned Machiavellian behaviour is apparent, to the cost of the organisation.

There is a triumvirate of learned Machiavellian behaviour types:

- *Big Mac*. This is the Machiavellian ruler, chief executive, or principal manager figure in the organisation. Such individuals are often highly egotistical, and are only interested in the exercise of power in order to increase their own authority and status. They tend to use organisations, rather than be used by organisations. The post that they occupy, even at senior levels, are often only a stepping stone to higher and greater things that they have planned for themselves. In achieving their own objectives they are utterly ruthless in promoting themselves and implementing change which will reflect well upon themselves in an organisation. They can exhibit sociopathic tendencies, caring little for the impact of their policies or approaches on others. However, and as envisaged by Machiavelli, such people do not care to be typified as Machiavellian in character, as it impinges upon their sense of self, and chances of career advancement. They therefore tend to attract to themselves the second of the triumvirate – 'Mack the knife'.
- *Mack the knife*. This was the role that Machiavelli saw for himself in relationship to Lorenzo d' Medici and was the job that he was seeking. It was that of the loyal subordinate to Big Mac, who equally ruthlessly carries out the policies and instructions of that individual within the organisation. In return for carrying out his duties Mack the knife looks to have a patronage relationship with Big Mac and to receive status and reflected authority in the organisation. This often is not paralleled by their position within the formal structure. Such people are often feared, because they 'have the boss' ear', and people know that they have protection which extends beyond their formal authority. Should Big Mac move on to another organisation they will quite happily ditch Mack the knife, although sometimes the patronage relationship is such that they will take that individual with them to the new organisation. However, if this is not the case, the Mack the knife character will often offer the same services to the new incoming boss. Mack the knife is generally not interested in being anything other than a subordinate – he or she seeks the role of the Consiglieri, to Big Mac's 'Godfather' role. This is unlike the third of the triumvirate – 'MacEvil'.
- *MacEvil* (the name is taken from a stock character, Machiavel, in Jacobean plays which builds on Machiavelli's notoriety and whose character, as

the name suggests, represents evil personified and ego unconstrained). The 'MacEvil' character is a subordinate to Big Mac, but unlike Mack the knife covets Big Mac's role. They are the usurper within the organisation. Ostensibly there are a loyal and willing subordinate of the Big Mac character, but they often build up a separate powerbase and authority and represent a permanent threat and challenge to Big Mac. Such people can often render the organisation unfocused, and can expend considerable resources in pursuing underhand policies contrary to those of Big Mac. The consequent frictions, outbreaks of bad behaviour, and tensions can derail effective service delivery. Ultimately either Big Mac or MacEvil will be successful. The senior management of organisations can therefore find themselves falling into two camps, placing psychological and personal bets on who will be successful, and whichever is can thus find themselves with alienated senior colleagues who backed the wrong side.

Where such egotistical and learned behaviour exists within the organisation this has long-term and serious consequences. Andrew Rawnsley in his book *The End of the Party* (Rawnsley 2010), which deals with the second term of the Labour Government administration from 1997 to 2010, describes a set of circumstances between the then Prime Minister, Tony Blair, the then Chancellor, Gordon Brown, and a leading figure Peter Mandelson that exemplifies some of the issues that arise when a Machiavellian triumvirate emerges. In our experience the senior management structures of some of the organisations that we have seen exhibited these tendencies and the costs to the organisation in a loss of focus, time taken to deal with emerging issues, and the long-term consequences for organisational behaviour are considerable. Trust in such organisations, which is fundamental to the psychological contract that underlies much of the legal contract based on job descriptions and person specifications which are essential part of a hierarchical bureaucracy, is in short supply when this kind of behaviour is in place. The effects can be long-lasting, in that senior managers who do not conform to the model of the Machiavellian triumvirate can often be driven out by their ruthless activities. The growth of the public sector and the increasing size of the hierarchical bureaucracies that deliver it may have given rise to the likelihood that these behaviours are more commonplace.

But this is not the only dysfunctional learned behaviour that can be promoted in large hierarchical bureaucracies. In recent years interest has been growth in the phenomenon of managerial and to an extent subordinate bullying within large organisations. In times when employment in organisations is at risk, where there is downscaling and austerity, and where inflexible performance measures are in place, then there is ample opportunity for those who believe, or have learned, that they achieve the results which they deem to be in their best interest by instilling fear into their subordinates (or in a minority of cases their manager) to demonstrate a bullying behaviour which becomes endemic in the organisation. Innovation, risk-taking, and efficient service delivery are impeded when bullying is an organisational norm to the extent that it becomes 'institutionalised bullying'.

However, it is not just these dysfunctional behaviours which can impede an organisation's efficiency and add to overheads. Large hierarchical bureaucracies are characterised by situations in which people typically are given high demands to deliver through performance management regimes based on the 'principal and agent' relationship, but where the work breakdown structures, job descriptions, and rules and regulations of the organisation give them little personal control over how the task is carried out. Situations where there are high demands and low personal control are known to be inherently stressful. Indeed, almost anyone reaching in middle or senior management post within a hierarchical bureaucracy will at some time have gone on a 'stress management course' to give them coping strategies for dealing with the stress which is assumed to be an inherent part of the organisational culture. Stress management techniques are generally only an approach to deal with the symptoms, the cause and the consequences largely remain unresolved in hierarchical bureaucracies. We identified two patterns of stress response which can impinge on the efficiency of delivery:

- *Loss of loyalty.* Sennett (Sennett 1999) draws attention to the personal and organisational implications when large, significantly rigid hierarchical bureaucracies are faced with a rapidly changing environment and thus create demands on their staff to be flexible. Despite thriving on clear and transparent task and person specifications, such organisations will often respond by demanding higher degrees of flexibility from employees. Particularly when there is the need to deal with changes of demand the use of temporary, call off, and part-time contracting will be widespread. Full-time employees may be expected to change their hours, location, and conditions of employment at short notice to deal with change. We've already spoken about the underlying psychological contract that underpins the legal and organisational regulatory framework for individuals. One of the essential underlying points of the psychological contract is a mutual loyalty to the organisation to the individual, and an expected loyalty in return from the individual to work in the best interests of the organisation. However, in many modern organisations the demand for flexibility is such that the organisation exhibits no loyalty to its employees, permanent or temporary, and as a result increasingly individuals who would naturally operate under McGregor's 'Theory Y' – that is the assumption that people will generally wish to do a good job of work and do not need heavy-handed supervision to do their best – find themselves squeezed into 'Theory X' environment. As a result Sennett suggests that they suffer a corrosion of character and their initial loyal and favour of the able disposition is replaced by a disloyal 'working to the job description' attitude. Such organisations lose flexibility long-term, essential business intelligence and communication, and an innovative edge from those who would otherwise prefer to do an efficient job but are compelled to do an inefficient job.

- *Burnout.* It has long been recognised that although people can suffer the consequences of a single traumatic event and can therefore exhibit the symptoms of post-traumatic stress disorder – loss of focus, disorientation, flashbacks, and anxiety – similar symptoms can often arise as a result of individuals being in a stressful situation for far too long. The damage done by a number of small stressful events can be as bad as the damage done by a single traumatic event. There are ample examples within military history (not because it is especially parallel to large organisations, but the experience of combat stress and its immediate consequences are often obvious and measurable) of situations where managers and leaders, exhibiting signs of PTSD, have taken rash decisions with disastrous consequences. Such individuals can often operate on the assumption that they and their subordinates are immune from further damage, and they can be heedless of their own safety and that of those for whom they have responsibility. The emotional damage created by high continuing levels of stress in organisation comes before the symptoms of more obvious consequences of intellectual loss and dysfunctional behaviour, and organisations led by individuals suffering high levels of stress are at risk. However the consequences of continual high levels of stress in an organisation are not always at the most senior levels. Front-line staff who are in difficult and stressful situations continuously will exhibit similar unresponsive personal behaviour and rash decision-taking which can have direct and immediate consequences for service delivery. The impact of this high organisational stress during a period of austerity is obvious. But there are also other long-term consequences. One of the issues that we addressed in Chapter 2 was a continuing problem of demographic change and longevity. As a result the UK Government and other Governments have to deal with the growing pensions' liability, and one of the policy proposals is to extend further the working life of individuals before they are able to draw on their accumulated savings as a pension (Pensions Commission 2010). This is a contentious area, and one of the long-term issues will be that if individuals are required to stay and work for longer in situations of stress and are unable to cope, then there may be unforeseen consequences in terms of efficiency, focus, and individual personal and mental problems that will add to the overall community cost.

Governance issues

Within the typical hierarchical bureaucracy in the public sector it may seem perverse to be asking the key question 'who is actually in control here?'

Surely such an organisation makes it obvious by its very nature that those at the top of the organisation are clearly in control. In practice it is not so simple, and the hierarchical bureaucracy can exhibit several paradoxes on governance issues.

For example, within local government the political and managerial parts of the organisation represent two potentially competing, but largely complementary hierarchies that need to work together effectively for efficient service delivery. At the top of the managerial hierarchy the Chief Executive Officer of the organisation will tend to have a direct and personal interface with the leader of the controlling political party at the head of a separate hierarchy which is not part of the constitutional or legal entity which is the public sector delivery organisation. The political and managerial structures will generally have different planning horizons; different standards for data and evidence to support decision-making; different values; different levels and patterns of technical expertise; and different rules and regulations for operation. Typically the managerial structures will have a longer timescale for taking action than the political structures which are tied to the cycle of elections. Decision-making on the managerial side will tend to be based upon business intelligence and financial analysis, whilst opinions, prejudices (rightly or wrongly held), and incomplete data based on personal and public experience are more dominant politically. Managerial values will tend to be less explicit, and more pragmatically expressed than the contrasting values within the political hierarchy, which are an essential glue that hold together the coalitions which constitute political parties and which have a tendency to factionalism and an unstable existence. Expertise in the managerial hierarchy will often be based on trained professional judgement, on the political side expertise may be entirely politically based, or transferred experience from other public sector or private sector organisations. Advancement within the managerial hierarchy will tend to be based upon merit and assessment, notwithstanding some possible dysfunctionality here arising from a patronage-based culture, whilst on the political side advancement tends to be as a result of a more explicit patronage culture.

The two hierarchies will interface most usually at the senior level, and particularly at the Chief Executive/Leader level. The personal relationship between individuals is often critical to an effective public service delivery. Yet, even if this is good, there is a tendency for the managerial hierarchy to believe that decisions in the public sector are the result of inchoate political values and the need to retain political power, so that strategic direction can be difficult to maintain and coherent policy-making is a struggle. On the converse side the political hierarchy will often express a view that the managers are in control of the organisation and that they are thwarted in their legitimate political ambitions by the foot dragging and technical nitpicking of the managerial hierarchy. Managers will often grumble to themselves that they could do a better job if 'it wasn't for the politicians'; while the politicians will argue that 'the managers are on top, instead of being on tap'! In some respects public sector organisations virtually operate in 'dual key' decision-making process. This can be incomprehensible to external individuals, organisations, or the private sector. These bodies sometimes believe that if they have successfully influenced the most senior politician then the decision is as good as done, or conversely that if the Chief Executive has been persuaded then the organisation's support will automatically follow. In practice both would need to be supportive, and this can generate delay and hesitancy in decision-making, particularly when significant change is proposed.

We noted in Chapter 2 the increasing dominance of managerialism as the primary focus for public sector activity, as against the professional or political bases. This increasing dominance has both clarified and confused the governance issues in public sector organisations. Increasingly the growth of the managerial approach to the delivery of public policy and public services has meant that senior managers and politicians have often been using the same language, technical background, and approach when discussing policy changes. This has reduced the level of friction between the political and managerial hierarchies, and the number of situations in the past where political decisions have been taken which have been strongly opposed on legal or practical terms of the managerial hierarchy, thus creating a significant organisational conflict, have been reduced over the past few decades. However, the competing roles of senior managers in the managerial hierarchy and senior politicians who are acting as 'super managers' has sometimes created greater confusion over decision-making and accountability. This is particularly the case where the political hierarchy becomes subdivided into those exercising an executive function – through Chairmanship of the Board, or membership of the Cabinet – and those who exercise a representative or scrutiny function. Increasingly the latter are dissatisfied with the overall control over the direction of travel for the public sector organisation, and perceive that they are either being sidelined into the unpopular and politically ambiguous role of scrutiny or being made to wait their turn in a collective 'executive waiting room' within the political party.

The lack of clarity that comes from two groups running public services within a single hierarchy means that in some cases organisational objectives can arise which apparently generate a life of their own irrespective of the occupants of the managerial or political hierarchies. The impacts of a separate organisation maintaining organisational integrity, and the dangers of producer culture, mean that organisational objectives can develop unchecked and provide a basic background against which the delivery of efficient public services is compromised. Organisations which end up believing that they have a right to exist and that, because of the value of the services that they provide, the interest of the public coincides with their own producer interest, can generate a set of policies that transcend the managerial or political hierarchies. These organisational policy norms tend to be resistant to either changes in either managerial control or political control. The same policies tend to crop up, in different guises, irrespective of who is in power.

The ambiguities over governance and public sector organisations has also meant that there is an increasing tendency, as the public sector has grown in size and the number of organisations has expanded, for these largely organisationally based strategies to create the scope for significant inter-departmental struggles. The competing hierarchies within the public sector have always struggled somewhat over resources. In their seminal book Heclo and Wildavsky (Heclo and Wildavsky 1974) describe how the competing hierarchies at central government level in the UK struggle between themselves to obtain resources as part of a competitive situation to ensure that their integrity and organisational objectives can be achieved, and how this is largely independent of political leadership. Their work dates from the early 1970s, but the continuing patterns of spending reviews, including the latest Spending Review of October 2010 clearly indicate that the coordination of overall government expenditure can be seriously impaired by inter-departmental wrangling over who will get the largest slice of new funds, or who will suffer the smallest of overall reductions.

Within such arrangements the struggles for a coherent and comprehensive public service delivery can get lost, and the dominance of resource management and financial control becomes paramount. In the past, political attempts to diminish the overall power of HM Treasury by hiving off some of its economic and regulatory functions have been largely unsuccessful. Harold Wilson tried using the Deputy Prime Minister George Brown to establish a Department of Economic Affairs in a co-ordinated attempt at economic planning in the 1960s. This was unsuccessful, and indeed under another Brown (Gordon) the Treasury became extensively involved in the development and delivery of welfare policy expanding its role beyond that which traditionally held in the first decade of the 21st century. This holding of the financial ring has given the Treasury a significant power position in Government, to the extent that it forms, with the Cabinet Office, two significantly competing hierarchies at the top of UK Government. The relationship therefore between the Prime Minister and the Chancellor of the Exchequer is, like the relationship between the Chief Executive Officer and political Leader of a public service organisation, the critical one to ensuring an effective service delivery. If they operate a broadly complementary role and support each other, they are a virtually an invincible combination against which major spending departments in Whitehall cannot prevail. If they compete, they can seriously impair the coherent delivery of public policy.

Conclusions – fit for purpose?

We began this examination of the characteristics of the common form of public sector organisation – the hierarchical bureaucracy – by asking if such organisations were likely to meet the three tests of capacity to change, driving out inefficiencies, and fairness that were going to feature as the 'age of austerity' bites in the future. Having now looked at the characteristics in some detail, we are in a position to draw a preliminary conclusion.

We have seen that the size of the change which is required of the public sector is greater than that which has been experienced in post-war Britain. The unique size of this challenge means that the inherent slowness to change and the difficulties in adopting and delivering significant alternatives implied by the H1/H2/H3 categories, by the hierarchical bureaucracy suggests that it's highly unlikely that all the changes which are required will be effectively delivered. The current plans of public sector organisations do not seem to be sufficiently forward-looking to achieve the change required. Figure 6.3 presents evidence from an Audit Commission study (Audit Commission 2010) which looked at the future planning documents of local government. It shows that a significant number are still operating on too a short timescale to be able to factor in the extent of change that will be required. There is an overall efficiency, and change capacity deficiency which the traditional form a public sector organisation seems unlikely to remedy.

The imperative of delivering efficient public services is not simply a matter of current financial necessity. There is a moral imperative that requires that if taxpayers' money, which is an in voluntary contribution, is to be used to deliver services then those services must be the most efficient level. However, we have seen that the traditional form of bureaucratic hierarchy carries a significant overhead in terms of its command and control costs, the costs of organisational integrity, and the costs of dealing with dysfunctional

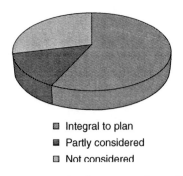

- ▥ Integral to plan
- ▨ Partly considered
- ▧ Not considered

Figure 6.3   Local authorities integrating longer term issues into planning

behaviour. It has been estimated from those involved in looking at alternative organisational structures that between 30 and 40% of the cost of an organisation may constitute the size of this overhead. This significant level of costs means that if there is a requirement to protect the front-line delivery, then improvements in these key areas are needed. Yet Figure 6.2 in this chapter showed not only that the plans of public sector organisations did not take into account the necessary partnership interactions with other complementary organisations, but also that in key areas such as the link between fixed and variable costs and the benchmarking of costs against other organisational approaches, there were considerable deficiencies. It seems unlikely that the traditional hierarchical bureaucracy would be able to reduce effectively this level of costs without a significant change in organisational behaviour, but as Deeming remarked you will not change behaviour without changing the system within which that behaviour is framed.

Finally, the impact of the organisation on delivering a fair and equitable outcome appears to be more a matter of chance than of design. Problems with the governance and control, and the persistence of the dysfunctional producer culture suggest that hierarchical bureaucracies often respond to the variation in individual needs by developing and delivering an equal and common service. Indeed, the media attention that is generated when there are variations in public service delivery – often described as a 'postcode lottery' – show that fair and equitable solutions are often equated with common and equal service delivery. People's sense of fairness extends beyond that and is more subtle. The relative rigidity of the traditional public sector hierarchical bureaucracy to deal with variability means that, if fairness results, it is not likely to be a matter of conscious planning.

There is no doubt that the system of public service delivery through hierarchal bureaucracies works. It has worked in the past, and there is no reason to believe that it may not work in the future. However, given the unique size of the challenge, and the imperative of finding fair and efficient solutions, the delivery through such traditional organisations may be at a price that we cannot afford in terms of the loss of public service delivery. The impact of such organisation in financial, human, and governance terms may also be too great a cost, and the danger is that the continued reliance on such organisations may only serve to widen the current disparity in public perception that exists between the general public, the users of services, and the executive that directs and controls service delivery.

7
UK Public Services – Attempts at Reform

The current UK model for planning and managing public services did not appear overnight. Neither is it really the product of one or more periods of radical and substantial change which might have taken place in extreme circumstances such as enemy occupation during wartime or major economic collapse. Instead the current model has largely evolved over a period of perhaps a hundred years or so as a consequence of a series of changes and reforms which have been implemented by successive governments.

In this chapter we consider the question as to whether the various waves of public service reform which have taken place over many decades can be regarded as successful or not, in improving public services in the UK. This is a daunting task but if the broad conclusion is that the past attempts at reform have not really proved successful then some other alternative kind of reform is really needed urgently to meet the extreme challenges of financial austerity.

In the chapter we will start by considering the main elements of what might be seen as the traditional UK model for the planning and management of public services and then try to summarise the various attempts at reform to this model that have taken place in the UK. It is a difficult exercise to try and summarise such a huge degree of change over such a long period and our attempt must therefore involve a fair degree of simplification. We provide an overview of the many changes and attempts at reform which have taken place and draw the key conclusion that UK public services change has rarely been dramatic but has largely been incremental, and that the constitutional weaknesses and centralised model have led to a process of 'muddling through' rather than a visionary and revolutionary change.

We will then consider whether the past attempts at reform have been successful, and if they have not, what are the main barriers to achievement. Having looked at the traditional approach and its strengths and weaknesses we will conclude that some of the worst consequences of the reforms undertaken might have been avoided because of the inherent inefficiencies in the traditional approach, rather than this being a desired outcome. Thus, paradoxically, it will be the inherent weaknesses of the traditional approach which will ensure that some of the dire outcomes currently being suggested may not actually come to pass. We will conclude, however, that this will not position the country to deal with some of the longer-term and more intractable issues set out in part one and that therefore a more radical alternative in line with the strategic analysis is called for.

The chapter covers the following themes:

- A summary of the traditional UK model of public service planning, management and delivery;
- The aims of public service reform;
- The different ways of classifying public service reforms;
- A summary of UK public service reforms classified by theme;
- A consideration of the degree of success of past attempts at reform;
- An analysis of the barriers to successful public service reform.

The traditional UK model

The traditional UK model for the planning, management and delivery of public services is inextricably linked to the constitutional, governmental and political arrangements which exist in this country. The key themes of this are discussed below.

Constitutional arrangements

As already noted and as every student of political science knows, the UK does not have a written constitution. It is usually argued that the UK does have an (unwritten) constitution which is largely based on precedent but also evolves to the changing needs and perceptions of different time periods. So whereas, for example, 50 years ago it was acceptable to appoint a peer to be prime minister such a thing would not be acceptable today and would be very unlikely to happen. However, in terms of constitutional law there is nothing to stop such an event taking place. This lack of a written constitution means that the UK does not have the constitutional safeguards and checks and balances that exist in other countries such as Germany and the USA. The sole principle of governmental authority is that 'the queen in Parliament is supreme'. This means that, in theory and sometimes in practice, there are virtually no limits to the power of a Government with a parliamentary majority and Parliament can ride roughshod over all other interest groups and public opinion in UK society – and often does. Thus, for example, in the UK there is no constitutional agreement concerning the duties and powers of elected local authorities vis-a-vis elected central government and central government can do virtually what it likes in relation to local government. Inevitably this usually means significant centralisation, detailed interference and so on. With the current Coalition Government it seems to mean declaring a belief in localism and the role of local authorities but in practice still trying to manage the way in which local government deals with the large funding reductions which it faces.

Strong executive power

Following on from the above, the supremacy of the UK parliament means that a prime minister and government with a healthy House of Commons majority and adequate political party discipline (which is usually available through Prime Ministerial patronage) controls almost everything and there are no constitutional checks and balances on the executive by the legislature which exists in, for example, the USA. Some might argue that the recent development of a Supreme Court in the UK imposes some sorts of checks on Parliament and the Executive but we suggest it is too early to make any serious conclusions about this.

Unreformed Civil Service

Government departments in the UK are staffed by members of the Home Civil Service. The UK civil service has much strength including intellectual ability and lack of corruption that would be envied in many countries. However, over the years there have been concerns expressed about the capabilities of the civil service to run the UK ship of state. In other words, is it fit for purpose in the current financial climate of austerity?

The most recent major report on the UK civil service, the Fulton Report (Fulton 1968) made a number of criticisms of the civil service, including that it was too much based on the philosophy of the 'generalist' or 'all-rounder', there were too few skilled managers and there was not enough contact between the civil service and the community it serves. Since the Fulton Report there have been many changes to the civil service concerning recruitment, training and sorts but still there are concerns that these are only window dressing and the ethos of the civil service remains unchanged. Some question what should be the optimal relationship between Ministers and civil servants and should civil servants be more concerned with protecting Ministers (as some may claim they are) or formulating robust policy? Others question whether civil servants are suitably skilled for the future (Talbot 2009)? Finally, the civil service (embodied in HM Treasury) is seen as a strong defender of the highly centralised approach to planning and managing public services, and constrains any ambitions new Ministers may have to get away from such a process. Linked to this is often an arrogance that central government knows best and everything would be fine if only local government and other agencies did what central government told them to do. It is difficult to see how this competency argument of central government can still stand when we see a public sector with a financial deficit of £155bn. It would be difficult to imagine a local authority getting into a financial mess of similar magnitude even taking account of differences of scale. It is not surprising that many politicians (including the former Prime Minister Tony Blair and the current Cabinet Office Minister Francis Maude) after originally embracing the civil service approach now seem to see it as a barrier to reform.

Poor decision-making at central government

There is often strong concern about the lack of effectiveness of decision-making about public expenditure within central government. At a specific and to some degree anecdotal level one only has to consider the implementation of the new general medical services (GMS) contract in 2004, designed to substantially change the way in which general medical practitioners were remunerated and aimed to provide incentives for GMS to improve performance in certain areas such as the vaccination of children. It was always expected that there would be substantial costs associated with the new contract but in the end the Department of Health spent £1.76bn (9.4%) more than it budgeted for on the new GMS contract between 2003 and 2006 according to the National Audit Office (NAO 2008). At the same time, polls of public opinion suggested that patients were not happy with the changes that had taken place in primary care services as a consequence of the new contract. Also, medical professionals in the hospital sector reported increased attendances at hospital as a consequence of changes in the out of hours GP services which were introduced.

Another specific example of such poor decision-making is that it was amazing to read an admission by the Cabinet Secretary (Public Finance 2009) that it was 'too early' to tell how much the creation of the Department for Business, Innovation and Skills had cost and that he was 'hopeful in time that it will be negative because we will have some synergies'. At face value, this seems to imply that no financial analysis of such a major Whitehall restructuring was ever undertaken, there were no budgets to control the costs of the restructuring process and that the whole reorganisation was an exercise in manipulating ministerial egos without any consideration of the best use of taxpayers' money. If this had been a hypothetical local authority carrying out a major restructuring without any consideration or budgetary control of the costs involved, critical comments and demands for action would have poured out of Whitehall, MPs, the Audit Commission, the Public Accounts Committee, the media and so on. However, when it comes to central government restructurings, it appears that no such rules apply.

At a more general level, a recent report (Centre for Social Justice 2011) heavily criticised decision-making processes about public expenditure within central government. The report argued that effective spending decisions require a fundamental change in the way public spending decisions were viewed. It stated that to achieve this required an important shift across the civil service: to a culture that values transparency and accountability, and incentivises cost-effective delivery and cross-departmental working. It argued that this required a change to the way government operates, as well as some institutional changes.

Lack of sub-national government arrangements

Most largish countries have some form of sub-national government arrangements which sit between central government and local government. Just a few examples will illustrate this:

- **USA** – elected state governments sitting below the federal tier;
- **Turkey** – non-elected regional tier of government with a regional governor;
- **Germany** – 16 elected federal state governments sitting below the federal tier;
- **India** – union of 28 states and 7 union territories alongside the federal government tier;
- **France** – although France is a unitary state the administrative subdivisions of regions, departments and communes have various legal functions, and the national government is prohibited from intruding into their normal operations;
- **Japan** – although a unitary state Japan has 47 sub-national prefectures sitting below the federal tier.

With the exception of the relatively recent developments of devolution to Scotland, Wales and Northern Ireland, the UK, in comparison with other countries, has no form of sub-national government for the 85% of the UK population which lives in England. Moreover, even these devolution arrangements are not constitutional arrangements and could, in theory, be reversed or amended by the UK Parliament should it think fit.

Regional government for England was proposed by the previous Labour Government but soundly rejected by the electorate in a pilot referendum held in North East England. The whole issue of English devolution now seems dead. Furthermore, even the small amount of administrative devolution undertaken through regional government offices will disappear with the abolition of those offices.

The lack of any form of sub-national government in the UK seems almost unique among largish countries.

Lack of local funding base

In 2008–2009, total sources of funding for UK public services (excluding borrowing) amounted to £575 billion. Of that sum less than 10% was raised locally through council tax and charges with over 90% being raised at the national government level through various sorts of taxes. The adage 'he who pays the piper calls the tune' comes to mind here. The fact that central government raise virtually all of the revenues used to finance public services in the UK suggests that its influence over those services will be dominant and overwhelming. This contrasts with the experiences of many other countries (e.g. USA, Sweden) where the raising of public revenues through locally based taxes changes the balance of power between the centre and the local parts of government.

In summary, the political and economic environment in which public services in the UK are planned and managed can be summarised as being:

- A very strong centralised government based on a Parliament with little control on the scope of its actions and a Prime Minister and an executive arm of government with little in the way of checks and balances over their activities;
- The absence of any form of sub-national government which might act as a counter-balance to the power of central government. At the very least the existence of devolved administrations in Scotland and Wales has shown that there are alternative approaches to public policy which can work;
- A public finance situation where over 90% of public funding is being raised at the national government level with the consequent power balance that goes with that.

As noted earlier the former UK foreign secretary (the late Robin Cook) once described the UK as the most centralised state in the EU (*Guardian* 2002) and the Economist magazine once suggested that the UK was the second most centrally funded state in the developed world after New Zealand which has a population smaller than Wales (*The Economist* 2010a).

Consequently, the model for planning and managing public services in the UK is a direct consequence of these constitutional and government arrangements. Key features of this model are:

- Public policy developed at central government level with limited consultation outside of government and little or no provision for regional variations to be applied;
- Public policies forced through Parliament often against public opinion, expert views, other stakeholders views and the views of other political parties, through the use of the Parliamentary whipping process;
- The vast bulk of public services being financed by central government with the consequent power that goes with that financial clout;
- Top-down planning of public services driven by HM Treasury which is one of the most powerful Ministries of Finance in the developed world;
- This top-down planning process involving centrally driven targets initiated at the centre of government through the use of Public Service Agreements and Departmental Strategic objectives. These targets are subsequently rolled out to local authorities and government agencies across the country, and performance against these targets is reported back to the centre;

- The views of local people and locally elected representatives being largely ignored;
- Sometimes, ministerial interference in relatively minor operational aspects of service delivery at the regional and local level – sometimes in response to questions raised in Parliament.

In the light of the above situation, all of the reforms of public service provision that we describe below must be seen as taking place in such a way that the features of the traditional model are not disturbed and any such reforms must fit in with this existing paradigm.

Aims of public service reform

The underlying aims of public service reforms may be to do with the services tnemselves, but may reflect power struggles within government or they may be part of a wider socio-political reform such as liberalisation, or they may be a symbolic response to a significant failure of government in the face of events such as natural disasters.

Before looking at detailed aspects of public service reform it is worth considering what the reform process is intended to achieve (the aims). An analysis of a variety of public service reforms suggests that they are primarily concerned with achieving some or all of the aims shown in Table 7.1.

Classifying public service reforms

There are a number of different ways of trying to classify the attempts at public service reform such as historical, service-based and so on. Possible approaches are discussed below.

Hierarchical reforms

Firstly it would be possible to analyse public sector reforms according to what level in the hierarchical structure of public services the reforms took place. Thus, for example, we could consider public service reforms according to the following:

- European level
- National (UK) level
- Regional level
- Local level

Consideration of reforms on this basis would necessitate consideration of the constitutional arrangements in a particular country since this could

Table 7.1 Aims of public services

Service aims	Political aims
Efficiency – Improved efficiency in the use of public resources. **Effectiveness** – Improved effectiveness of service provision in relation to strategic objectives. **Consumer satisfaction** – improved levels of satisfaction with public services from the users of such services. **Choice** – provision of increased choice to consumers about the type and location of service they required. **Access** – improved access to public services particularly in relation to the timing and reduction in waiting times. **Flexibility** – greater flexibility in the delivery of public services and the improved tailoring of service provision rather than a 'one size fits all' approach.	**Public sector monopolies** – many public service organisations are often described as being state monopolies. Reforms may be concerned with breaking up such monopolies. Recent UK Governments had a clear policy of expanding the role of the private sector in health service provision since the NHS is often seen as one of the last state monopolies in the UK exhibiting such negative characteristics as inflexibility, unresponsiveness to customer needs etc. **Reduce restrictive practices** – many politicians were of the view that the public sector was rife with a large number of restrictive labour practices deriving from trade unions and/or professional bodies. Many of the reforms were concerned to loosen such restrictive practices as a means of delivering on the service aims described above.

affect the impact of those reforms. However, it is not clear how useful this might be because we would see certain aspects of reforms taking place at many different levels in the hierarchy.

Service-based reforms

A second approach to classifying public service reforms would be to do this according to the particular public service concerned. Thus, for example, we might consider reforms that have taken place in relation to:

- the NHS
- post-16 education
- economic development

The problem with this approach of course is that it provides no analysis of the application and impact of a particular type of reform (e.g. market testing) across a range of public services and does not permit one service to learn from the experiences of another.

Thematic reforms

A third approach to classifying public services reforms is to do it by reference to a particular theme. Such themes often cover several different public services. We have concluded that it is this thematic approach which is the best way of describing and discussing the types of public sector reforms which have taken place in the UK (and other countries), and we have used the following categorisation:

- Structural change
- Competition and contestability
- Mixed economy of provision
- Consumerism and choice
- Audit, inspection and regulation
- Reforms to joining up service provision
- Financing reforms
- Managerial reforms

Analysis of thematic reforms

In this section, we briefly discuss some of the thematic approaches to public service reforms that have been applied in the UK and other countries.

Structural change

Many reforms are concerned with changing the structures of organisations concerned with the planning, management and delivery of public services. Over a long period of time many different types of structural reform have taken place in almost all parts of the public sector. In doing this public sector organisations may have been formed, abolished or changed in some way. Some of these have just involved changes to organisational arrangements with little impact on the underlying operational procedures or cultures of the service. For example, in 1974 the NHS underwent a major reorganisation involving the replacement of Regional Hospital Boards and Hospital Management Committees with a series of Regional Health Authorities, Area Health Authorities and District Health Authorities. While such a reorganisation impacted greatly on the administrative arrangements of the NHS there is little evidence of change taking place within individual hospitals or community health units.

Some examples of structural reforms which have taken place in many public services concern the following:

- *Simplification* - in many parts of the country the local government structure has been simplified from a two-tier structure to a unitary structure.
- *Merger* – many organisation mergers have taken place in the public sector including NHS Trusts and FE colleges.

- *Abolition* – the Coalition Government has recently announced the abolition of RDAs and their replacement with local economic partnerships.
- *Creation* – new public sector organisations have been created in response to specific concerns (e.g. Food Standards Agency).

Another more profound example of organisational change has concerned the separation of service commissioner and provider. In many parts of the public sector, this has involved the separation of the policy-making and planning functions from that of actual service delivery. The former would be responsible for defining what type of services are required while the actual provision of those services would be undertaken by a separate unit or organisation. Some examples of where this approach has been applied are as follows:

- *NHS* – the NHS internal market involves separation of the commissioner function (PCTs, GP consortia), responsible for deciding which services should be provided, from that of service provision via NHS Trusts or other types of provider.
- *Executive agencies* – within central government departments there has been a separation of the policy-making function from that of service delivery through the creation of separate executive agencies with responsibility for service provision. Thus in the Department of Work and Pensions policy-making is retained within the Department itself while the actual tasks of assessing and paying benefits to individuals is undertaken by an executive agency entitled the Job Centre+.
- *Local government* – for certain specific services (e.g. leisure services, waste collection) the relevant local authority department (the client department) would define what types, volumes and quality of services should be provided. The actual provision of those services might then be provided by a separate contracting unit of the council known as a Direct Service Organisation (DSO).

Such changes can have profound impacts on the operational procedures and cultures of the organisations concerned.

Competition and contestability

One of the key themes of public service reform (as exemplified in the term New Public Management) was that of exposing public services, traditionally provided in-house, to external competition via some form of market testing exercise. One possible outcome of such an exercise could be that service provision might be outsourced to an external body, but there are also many examples where in-house units improved their cost and quality performance to such an extent that they were successful in retaining the contract for service provision. In all of these types of market testing exercise the external competitors may be other public sector organisations, private sector organisations or third sector organisations. Market testing exercises need not just apply to in-house service provision. Where a public sector organisation has already outsourced service provision to an external organisation they may still conduct periodic market testing exercises to ensure they are getting the best deal. If current provider is already external (i.e. outsourced) then market testing exercise may result in a re-insourcing of that service.

Contestability is not the same as market testing and competition. The concept of contestability was originally developed in the 1980s, by the American economist William Baumol in relation to industrial markets (Baumol 1982) and was concerned with the position and behaviour of monopolistic providers of goods and services in such markets. Baumol suggested that monopolistic providers did not need to be exposed to actual competition in order to make them responsive and competitive – the mere threat of competition might be sufficient to achieve these ends. Thus contestability is not a synonym for competition, but describes a situation where a provider faces a possible and credible threat of competition. In this context, contestability could involve, for example, the creation or encouragement of a credible alternative provider of goods or services. Contestability is fundamentally different to 'market testing', as it does not require every individual service to be competed only for a threat to be created.

Contestability has been subsequently extended to cover public monopolies and public service delivery. An example here would be the prison service which although largely publicly provided has some small element of private provision. The existence and operation of this private element provides a real and credible threat that, at some future date, and if deemed necessary, yet more of the prison service could be transferred to private provision. This inhibits the existing public provider from displaying strong monopolistic tendencies of inflexibility, resistance to change and so on. Contestability has been applied to many other public services and may be extended even further in the future (Prowle 2008).

Mixed economy of provision

Traditionally most public services were delivered primarily by public sector organisations. However, over the past 20 years or so there have been substantial changes in the mix of public, private and third sector provision. Such trends undoubtedly reflect changes in political perceptions of the role of the state in service provision with an increasing emphasis on the state as an enabler rather than a direct provider. Also it must be noted, that although many traditional public services are now delivered by the private or third sector they are still financed by public funds. This enhanced involvement by the private and third sector has taken several forms:

- *Market Testing and Outsourcing* – as discussed above many parts of the public sector, have been required or encouraged to subject large parts of their in-house operations to market testing and external competition. Frequently, the result of such a market test exercise was for the in-house service to retain the contract (often as a result of internal efficiency improvements). However, a significant amount of service provision was also transferred to private sector contractors or third sector providers via this process.

- *Private Finance Initiative (PFI)* – The involvement of the private sector has been further extended through the application of the private finance initiative (PFI). Basically the PFI involves private contractors (or more usually a consortium) bidding for a contract to construct a public sector building (e.g. a hospital) *and* to provide a wide range of services to support that building. In turn the private contractor would charge the public sector an annual unitary payment for the use of the building and for service provision. Although the private contractor is involved in financing large-scale capital expenditure it is important to emphasise the role of the contractor in providing services and not just in constructing a building. Treasury rules inhibit an arrangement whereby the private sector merely finances and constructs a new building and leases that building back to the public sector organisation.
- *Private service contracts* – In some situations, contracts for the delivery of new services have been let to private contractors rather than by enhancing in-house provision. One example of this was the Independent Treatment Centres initiatives in the NHS. These involved the Government entering into contracts with private companies to deliver additional surgical and diagnostic services rather than by expanding the NHS capacity.

Consumerism and choice

A strong theme in public service reform has been that of consulting the users (and prospective users) of services concerning their views. It may seem strange today to imagine that 30 years ago most public service organisations undertook little consultation with service users about the services being provided, but today, through consultation, the views of service users should shape services for the future. Such a consultation could be ex-ante in terms of the consultation about changes to service provision or ex-post in terms of the degree of satisfaction with services received. Such consultation would take the form of consulting with individual citizens or with whole communities and various techniques might be deployed such as questionnaire surveys, focus groups and citizen's juries.

However, the situation is not always that simple for a number of reasons:

- The public service organisation may be in breach of the law or Government policy by applying the views of consumers (e.g. weekly or two weekly refuse collection);
- There may be insufficient resources to apply the views of consumers;
- There may be lack of clarity about who the consumers actually are and there may be divergences of view. For example, in a school are the consumers the parents or the children.

Perhaps the key to this is to give feedback to service users and information as to why how views about services could not be applied. In this way the consultation exercise will not be seen as pseudo-consultation.

A natural extension to consulting the users of services about the services they receive is to give them greater choice of the services they receive. This could involve a variety of choices such as choice of service required, choice of location of service, choice of timing of service and so on. Choice was a key policy plank of the previous Labour Government. One example of this was the policy of Patient Choice (Appleby and Dixon 2004) in the NHS where patients choose the hospital where they will receive their treatment from a list of possible providers (public and private). Other examples of extended individual choice include a major expansion of specialist schools and the introduction of light rail systems improving transport choice in some parts of the country. An example of choice which goes even further is that of personal social care budgets where the service recipient can decide not only who should be the provider of services but what types of services they wish to purchase from their personal budgets.

Audit, inspection and regulation reforms

Over a period of years Governments have made significant extensions to the range of audit, inspection and regulatory arrangements concerned with public services. Some examples are as follows:

- *Audit* – the Audit Commission was created in 1983 with responsibility for the audit of local authorities (and subsequently for the NHS). In addition to traditional audit work, the Commission had an expanding role in promoting VFM. Similarly, in other parts of the public sector the National Audit Office (NAO) has been active in promoting improved VFM through its audit activities. The Coalition Government has indicated its attention to abolish the Audit Commission.
- *Inspection and regulation* – many public services are subject to an independent review of services they provide. Some key examples of this are OFSTED (schools and other education functions), Care Quality Commission (health and social care) and the Audit Commission inspection functions (local government). Although the precise form of inspection and regulation will differ between agencies (some make greater use of data analysis while other make greater use of inspection visits), the aim is the same. It is to identify what the organisations are doing well, what they are doing badly and how standards can be raised and performance improved.

Many will criticise the range and power of these bodies and see them as just another arm of central control of public services. Others have suggested that the activities of these bodies inhibit the effectiveness of governance and management within public sector organisations themselves.

Joined up working

The previous Labour Government placed great emphasise on improvements in what was termed 'joined up' government. This implies greater joint working between government departments and agencies in order to deliver. At the central government level a number of changes were made to foster joined up government. These include structural changes such as the creation of Cabinet committees and inter-departmental committees of civil servants to address cross-departmental issues such as basic skills, environmental issues and so on. In addition the creation of Public Service Agreements which covered several departments and which got those departments signed up to a shared set of service objectives aimed to foster improvements in joined up working between departments.

At the local level, multi-agency partnerships were created which involved statutory agencies, such as local authorities, NHS bodies and police authorities, and third sector organisations and which aimed to plan and deliver services in a more coherent and co-ordinated way. These partnerships were then supplemented by the requirement to produce Local Area Agreements (LAA) which set out how the various agencies might contribute to service delivery in a coherent manner. Other developments which have fostered this joined up working at the local level included the use of common need assessment processes, the provision of joint training for staff from the various agencies and the sharing of information resources between agencies and so on. The Coalition Government is in the process of dismantling much of this partnership architecture.

Financing reforms

If we consider reforms to the methods of financing public services then it is difficult to see that there have been many significant reforms in this area. Clearly there have been changes to such things as the detailed methods of distributing public funds between competing public expenditure programmes and organisations and changes to the balance between specific grants and general grants to local authorities, but these don't constitute significant changes in terms of the means of financing services and the balance between national taxes, local taxes and user charges.

The National Assemblies for Wales and Northern Ireland have no tax raising powers and while the Scottish Parliament does have the power to raise funds through a local income tax, this power has never been used. Thus the funds raised by local authority's remains the only source of local taxation. The type of local tax on individuals has been changed over the years going from a property tax termed domestic rates to a flat rate tax termed community charge (or poll tax) and back to a different property-based tax called council tax. The process of distributing business rates has been changed away from a system where locally raised rates were used locally, to one where locally raised rates were pooled into a national fund and then distributed back to individual local authorities. This change broke the link between tax and spend but the Coalition Government may reverse this arrangement to allow local authorities to keep, at least, some of the business rates they collect. Also, there have been changes in the scope and level of user charges for public services but at a level which does not disturb the traditional pattern of financing.

Over the years there have been calls for the introduction of a new local source of taxation (e.g. local income tax) for local authorities and at one time the Labour Party advocated the introduction of a local income tax to finance the NHS. All such ideas now seem to have been forgotten in the interests of central control. Although the detailed make up of centrally raised revenues has changed over the years with the introduction of new taxes and the amendment of existing ones, the reality is that public services are now more dependent on centrally raised funding than they have ever been.

Managerial reforms

A whole host of managerial reforms have taken place in public services with the aim of improving management practice. These have covered a wide range of areas of management including strategy, finance, human resources and sorts. Just a few examples listed below will illustrate what has been taking place:

- Financial management initiative
- Leadership development
- Strategic planning
- Performance management

Success of past attempts at reform

Public sector reforms have taken place in the UK over a wide range of services, over a long period of time and, as discussed above, have taken a wide variety of forms. Thus it is very difficult to provide a simple answer to the basic question of whether such reforms have proved successful. If we look at specific reforms we will probably find that some reforms were more successful than others even though their impact was not even over the whole of the country. For example, let us take the reform of market testing. In some parts of the UK there is evidence that this policy has improved the efficiency of service provision while in other places it has had a negative impact on service standards. However, looking broadly, there is evidence to suggest that overall this policy was successful and still continues.

In trying to answer the big question of whether the huge range past approaches to public services reform have proved generally successful, we refer to four assessment themes:

Magnitude of public spending

In Chapter 2 we discussed the long-term upward trend of public spending in the UK over the past hundred years or so. The past few decades have seen a considerable increase in public expenditure with billions of pounds of additional spending being committed to public services such as education, welfare, social services, health, and programmes intended to address the causes of social breakdown. This spending has resulted in a continuing increase in the tax burden on UK citizens. Moreover, much of this spending in recent years was financed by vast Government borrowing to the extent that the UK is now in a serious fiscal state and is having to implement austerity measures by increasing taxation and reducing public expenditure.

Value for money

In spite of this large-scale growth in public expenditure, in many cases, there remain grave doubts as to how well the money has been spent. While recent governments have placed more emphasis on the management and monitoring of public services, it is not obvious that this has delivered better value for money because the true effectiveness of most policies is still poorly understood. If government cannot determine where public spending delivers results and where it does not, both the taxpayer and society as a whole will continue paying for ineffective and inefficient programmes.

Let us just take a few examples:

- *Health* – spending on the NHS in England has grown at an unprecedented rate over the past decade but NHS productivity has fallen (House of Commons 2011).
- *Schools* – between 1999 and 2007 Government spending on schools almost doubled but productivity fell by an average of 0.7% per annum (*Financial Times* 2007). Also the extra spending produced an average increase of just one extra GCSE per pupil every five years. The analysis came as results in tests showed that standards in English and mathematics are falling in more than half of primary schools and four in ten pupils leave without a basic grounding in numeracy and literacy.
- *Defence* – A report commissioned by the Secretary of State for Defence in the last government, which was never published but was leaked (*Spectator* 2009), concluded that the Ministry of Defence's equipment programme was £35 billion over budget, five years behind schedule, and could not be afforded in the long-term. The report also commented that the problems were so severe that they were 'harming our ability to conduct difficult current operations'.

We have to ask whether such failures in achieving value for money in the use of taxpayer's money would be tolerated in any other kind of organisations.

Satisfaction levels

As already noted in Chapter 2, in the UK, in spite of the various public service reforms that have taken place over the past 30 years and the substantial growth in public service funding, there still appears to be a considerable degree of dissatisfaction among UK citizens with public services in general (Cabinet Office 2001). Using health as an example, available data shows high degrees of consumer satisfaction in countries such as Denmark and Sweden and low degrees of satisfaction in countries such as Italy and Greece. Satisfaction levels in the UK fall well below that in the Scandinavian countries even though the NHS has had huge increases in funding.

Status indicators

By status we mean measures which may give some indication of the effectiveness or otherwise of public services. If we consider where the UK stands in terms of status indicators we will find that in spite of the additional billions of pounds of public spending and the almost constant stream of reforms we are not making good progress. Some examples of this are:

- *Education* – in the recent PISA rankings published by the OECD (OECD 2009) the UK was well down the rankings and behind its main competitors with regard to reading, mathematics and science. A recent report for England showed that only 16% of school pupils leave school with five A-C passes in their GCSE examinations.
- *Health* – international comparisons of a range of health status indicators (such as life expectancy, mortality rates) suggest that the UK does not compare well in a number of areas with comparable European countries such as France, Germany, Sweden and Denmark (Mladovsky et al. 2009).

Taking the above four points together suggests that there is something seriously wrong with UK public services. Despite huge growth in spending there are large areas where productivity has declined, customer satisfaction is, to say the least, not glowing and there are serious questions of effectiveness. Our overall conclusions from the above are that despite a raft of public service reforms which have taken place over a long period of time, the fundamentals remain unchanged. Hence we must seriously question how effectiveness past attempts at public sector reform have been and how the current public service model can possibly cope with the challenges of austerity.

The approach to planning and managing public services in the UK remains largely a heavily centralised command-and-control approach driven by a central government apparatus based in London. There is limited regional or local decision-making regarding the raising of local funds or the use of centrally provided public funds. Furthermore, even though newly elected governments usually promise to implement some form of localist agenda, once they have been in power for a while the localist ideas usually become minimalist or disappear completely.

Barriers to change

If the centralised command-and-control system of planning and managing public services in the UK 'delivered the goods' in terms of having highly effective and efficient services with high levels of customer satisfaction, then there would be arguments for its retention. However, we have argued that the opposite is the case and that the evidence suggests that there are huge problems with UK public services. In this situation one may wonder why the highly centralised approach hasn't been modified and what are the (obviously very strong) barriers to change. We suggest the following:

- *The dominance of London* – hardly anywhere else in the developed world does one city dominate a country to the extent that London does in the UK. London dominates politically, economically and culturally. The vast bulk of politicians, senior government officials, business leaders, the media, and heads of professions, all locate themselves in or around London. Consequently, whatever the merits of the case it is difficult to persuade these opinion formers of the imperative of equalising influence around the UK (Latham and Prowle 2010).
- *The nature of politics* – as we noted earlier, the nature of politics has changed. The lack of a regional tier of government (outside of the Celtic regions) means that an ambitious politician wishes to become a Member of Parliament. Since politics is now very much a lifelong profession most MPs now wish firstly to retain their seat for a long period of time and secondly to make progress up the ministerial (or shadow ministerial)ladder. This means being based in London and developing a high enough profile for consumption both in Westminster and back in their constituency. In these circumstances they have every reason to retain decision-making power in parliament and in the Executive branch of the UK Government rather than devolve it to the regional and local levels.
- *The failure of opposition parties* – we suggest that one of the barriers concerns the failure of opposition parties to be effective and there are a number of aspects to this. Firstly, our observations are that despite long periods in opposition and for whatever reasons, parties come to power with very little preparation for government. They have manifestos and policy papers, but often these lack rigour. The former Prime Minister Tony Blair virtually admitted that his government's first period in power was wasted with regard to public service reform because of lack of preparation. Secondly and linked to the above, for electoral purposes, parties often pander to the prejudices of the electorate in adopting naïve policies which they then have to reverse in government in the teeth of public opposition. Let us

take the NHS as an example. Our observations are that most opposition parties focus on three policies: reduce the numbers of administrators, give more power to doctors and nurses and protect the NHS budget for the simple reason that this is what the general public has been led to believe are the solutions. Once they get into power they find that the NHS is a complex organisation where the problems and solutions are also complex and where simple solutions won't work. They often require major changes in the configuration and methods of operation of the NHS. However, the same party in opposition has led the public to believe that their simple proposals will provide a solution to the NHS and they then have to try and implement new solutions in the teeth of the public opposition they created. The media also has a role to play here although, as already noted, it is a point of debate as to whether the media leads public opinion or reflects what already exists.

- *The Civil Service Culture* – firstly, the reality is that the vast bulk of senior civil servants involved in policy-making are located in London offices somewhere close to Whitehall. This indicates that the main sources of power (ministers and senior civil servants) are in London. Secondly, the Civil Service has an inherently centralising culture with a sometimes disdainful view of the merits of regional bodies and local agencies and their capabilities in policy-making. Thirdly, the Civil Service has a predominant view which separates policy-making and implementation into two separate categories with policy-making being the province of Whitehall and implementation being the job of agencies, local authorities and so on. Unfortunately this separation often means that policy-making is undertaken without any serious consideration of the difficulties of implementation and this is where problems start. Lastly, of course, in spite of the Fulton Report many would argue that there have been minimal changes to the Civil Service culture. Most senior civil servants are recruited and spend most of all of their working life in the Civil Service. The lack of contact with people from other types of organisations and culture (e.g. the private sector) means that the prevailing Civil Service culture is reinforced with each generation.

Conclusions

The overall conclusion must be that in spite of large growth in UK public spending, which most recently has resulted in the country being left with huge amounts of public debt, the state of public services in the UK is not good. This is in spite of an almost continuous and varied programme of public service reforms which have taken place over the past 30 years or so. The situation is such because, in spite of all the reforms that have taken place, the centralised command-and-control system for planning and managing public services has remained broadly unchanged. Moreover, there are significant barriers to changing this situation.

Part III

Radical Alternatives and Charting the Way Forward

8
A New Paradigm

Paradigms can be seen as the constellation of beliefs and values and techniques which are shared by the members of a given community. Most organisations that have a coherent focus will have a paradigm that is either explicit or implied. The paradigm of an organisation is supported by a number of elements that can be measured and evaluated. These elements tend to be mutually supporting, and reinforce the overall shape of the paradigm – which can be broadly described as 'the way we do business round here'. The most common ones are illustrated in Figure 8.1, and are self-explanatory.

Breaking out of a paradigm requires significant effort, and a clear willingness to sustain change even when all the existing pressures are pushing you back to doing things the old way. It requires a significant change of mind, and is often enforced because the existing paradigm ceases to provide a reasonable explanation of experienced reality. In this part of the book, we examine alternatives to traditional approaches to see if they might be more successful in current circumstances. In the light of Chapter 4 the proposed alternatives are definitely in the H3 category, in that they require a revolutionary change in thinking amounting to a paradigm shift. Because such changes are necessarily long-term, we would not suggest that adopting a new approach on its own would provide a successful strategy. In line with the thinking outlined in Chapter 4 any H3 paradigm shift would necessarily need at least some H1 coping strategies, and perhaps even some H2 project-based reforms depending on the time scale and resource availability. So, although we concentrate on the substance of the H3 change, it's important to recognise that this does not mean that either some of the current proposals to deal with the immediate financial issues or some of the reforming changes would not also be required.

In looking at the paradigm issue we consider a number of things. Firstly, how paradigm changes have occurred in the past, using an example of that of the Copernican revolution, to draw out some key features of paradigm shifts. We'll then look at two significant changes in thinking from the 20th century which provide significant underpinning for the paradigm shift in

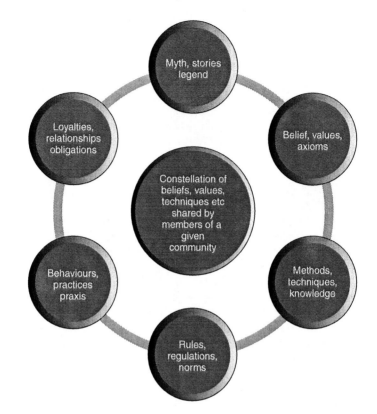

Figure 8.1 Diagrammatic representation of the thinking behind a paradigm

public services that is required. The first of these changes centres around the insights of Chaos Theory and Quantum Theory which provided a better understanding of issues to do with complexity and uncertainty. The second of these insights is the shift away from thinking about economies and organisations as machinelike arrangements to structures which are closer to living entities and biological forms. We then consider paradigm shifts in relation to the two most significant issues:

- Political economy
- Organisational forms

The nature of paradigm changes

The Copernican revolution

With very few exceptions most informed people currently accept that Earth is part of the solar system, that it is part of a heliocentric arrangement where the Earth circles the Sun. Since the discoveries in astronomy of the 20th century, most would also accept that our Sun is an ordinary star located in a relatively insignificant part of a galaxy which is only one of billions of galaxies in the universe. This view, though originally put forward in the 3rd century BC by Aristarchus of Samos, was not generally accepted until the 16th century following the work of Copernicus (Wikipedia b), and it took until the 17th century before the works of people such as Kepler and Galileo provided refinements and observational data to back up Copernicus's views. Copernicus's original views were in circulation in the 1530s, and were referred to in lectures from 1533. However he did not write his definitive version until 1543 and immediately came into conflict with the Catholic Church, and with Protestant reformers who held that his views were not scriptural. Attempts were made by Tycho Brahe in 1587 to synthesise Copernicus's new approach with the older Ptolemaic geocentric system. Galileo's development of the telescope led to his publication in 1610 which supported Copernicus but led him into direct conflict with the Catholic Church which required him to recant his views. Kepler, in publications from 1609 onwards, refined Copernicus's views by introducing the elliptical orbit and provided predictive capacity for the position of the planets. Despite the fact he was a Protestant his writings were also proscribed by the Church. This opposition continued until 1758 when the works of Kepler, Copernicus and Galileo were finally removed from the index of prohibited books, although the heliocentric approach was not fully approved by the Catholic Church until 1822.

This very brief chronology establishes a number of learning points about paradigm changes:

1. The original conceptual ideas for a paradigm change often goes back way before the proposed alternative view is thoroughly explored. Many such changes have often been hunches, but the speculation often lacked sufficient observations, predictive capacity, or detailed work to stand as an accepted view of reality. The early speculative pioneers were often right, but sometimes could only come to their conclusions by analogy and intuition rather than by detailed factual analysis.
2. Paradigm changes take time. From Copernicus's earliest writings to Kepler's thorough analysis and predictions took almost 100 years, and to become accepted as the orthodox view of reality took a further hundred years. Niels Bohr, speaking of Quantum Theory, suggested that it takes three generations for new thinking to become accepted. The first generation develops the thinking and coherence of the idea, the second generation learns it as an alternative alongside the more traditional approach, and only in the third generation does it come to be accepted as the new orthodoxy.
3. The simplest changes often meet the greatest resistance. Challenging orthodoxy is not easy, and although it may seem a relatively simple step to change thinking from a geocentric to a heliocentric universe, the

proposals of Copernicus ran into substantial resistance not only from the Catholic Church but also from the more reforming Protestant authorities. Whilst some authorities encouraged debate and discussion, the general approach was to shut down debate, proscribe the thinking, and, in some cases, use bullying or threatening tactics to prevent change.

4. Once the ideas of a new approach has been published, there is often a phase of very rapid thinking development as the principles and possibilities are considered and expanded. However, resistance from within the scientific and philosophical community to accepting in full the new proposals can also arise. At some point there is generally an attempt at a synthesis between the existing traditional approach and the new thinking. This is generally unsuccessful, as the principles, and implications of the traditional orthodoxy and the new view are generally incompatible.

5. One of the key questions of debate as a new paradigm develops is whether it represents a better description of reality, or simply a more convenient way of measuring and predicting outcomes of events. This balance between positivism – it represents a better predictive theory – and realism – this is actually how things operate in reality – often remains unresolved among those who adopt the new approach from a technical point of view, as opposed to those who believe it is true.

The traditional paradigm – the Newtonian World

The development of Copernican thinking, which looked at alternative explanations of observable phenomena and asked for the simplest set of assumptions to explain them (using the principle of Occam's Razor), was a precursor to the wider development of scientific thinking which found its expression in the Enlightenment. To a very substantial extent we are all living in a post-Enlightenment age, where scientific method has been used extensively to develop technical and predictive capacity, replacing earlier dogma and belief-based systems. In the development of Newtonian physics, we were given a set of tools which were used in the post-Enlightenment age for the development of our economy, and our organisational systems, as much as they were used in the development of science and technology. These basic principles substantially underlie the traditional hierarchical bureaucracy that we've already examined. Before looking at the challenges that modern Quantum Theory and Chaos Theory have given in both the scientific and in the larger world of human knowledge, it's worth restating very briefly those basic principles, which we summarise, perhaps unfairly, as Newtonian:

- The approach is reductionist. That is to say when presented with a significant large problem the approach is to break it down into smaller units or sub-problems and solve each independently putting them together again at the end to create a wider and complete understanding. The underlying principle is that of independence, that is, individual units within the universe operate independently, and therefore the change in any individual part can be summed to provide the change when all the individuals are considered together.

- The approach is positive. That is as we delve deeper and deeper into the subsystems we find each one of them is increasingly mechanistic and devoid of value attributes. The conclusions deal with facts – what is – not with opinions – what ought to be. David Hume, the Enlightenment philosopher was careful in his analysis to show conclusively that you cannot derive 'what ought to be' from 'what is'. The scientific approach is therefore amoral, it makes no judgement, and it simply determines what is.

- The approach is linear and deterministic. Changes have an obvious cause and effect. Newton's three laws of motion expressed this most succinctly. Although the interaction of cause and effect can be complex, it is possible to calculate and predict both preceding system states, and final outcomes. Consequently this implies that outcomes are:
  - *certain* – Laplace is said to have boasted that if he had sufficient knowledge of the original conditions, and enough computing capacity and knowledge of the principles of change that he could predict the outcome – both forwards and backwards – with certainty for any system,
  - *scalable* – If you want to double the outcome then you double input. Things act proportionately and to do something bigger or better, you simply need to scale it up,
  - *monotonic* – For a single set of initial conditions and a change there is a single predicted outcome which leads on to others and so on so there is only ever a single solution.

Step 1 of the new paradigm: insights from Chaos Theory and Quantum Theory

These underlying Newtonian principles which served well for a long period of time fell apart when scientists came to investigate the phenomenon of light and the subatomic structure of matter. The development of Quantum Theory (Kuman 2009, Polkinghorne 2002) shows many of the characteristics of the Copernican revolution:

> it took almost 100 years for it to become largely accepted; there was considerable resistance internally and externally to some of its conceptual outcomes; although it had substantial predictive capacity the question about whether or not it represents reality is still in debate.

Attempts were made to synthesise the quantum approach with a more deterministic approach of Newtonian physics and although there were some brilliant insights it often took much longer before successful experiments could show that the speculative thinking had some basis in reality.

However, the Quantum approach and the development of Chaos Theory (see Smith 2007) have contributed to a changed understanding of complex reality and uncertainty, have developed new thinking that contrasted with the more deterministic solutions of Newtonian thinking, and have subsequently greatly influenced our modern understanding of the world.

Thinking about physical systems in the world, from subatomic particles upwards, has tended to be dominated, the last half of the 20th century, by the developing insights of Quantum Theory and Chaos Theory. Subsequently, much of the predictive capacity of meteorological forecasting and climate change analysis has been heavily influenced by this kind of thinking. In the world of evolution these developments have given rise to the concept of 'punctuated equilibrium' – the sudden and rapid change of life forms following a perturbation in ecological systems after a period of considerable stability. This has developed thinking about a 'new catastrophism' that supplemented the more Newtonian uniformitaranism gradualism of early geological and paleontological thinking.

Chaos Theory is a mathematical method based on mapping input variables into outputs based on simple rules as a means of explaining apparently complex systems. However it tends not to be reductionist, in that it does not attempt to break down the problem into a series of small problems, solve them individually, and reassemble the whole. It is holistic in nature. Nevertheless, as a deterministic system it deals with what is not what ought to be. As such, it has no ethic or moral values to assert. The rules and maps of Chaos Theory tend to be non-linear, and based on systems in which the outcomes can be impacted significantly by small variations in the initial conditions, often giving the impression of randomness. Chaos Theory tends to produce results which are subject to phase shifting – that is, moving quickly from one condition to an alternative without any significant intermediate transition state. This gives rise to the phenomenon of 'strange attractors' when the variables cycle around alternative states without ever reaching any specific state, or reaching a point of equilibrium, thus implying virtually continuous cyclical motion.

Figure 8.1 shows how the existence of these 'strange attractors' might give a pattern between economic output and resource utilisation which matched the insights of John Maynard Keynes. He (Keynes 1935) felt that the economy was capable of being in equilibrium at a lower state, but in this case no equilibrium is actually ever reached, indeed it may not exist at all, but simply becomes an attractor around which the economy endlessly circulates.

The concept that there is a natural level of uncertainty and improbability features strongly in the understandings of quantum mechanics, as does the idea of phase shifting. Within quantum mechanics there are only certain positions that subatomic particles can take and they have logically limited alternatives. If an electron occupies a certain position, then another cannot.

Output

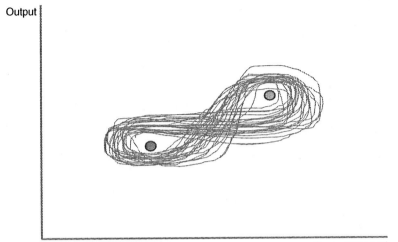

Resources used

Figure 8.2 Strange attractors and the economic cycle

The overall conclusions from quantum mechanics suggest not only logically limited phase states, but also interdependencies within the elements. These ideas have developed within the new economics from the understandings of writers such as Piero Sraffa who considered that economies could have sets of outcomes which were logically possible, but couldn't occupy any intermediate position between them. Nor was it necessary to assume, as economic orthodox theory had it, that moving between one pattern of the economy and a second pattern that inputs or outputs will be changed in a predictable way.

Much more significant however is the whole issue of uncertainty. Uncertainty is inherent within quantum mechanics. We simply cannot know what the outcome is going to be, which limits in some respects the ability of new economic thinking to predict accurately future pattern of the economy. The difficulties of measurability may also emerge in the economy, much in the same way that Heisenberg's Uncertainty Principle in quantum mechanics determines that the minute you measure the mass of a particular particle you can no longer determine its position. In the same way the minute you set out to measure some element of the economy you cease to be able to use that measure as a determinant of the state of the economy. In the same way the ability of the economy and economic agents to adjust behaviour individually and collectively may both create the circumstances which were predicted or its opposite. You cannot be certain of which would be the outcome, but if you set out to measure it, you may end up by not being able to measure the true position at all.

The insights from Chaos Theory and Quantum Theory would begin to give a whole new dimension to the question of future economic prediction from the new economics. But these insights have also begun to be applied towards new forms of organisation giving rise to new thinking about the way that organisations actually work. Some of the early thinking about this was developed in a groundbreaking work by Margaret Wheatley (Wheatley 2001) who took some of the insights around Quantum and Chaos Theory and began to apply them to the way that organisations functioned. Then, in one of those 'hunches' that prefigures paradigm change she, and others, moved from applying the outcomes of Chaos Theory and Quantum Theory as simply better post-Enlightenment scientific explanations of the more complex world of organisational behaviour and outcomes on to another level. The substantive change can be summed up in the change of metaphor from organisations as a machine to organisations operating as living organic entities. The Newtonian way of thinking considered organisations by using the language of machines. Quantum and Chaos Theory gave holistic insights into organisations. As organisations are essentially voluntary associations of individual autonomous agents, suggested they might function much in the way that herds of animals or flocks of birds did in the natural world. Information about the way that the natural world functions suggested that this approach would give fresh insights.

Step 2 of the new paradigm: autonomous agents – herds and flocks

If some of the nonlinearities of the new paradigm can be derived from Chaos Theory, then a greater understanding of the implications of those nonlinearities comes from the behaviour of autonomous agents. Stuart Kauffmann's work on what constitutes the minimum conditions for an autonomous agent is based solidly in biology (Kauffman 2000 and 2008). For him autonomous agents represent entities that are capable of reproducing themselves and doing at least one thermodynamic cycle of work. From one point of view this relatively minimal level of understanding of autonomous agents is not particularly helpful, but the third element in his definition is. Autonomous agents have to have the ability to receive information, to have choice in determining the course of action, and carry out that action. The whole thrust of the market economy is that it is full of autonomous agents, individuals, governments, organisations, economic enterprises, investors and stakeholders, and so on. It is less a deterministic machine, more a living social entity. What emerges from the thinking about autonomous agents, particularly when those are gathered together in organisational forms as herds and flocks, is as follows.

Firstly, they are self-organising. That is they are able to process information without a command structure that controls actions, to come to a reasonable decision and take action as if the group had a single mind and purpose. The self-organising nature of groups is an important aspect of the new paradigm. Although herds and flocks might appear chaotic when first seen, in fact careful observation shows that they are largely self-organising groups that achieve collective objectives – protection from predators, safety from environmental hazard, protection of young, provision of a gene pool for adaptive development and perpetuation – that would not be achieved by individuals operating alone. Herds and flocks also show different patterns of leadership, and alternative approaches to structure and power that give insights into the ways in which organisations function. Herds and flocks are also not simply collections of random individuals. There are within them families, teams and subgroups with extensive social and technical networks within which individuals function and to which they contribute. So organisations, considered holistically, are not simple organic entities; they are also patterned by networks of relationships. It is thinking about organisations in this way that provides the simple, but revolutionary H3 alternative to the way public sector organisations might be organised for the future. In his book *Smart Swarm* Peter Miller (Miller 2010) gives some examples of the ways in which approaching business problems from an organisation based on a 'herds and flocks' approach has enabled a number of businesses to serve some difficult operational issues that defy more traditional methodologies. Using three basic mechanisms of decentralised control, distributed problem-solving, and multiple interactions between independent agents has created greater efficiencies in organisations. For the most part these have involved the use of relatively simple decision rules repeated via computer simulations – an approach which bears a very close resemblance to Chaos Theory. Not surprisingly complex issues can be analysed thus and apparently chaotic behaviour begins to develop periodicities and regularities the hierarchical, Newtonian, type of approach could not resolve. This operates even where the independent agents – such as ants and bees – do not possess a particular high individual intelligence, but as colonies or hives exhibit efficient and effective behaviours. To speak of the leadership in such contexts is fallacious, but other examples can show that leadership models that rely on individuals following the leadership of others physically close to them can ensure that, in the long-term, the herd or flock learns techniques of predator avoidance, migration or pathways, or strategies for dealing with uncertain conditions such as flood or bad weather. Similar leadership strategies can enable organisations to cope with long-term learning, uncertainty, and adverse circumstances.

Secondly, autonomous agents make choices so the possibility of value, purpose, and moral intent emerges. The activities of autonomous agents cannot be determined as part of a reductionist system. The group as a whole behaves in self-organised ways which are sometimes beneficial to its continued existence, and sometimes not. So, for example increasing densities of insects or fish, which have relatively limited reasoning capacity, can result in them adopting techniques which enable them to avoid a predator which is beneficial to the group's continuing existence. In like manner, groups can be beneficial or not to their environment. Autonomous agents both respond to the environment they face and modify their environment. In the cases of social insects this can result in them creating significant structures above and below ground which do not just modify the environment for themselves more favourably individually and as a group, but can actually alter the macro environment as well. However when locusts get above certain densities their effect on the environment can be disastrous stripping it of all resources before moving on as a swarm to destroy crops and vegetation elsewhere. Interestingly, in the case of locusts, this arises because, faced with a short-age of individual resources, locusts will resort to cannibalism of their neigh-bours, and it is trying to avoid being attacked by others in the swarm that causes the locusts to move from eating to swarming as a major phase shift, to find alternative food sources. Whereas ants and termites as social insects may show clear evidence of co-operative behaviour, it is the excessively com-petitive behaviour of locusts which causes their destructive activities.

Finally, in this area of autonomous agents there is the issue of Time's arrow. Reductionist deterministic systems have to deal with the fact that although technically they predict that, by reversing causality, they could show the initial conditions which gave rise to the final outcome, in practice time it does not permit you to go backwards; you can only move forward. Autonomous agents are operating in a world where the decisions that are taken set the pattern for the future. So, as a result of individual and col-lective behaviour and organisation, a group of individuals, and economic enterprises, can influence and modify the environment for good or ill. More importantly it is not possible to predict what the outcome of these collective decisions will be, because it is not possible to put boundaries around all pos-sible outcomes and associate probabilities with those outcomes. The inevi-table consequence therefore of autonomous agents is that there is inherent uncertainty going forward. The only absolute certainty would be in terms of looking back, and even then it would be limited in that it will become tech-nically impossible to answer the question of what would have happened, had what did happen, not happened. This inherent uncertainty needs to be distinguished from that of risk, in which a number of alternative outcomes can be predicted or estimated with a certain level of probability, and where it becomes mathematically and technically possible to minimise the overall risk level from a group of probable outcomes. It was a failure to distinguish between risk and uncertainty that led a number of financial institutions to assume that their complex risk reducing CDOs and CDS instruments meant that they could ignore the implications of an uncertain economic future. When the economic downturn occurred, the implications of their 'riskless' positions became all too apparent.

The insights drawn from this thinking – the greater complexity and uncertainty developed by Chaos Theory and Quantum Theory even within deterministic systems – and the insights drawn from thinking of organisations and economic systems as essentially composed of autonomous agents in a biological sense are the key changes that underpin the new paradigm. We'll now see how this paradigm change has implications for the way we approach political economy and organisational forms, and provides an alternative to traditional orthodoxy for both.

The impact of the new paradigm – political economy

We have seen how, in thinking about the new paradigm, we've moved in two stages beyond the simple, mechanistic and Newtonian world:

- Stage1 used the insights of Chaos Theory and Quantum Theory to provide a better explanation of the complexity that we see.
- Stage 2 moved to consider systems not as machines, but as living entities and gained further insights into their uncertainty and complexity.

In Chapter 3 we introduced the two principal poles of economic thinking to help explain the alternatives for public services policy. In this section we apply the same two-stage thinking to the development of a new economics that challenges the orthodoxy of the post neoclassical endogenous growth theory.

The development of this particular economic theory, and its later development into monetarist economics, goes back to the term of the 20th century. Utility theory (Walras 1874, Marshall 1890) led to the development of the neoclassical approach to economics that substantially separated it from its social roots and political origins. It set out economics as a specifically quantitative social science with the emphasis on the scientific method. It became the dominant economic theory and its post–Second World War development through the work of Samuelson, Solow, and Friedman was substantially US led.

The development of this economic orthodoxy was not without challenge. The concept of an individual acting independently to maximise his/her own welfare or utility was challenged by thinkers such as Thorstein Veblen (Veblen 1899) who perceived the social aspects of consumption. The impact of a free-market economy on wage rates and the distribution of income and the employment of labour was the substance of the Marxist critique, suggesting that the capitalist system would collapse and be replaced by the more equitable Communist system. The role of technology change and long-term economic cycles developed as part of the thinking of the Austrian School and by Joseph Schumpeter (Schumpeter 1934) with the proposal that any significant technology shift will be accompanied by a process of 'creative destruction' with consequent asymmetrical impact on employment. Following the experience of the 1930s depression when economies followed the economic orthodoxy and engaged in 'beggar your neighbour' strategies, Keynes proposed an alternative understanding of the economy which principally allowed the possibility of there being a phase shift towards a lower level of equilibrium in which resources remained unemployed, in contradistinction to the predictions of economic orthodoxy. Finally, as the growth theory of economic orthodoxy came under attack other economists of the Cambridge School, such as Piero Sraffa (Sraffa 1972), suggested that economies might show significant phase shifts in which the changing technology base did not exhibit the smooth transition from labour to capital, and the convergent growth predicted by the more orthodox thinking.

One of the difficulties with the description of the new economics is that whilst there is a clear cluster of economists supporting a broadly coherent group of theories around the post-neoclassical endogenous growth theory, the radicals represent a far more disparate group and it is difficult to establish a common set of principles or understanding that would bind together the critique that they independently make of orthodoxy (Coyle 2009, Ormerod 1997 and 2008, Boyle and Simms 2009). In one respect the champion of the radicals has tended to be John Maynard Keynes – and there are grounds for generally describing the alternative approach as neo-Keynesian. It was Keynes who identified the possibility of the economy being in equilibrium in a different state from that of full employment as implied in orthodoxy; it was Keynes who identified the significant impact of confidence and the existence of 'animal spirits' in driving changes in the economy; and it was Keynes who incidentally through his work on probability drew attention to the issues around uncertainty within the economy. All these aspects – phase shifting, behaviour, and uncertainty – are key underlying parts of the new economics.

Nevertheless, these do not exhaust the current critique of orthodoxy from a new economics standpoint. Challenges to the assumption of continuous economic growth and sustainability have been a pole of criticism from Ruskin (Wikipedia c) to Schumacher. With the rise of the environmental and green agenda increasingly challenging questions are being asked as to whether the overall pattern of economic development can be sustained except for a very small minority of countries (see Figure 8.3). The collective consequence is that if all economies operated on the same basis of resource consumption as Europe we would need 8 planets to meet the demands, and if in the case of the United States, 16 planets.

The reasons why economic growth in terms of GDP per capita has been such a driver are now being questioned. The impact of interest-bearing debt on the world economy, repaid out of additional surplus gained from growth, is being challenged as an unacceptably onerous overhead to economic activity. In much the same way David Ricardo (Wikipedia d) challenged the level of rent from land as being unacceptable burden on economic activity, so the questions of the burden of interest payments arising from increasing level

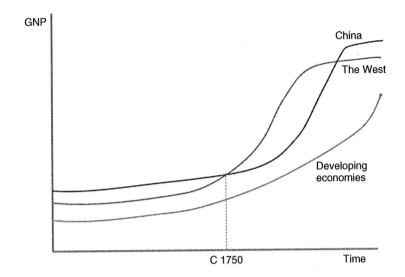

Figure 8.3 The growth of world economies

of international, national and personal indebtedness is being questioned. People are increasingly beginning to look at the implications of adopting Islamic style methods of finance, or the reinvention of the late mediaeval prohibition against usury, as a radical alternative to levels of activity in international finance which are now many times greater in volume that is necessary for either investment, regular financing, or trade purposes. If debt drives the necessity for growth, it also becomes a key driver of over-consumption, as products and services need to be consumed by a greater and greater number of people and in greater and greater quantities in order to provide effective demand to support economic growth. The extent to which this is being fuelled by marketing, fashion, and modest improvements on existing technology, rather than real innovation, has international implications in steepening the gradient between rich and poor; creating dissatisfaction through artificial and unsatisfied wants; and leading to problems of redundant items which are thrown away before they are worn out.

Of course within the traditional orthodoxy the assumption is that GDP represents the sole measure of economic performance. This assumption has been heavily criticised in the new economics as not representing an adequate description of economic activity, or indeed of activity which is publicly valued. So, for example, the development of approaches around measuring an index of welfare, well-being, or happiness has begun to be developed as an addition to GDP. The current Coalition Government is already conducting an investigation to determine whether or not such a

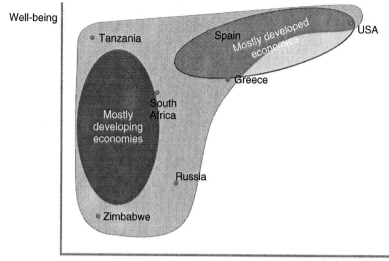

Figure 8.4   Relationships between happiness and national income levels

composite measure might not give a better understanding of public well-being. Cynics suggested this is to draw attention away from the fact that the GDP element will inevitably decline under current economic circumstances of austerity, and reflects the fact that the linkage between GDP per capita and personal happiness and well-being is a weak one for developed economies. Within underdeveloped economies more personal income is generally associated very positively with individual and community well-being, but within developed economies there is little variation. (See Figure 8.4)

We now turn to look at these issues in more detail as well as introducing the second stage of considering the economy as a living organic system that lies behind the development of the new economics. Looking at the new ꞈconomics overall, this section seeks to clarify the linkages with the other key thinking that underpins the new paradigm, that is the developments around Chaos Theory; autonomous agents (herds and flocks); and the nondeterministic elements of Quantum mechanics. Finally, we return to the question about whether the new economics, or the old orthodoxy, represents just a better methodology or whether it could be seen as a better understanding of reality.

Chaos Theory and political economy

If we compare the use of the basic principles of Chaos Theory within the new economics and look at the orthodoxy there are some immediate points of variation. Like Chaos Theory, the orthodox approach is based on a firmly deterministic model, but one which is reductionist in nature. It suggests that better and better explanations of the economy can be gained from looking at smaller and smaller segments of markets, enterprises, and individual behaviours. It implies that if one had a full understanding of the initial equilibrium conditions, and all subsequent individual behaviours and responses, then we'll be able to predict with accuracy economic outcomes, much along the lines of the boast of Laplace's daemon. This deterministic approach is carried forward into the concept of 'positive economics' in the orthodox model, that is, economics is a scientific approach that determines 'what is', and, consistent with Hume's analysis, from 'what is' you cannot derive 'what ought to be'. Compared to the Chaos Theory approach the orthodox economic model is one which is linear, and where the single measure of GDP, broken down into volumes and prices of market outcomes, is the sole valid measure. The economy will be at equilibrium, unless something changes in which case it will move smoothly to a new equilibrium. Given that things are pretty consistently changing, the orthodox theory predicts the market in transition to an equilibrium which is never reached, but which is always the goal. The path of change from one equilibrium to another is monotonic, that is the economy can adopt any number of intermediate positions and the path of change can only be made into a pattern of cyclical behaviour that is observed by the use of some form of boundary condition to contain the pattern of economic activity. This contrasts with Chaos Theory in which there may not be an equilibrium point at all.

The great contribution of Chaos Theory, therefore, towards the development of the new economics lies in replacing a reductionist approach with a holistic one; replacing the simplicity of linearity with non-linear functions; and replacing the idea of point equilibrium to point equilibrium changes by one of continuous activity around 'strange attractors'. Nevertheless, by adapting to the basic assumptions of orthodox economics to these new approaches more meaningful understanding of the nature of economic cycles, and of the implications for the economy of behavioural changes can be accommodated, and the inherent complexity of economic outcomes better understood.

Autonomous agents and political economy

Comparing the thinking behind autonomous agents with the thinking behind neoclassical orthodox economics reveals some inherent problems in orthodoxy. First, it is clear that the market economy, consisting as it does of a series of autonomous agents, is a self-organising entity. Adam Smith recognised this in his Wealth of Nations when he spoke of individuals maximising their own self-interests as being led by an 'invisible hand' towards an organised, efficient, decision that provided a solution to the key issues around the provision and distribution of goods, services, and resources.

Yet this self-organising system is at odds with the scientific reductionist approach of conventional orthodox economics. The assumption of orthodox economics is that the independent agents do not in fact organise themselves properly, but are genuinely independent, possess all necessary information and operate without any linkages between them at all. The simplicity of this assumption needs to be seriously questioned. If it is true, even as an assumption, then there is no place for fashion, or advertising, or any indication that goods have a utility other than their intrinsic nature. The concept of conspicuous consumption does not have any validity under such an assumption, which caused Veblen to question the validity of the assumption in the first place. Similarly, the assumption that all parties within the market are in possession of all relevant information, and that there is no false trading – that is no trading at all except at the equilibrium price – seems to fly in the face of what is clearly the case where there are a great many market-based relationships where there is clearly information asymmetry, and false trading. Indeed, much of the volumes of finance and debt transactions would not be profitable unless they did exist. The assumption that there are only contractual relationships because of perfect information also underlies the misunderstanding and importance of trust relationships for many organisations. In respect of their consumers, information asymmetries mean that professional and major service and product providers have a trust or quasi-trust relationship with their consumers, not a contractual one, which accounts for the distrust with which many large organisations are viewed by their consumers, and the constant call for government regulatory activity. Finally, the nature of 'positive economics' and its insistence on scientific accuracy of 'what is' as compared to 'what ought to be' flies in the face of the self-organising nature of the market. If the positive economics of the orthodoxy is correct then greater understanding lies in seeking explanations that are further down the explanatory chain so the arrow of explanation points down, and as it does so it is increasingly meaningless. However, the implications of this in terms of the boom and bust cycle, speculative bubbles, decisions made by organisations that affect individual well-being, communities, and the environment is to suggest that these important and value-laden decisions are in fact value-free ones. Suggestions that 'you cannot buck the market' and that 'there is no alternative' are driven by an orthodox economics which is at odds with the experience of outcomes. This has been recognised as a deficiency for a long time; Ruskin in his famous article 'Unto This Last' (Ruskin 1860) was specifically critical of the failure of the modern capitalist market economy to take into account the moral implications of what it was doing.

Quantum Theory and political economy

A greater understanding of the theory of autonomous agents and the understanding of complex systems from Chaos Theory drives much of the critique of orthodoxy from the new economics. However, there is a third element that needs to be addressed. Both the new economics, derived from Chaos Theory, and orthodox economics, derived from Newtonian thinking, have an element of determinism. We have seen how the ideas of autonomous agents give rise to the concept of uncertainty – and that this is inherent in a process which is driven forward in time and is not reversible as a reductionist approach would have it. The great contribution of Quantum Theory to economics lies in reinforcing the state change implications of Chaos Theory, and in reinforcing the inherent uncertainty that is a feature of autonomous agents.

A better mousetrap or greater truth?

Given the relative failures of the neoclassical orthodox economic theory to explain economic growth satisfactorily, or the pattern of business cycles as an integral part of its analysis, and given the failure to predict with accuracy the significant economic risks run by the speculative financial activity in the run-up to the financial crisis of 2007, it is not at all surprising that the number of economists have seriously begun to ask whether or not a fundamentally radical review of orthodox theory is called for. Equally, there has been a defensive reaction on behalf of a number of economists who have sought to defend the orthodox approach in two ways:

Firstly, a number have begun to look at some of the technical assumptions that underlie the neoclassical theory, particularly in the areas of perfect markets, information, and the possibilities of 'false trading' and expectations. Not surprisingly these adjustments to the basic assumptions, whilst keeping the reductionist and deterministic nature of economic theory, result in more variable and 'policy uncertain' outcomes and, it should be said, a much greater complexity in understanding the lower-level constituent parts of the wider theory. Secondly, a more generalist response is to acknowledge the validity of some of the criticisms from the group of economists that constitute the radical alternative of 'new economics', but to maintain that the neoclassical theory still has validity because it represents important 'first order' assumptions, and that the linearity that is assumed is a broad approximation of a more complex reality. This first order approach permits economists to arrive at policy conclusions and analysis that is clear and simple for policy-makers to follow, and which whilst it might not deal with the whole of the truth behind the economy, nevertheless provides a good enough description of reality to be good enough for policy purposes.

We are not persuaded by these attempts to rescue neoclassical economics. The vastly different outcomes that emerge even from regarding the economic system just as a complex system within the definitions of mathematical Chaos Theory (sensitive dependence, deterministic, and non-linear) do not support an idea that simple linear assumptions give conclusions which mirror the consequences of nonlinearity and sensitive dependence. And this does not take into account the wider, nondeterministic and uncertain outcomes that come from looking at economic behaviour as the self-organising outcome of autonomous agents. Instead we believe that there are strong reasons to adopt the new economics approach even on methodological basis. There are three basic reasons for our conclusions.

Firstly, it is possible to regard the neoclassical theory as representing a 'special case' of a wider new economics, applicable in certain very limited short-run changes over a limited period of time, and within a single market. However the simplified assumptions of neoclassical economics are not valid when universally compared to the actual experience and are not supported by economic activities and outcomes – such as status goods, fashion, or advertising – that are seen to have validity. The theory simply misses out too much which is deemed to be valid activity. As Joseph Stiglitz has said 'only what is measured is the focus of importance', and it is the omission of whole areas of valid economic activity that are extra market (such as economic activity within families, charities, or other voluntary activity, not to mention the implied dualism and hostility towards much of the nonmarket public sector activity funded by taxation whose existence is deemed to be an 'necessary evil' because it cannot be denied); the omission of economic outcomes which have implications that go beyond the immediate contractual situation between supplier and consumer (the externalities problem and community impacts of economic activity); and the simplification of the utility of human endeavour to value that which is measurable in monetary terms, that reduces the overall scope of economic analysis and advice, and leads to the undoubted criticism of economics as 'the dismal science'.

Secondly, somewhere around the end of the 19th century neoclassical economics made a decisive break with the areas of psychology and moral philosophy which had been the founding philosophical areas from which it emerged. This so-called 'Paretan turn' has led economics into an area of greater complexity, mathematical analysis, and the whole panoply of post-Enlightenment scientific endeavour that has divorced it from its natural allies in areas of human knowledge such as psychology, accounting, organisations and behaviour, and projected it to a rarefied atmosphere of complex and largely unintelligible analysis. It is no surprise that the development of mathematical analysis of risk in the 'Black–Scholes' equations led a number of decision takers in financial institutions to back the idea that they could absorb derivatives and swaps and collateralised debt without it having any significant impact on their viability in the long-term. The fact is that many decision-makers confess that they did not understand the mathematics that lay behind these seemingly bizarre conclusions of their quantitative economic analysts, but nevertheless followed the assumed validity of outcomes to their individual and collective disaster. We believe that the Paretan turn was a mistake. It divorced economics from values. It led economics into a cul-de-sac which concentrated on explanations of 'what is' on the assumption that this neutral analysis would avoid discussions of 'what ought to be'. It led to the jibe against economists that they were people who knew 'the price of everything and the value of nothing'. However, both economists and politicians could not avoid the fact that values are important. This turn of economics was protested at the time by commentators such as Ruskin who clearly identified the community effects of an unregulated capitalistic market economy in his suggestion that opposed to wealth there was also the detrimental effects, which we might now describe as externalities. Similarly, the outcomes of the neoclassical 'positive economics' approach to poverty and the distribution of income, which emerged as an outcome from the analysis, rather than input to policy, has led to significant impacts on the delivery of public services and the sustainability in the current crisis. We will return to this question in more detail in the next chapter. Finally, the failure of neoclassical economics to explain adequately three principal areas of experience in the economy cannot simply be put down to the consequences of simplification. If we simplify something to the point where it no longer provides an adequate explanation of what happens, then we need to question the validity of the methodology itself. The historical pattern of economic growth has been one of a period of slow and steady increase followed by a sharp upturn in the levelling out in the future period (see Figure 8.3). It is the explanation of this 'take off' of economic growth which is essential if economics is to be meaningful. However, the neoclassical growth theory makes assumptions, and predictions, which are simply not borne out in reality. It implies growth convergence between economies, but often there is none; it implies an increasing level of capitalisation, where this need not be the case. The application of policy advice derived from this analysis created signal failures in developing economies during the 1950s and 1960s, and led to the development of a whole new area that looks at institutions and behaviour as essential precursors to the development of the market economy. Again neoclassical economics needed the application of ideas drawn from the new economics in order to arrive at even remotely meaningful outcomes. Similarly, the pattern of neoclassical economics does not adequately explain the shifting nature of the economic cycle, except by creating complex set of boundary conditions, and in no way matches the simplicity and explanatory power of the more complex, chaotic, and non-linear systems of the new economics. Finally, in the key area of the repeated speculative 'boom and bust' situation neoclassical economics provides no adequate explanation. Such speculation is deemed to be an aberrant nature of the economy, where 'bulls' and 'bears' cancel each other out, and where the drivers of demand and supply are entirely based on rational calculated decisions. Instead, experience suggests that speculative bubbles are commonplace, though often they may not develop particularly significantly before they are checked, yet when they are checked there is always a re-distributional effect in terms of wealth and income. It is on the area of autonomous agents, behaviours, and the potential runaway effects of sensitive dependence that the explanation of speculative bubbles depends.

The weaknesses of neoclassical economic orthodoxy go beyond simple methodology. The emerging area of the new economics not only provides a better methodology, but a better explanation of reality – of what is actually experienced in the economy. The neoclassical orthodoxy is hopelessly internally conflicted. Its reductionist, scientific, approach to an explanation of the pattern of the economy does not adequately deal with the fact that economic outcomes only emerge in the future, and then only with uncertainty, and cannot be adequately predicted by determinist approach. The pattern of economic change is essentially a historic analysis, whose emerging possibilities can only be seen in hindsight and analysed as such. The idea that in any way the pattern of change in the economy can be repeated as if it were a chemical or physical experiment is not valid. We constantly look back to understand what happened, but in looking forward we can only suggest possible outcomes at a level of attached probability. This is an uncomfortable position the political decision-makers find themselves in, they would prefer certainty, but the outcome of new economics would suggest that such certainty is a chimera sought by 'madmen in authority, who hear voices in the air', as Keynes put it, and who 'are distilling their frenzy from some academic scribbler of a few years back'. The whole area of analysis of autonomous agents not only leads us to this view of uncertainty, but also points to the inherent conflict within neoclassical economics which purports to be a valueless scientific endeavour, yet regards that the economy is being led by an 'invisible hand', a clear 'self-organising' system that is fully consistent with the non-reductionist implications of autonomous agent theory.

Adopting a new economics approach not only gives us a powerful new radical explanation of economic reality, but also allows us to significantly shift behaviours within the system. It gives us the possibility of looking primarily to holistic solutions to major economic problems, ones that will require the inevitable imperative of international solutions to wider economic issues instead of ones that pursue the assumption that purely nationalistic economic outcomes are in any way achievable. It is the significant possibility that key issues around climate change might be properly addressed, instead of the relative failures of climate change discussions in Copenhagen and Cancun to reach decisions because they are tied up in seeking to achieve national economic objectives based on a deficient theoretical base. The demand will be towards much more co-operative compromises rather than nationalistic competition. Anecdotally we perhaps need to remind ourselves that whilst co-operative insects such as ants and bees apparently are capable of taking good collective decisions, it is the ultracompetitive locusts that progressively and repeatedly strip their environment without solving the underlying population problem. Adopting the new economic approach would also imply that we would seek to measure a wider measurement of valid economic activity that has value and not just simply those things which were artificially adding to GDP. So, for example, if a couple decide to start a family and one of them decides to stay at home and look after the child then in GDP terms this is detrimental because it creates a drop in measured GDP. However, if the couple decide to divorce and the partner having custody of the child chooses instead to employ a full-time nanny then GDP is boosted as a result. However, in value terms it is difficult to argue that the stable relationship looking after the child is inherently of less value than the unstable relationship where the child is looked after by strangers. The impact that changing economic thinking might then have on key issues such as organisational structure, accounting, and preventative healthcare could be profound, flowing from a much wider inclusion of human activity that is economically measurable.

The development of this thinking is at a very early stage, and it is by no means certain that those who are propounding the adoption of these new approaches towards economics will ultimately be successful. As we have seen with other paradigm shifts, economics has also dealt with the critique of contrarian thinking by attempts at synthesis, operating both theories as models of reality but at different scales – the micro- and macro-economic split – or by using the contrasting methodologies not as descriptions of reality, but simply as useful tools for developing policy. There has been, and continues to be, a considerable reluctance to move away from economic orthodoxy, and it's clear that a number of policy-makers are proposing to further develop and create more complex theoretical models to continue to support the basic economic orthodoxy. This is despite the fact that the existing orthodox model, whilst being good at explaining individual markets and in the very short-term, has shown itself to be very poor at explaining economic growth, the clear periodicity of the business cycle, and predicting long-term economic changes. The new developing economic thinking gives a better explanation of economic growth and business cycles, given its basic underpinnings, and its greater integration with organisational thinking, politics, and the social underpinnings of economics gives it greater scope and usefulness, yet because the policy guidance that emerges can be fraught with uncertainty which may be observational or inherent, it makes it more difficult to use the thinking in order to drive policy.

At present the current state of political economy feels to be at a turning point. The current orthodoxy has clarity, even though it is clearly wrong in its predictions. And the monetarist conclusion that the best public sector intervention in the economy is the least public sector intervention is politically convenient to the 'small state vision' of some politicians without being particularly helpful in dealing with the important issue of the distribution of income which, whilst being an outcome of the orthodox model, is seen as an important policy tool within the developing alternatives.

The impact of the new paradigm – organisations

The works of Margaret Wheatley, Peter Senge, Stephen Covey, Daniel Goleman, and others have analysed the characteristics of an organisation based on organic rather than machine forms to see what makes it tick. Margaret Wheatley (Wheatley 1997) summarises it as having four characteristics.

Vision

Any organisation has to have a sense of purpose that is clear and understood by those participating in it. However, the nature of the vision for the organic form of organisation differs from that of the normal machine-like organisation. Such a vision will be aspirational; it will go beyond the current capacity of the organisation to deliver and will be stretching. It will have an ethical and moral purpose that extends beyond the simple continued existence of the organisation, or a statement of its commercial objectives. It will define what is special about the organisation that gives it identity. Within the public sector such statements of vision tend to be somewhat easier than those that are developed within the private sector. Private sector organisations often spend a considerable amount of money in developing complex vision statements to give their organisation a specific moral or ethical purpose, and in communicating that to the wider public, stakeholders, customers, and staff. Within the public sector the existence of the 'public sector ethic' of altruistic service to the community, though often derided, is a strong single motivating force that many of those who work at all levels within public sector organisations subscribe to. The concept of public service is a strong unifying force. Nevertheless, within some public sector organisations this critical statement of identity can be, and is, undermined. Organisations can exhibit displaced objectives, as we have already seen in our discussion of the hierarchical bureaucracy and the rise of producer culture. Such displaced objectives can often have terrible consequences for the delivery of quality public service, efficiency, and the relationship between citizen, client, customer, and the public sector. When public sector organisations find themselves under organisational pressure to reform and reorganise, even though this may be in the public interest, they often substitute the most primitive of displaced objectives – that of structural survival – above all other statements of purpose. Often, for public relations purposes, this is glossed over in terms of a wider community or social value, but it becomes difficult to disguise the self-interest. Within public sector organisations, particularly hierarchical ones or ones which are organised on professional lines with clear divisions of status, the overall sense of vision for the organisation can be undermined by individual team, departmental, or professional loyalties that override the ultimate purpose of the organisation. The introduction of inappropriate private sector management techniques into the public sector has, to some degree, exacerbated a tendency towards this fissiparous nature for organisations, and undermined the unity of purpose, often by the introduction of inappropriately competitive arrangements in what should be co-operative partnerships. As a consequence there has been a growth in the public sector of internal culture change management programmes which often have at their heart an attempt to reconnect the staff of the organisation with its overall purpose.

However, it is not the case that any statement of vision, identity, and purpose will do. Ownership of that is critical. Many of the campaigns that we just referred to are based around getting staff to buy into a statement of vision and purpose that has been prepared by senior management sometimes with external support and advice. The better cultural change campaigns get the staff involved in developing the final version of the vision statement for the organisation. Yet even these do not go far enough. Staff who have been involved in culture change campaigns around a corporately produced vision statement will not own a statement in which they have not been deeply involved, and which does not reflect their own views. The same is true of any public sector organisation which seeks to make a statement of its vision and identity for the communities it serves. The vision and purpose will not be recognised by a community that has not been involved in developing that statement. We will see in later chapters the practical outworking of this in the development of Sharmer's 'Theory U'. The statement needs to recognise and reflect the values and aspirations of the community if it is to have meaning. Public sector organisations have to become the collective means by which the community can take action to achieve its common and agreed purposes if it is to command support. However, this creates some particular issues for public sector organisations which typically serve not one but several communities of interest – geographical or subjective based. It will be particularly an issue for those organisations which are locally democratically based, as against those organisations which are the service delivery agent of central government. The situation is particularly complex where a local organisation is both, and has become more significant in recent years with the increasing centralisation of the UK public sector. The critical question becomes 'whose vision is this?' So it is unlikely that a single organisational vision statement can be prepared, except at the highest and least effective level, and it follows that an organisation needs to be able to reflect diversity and variance in community needs and aspirations, and that implies that it will be developing, working with, and seeking to deliver to a number of vision statements. Overall, the organisation can, to some degree, hold the ring by ensuring that the individual statements of communities are not competitive, or contrary, but hopefully are complementary or, at least, neutral as against each other. When this is not the case, then the democratic organisation has perhaps a higher objective of ensuring complementarity and has some work to do with the constituent communities. It is highly likely that multiple visions, which have to be held in tension and in priority, will be the lot of a genuinely locally focused public sector delivery organisation under the organic model. It is more complex and more challenging. However, it represents the balance that often has to be held in a representative democracy between representatives sponsorship of, and service to, the communities that have elected them, and the overall responsibility of the collective of those representatives sitting together to balance the needs of one community as against those of another.

Information

We have already seen how in the traditional hierarchical bureaucracy delivery organisation in the public sector the tendency is to use information in inappropriate ways by sophisticated 'games playing' for status or power; withholding or disclosing information as a means of exerting power and influence; and the use of performance measures and control indicators to assert objectives from the top, and to control the flow of activity in the organisation. We have also seen how in the traditional hierarchy, information is distorted or lost in transmission up and down the organisation. In 1989, Peter Drucker (Drucker 1989) described managers as 'relays – human boosters for the faint, unfocused signals that passed information in the traditional pre-information organisation'. Within the organism and networked organisation information operates on an open rather than closed model. Such organisations are essentially learning organisations. They are prepared to take risks and experiment, and to learn from their mistakes as much as their successes, and to be open to admitting failure as well as success. Within the traditional learning cycle pattern of plan, execute, and reflect, they are careful not to lose the opportunities for reflection which so often lost in more traditional organisations which goes straight from planning to doing and back to planning without there being any intervening consideration of outcomes and what has been learned thereby. As we shall see later, in trying to implement the new kind of organisation this basic pattern of learning cycle has also to be expanded to take into account the openness that is required to the organisation to effectively learn in the face of an unknown or rapidly changing environment. Furthermore, the information within the organisation has genuinely to empower those who have the responsibility for direct service delivery to deal with the variance of demand, and to adjust the pattern of service to meet the changing environment without the need to either seek permission or pass a problem up the line for solution. Such organisations will have a highly devolved arrangement and will be the antithesis of the hierarchical machinelike bureaucracy. So, for example, front-line staff who work on the production line in the Toyota Company are empowered to stop the line if necessary in order to rectify a problem that exists.

Self-organisation

'Organic' organisations often exhibit a unity in action that derives from relatively simple behavioural rules on individuals operating within them. Consider, as an analogy, a flock of starlings. As a flock they seem to move as one with several hundred birds turning and changing direction while still retaining an almost cloudlike shape as a flock together. The starlings are not moving according to a pattern that has been set out by a Chief Executive Starling and Management Team! Instead each bird, it has been observed, is looking at, on average, seven other birds located around it and as they move, so it moves. The organic form of organisation will tend to change direction in a very similar pattern with each person, operating within a team, learning from, and changing with the overall pattern of the team in a purely natural form of behaviour. Similarly, to extend the bird metaphor, a skein of geese migrating on a long journey will interchange the role of leader at the front, taking all the buffeting of the elements, with that of the bird at the tail of the V who is in some senses protected by the other birds. They will cycle from the front to the back and move up the arm of the V step-by-step to take on the role of leadership on a rotational basis. In organic forms of organisation, leadership will often operate on a rotational basis depending on skills required, the task in hand, and the abilities of individuals within the team. Structures will reflect needs and are not necessarily permanent. Such organisations will react to the changing environment as they move together, like a herd. Within a herd some animals may be grazing, whilst others take an observational and protective role against the danger of predators. Other animals may be foraging ahead to seek suitable food sources. Herds do not move randomly, but with purpose, and with animals taking different roles at different times. There is, in a sense, a combined sense of purpose and unity as they operate together.

Relationships

Not surprisingly in an organisation which is based on the concept of an organism, relationships between individuals are critical to the efficient functioning of the organisation. The traditional hierarchical bureaucracy describes their organisation by giving you an organisational chart in pyramidal form. Most people, however, recognise that the information conveyed by this chart does not set out how the organisation actually functions. In astrophysics it is recognised that all the visible matter in the universe does not explain how the universe actually functions. There is what astronomers call 'dark matter' which exerts influence without being visible. There is within any organisation similar 'dark matter' – factors which affect an organisation's efficiency and delivery but which are not immediately obvious. Organisations will tend to have a significant pattern of networks of trust which individuals who join an organisation rapidly learn to appreciate, understand, and join if they are to fit in. The most obvious of these is the world's best communication network – the grapevine. Many internal communication campaigns are derailed by the speed and consistency of message from the office grapevine. Myths, rumours, stories, and legends are conveyed by a random interaction of individuals trading information and knowledge. Most organisations can identify at least seven of these networks of trust:

- *The work network* – such as the grapevine, whom do you swap information with on a day-to-day basis, within the organisation?
- *The social network* – whom do you acknowledge as friends?
- *The innovation network* – do you bounce a new idea off to test it out?
- *The expert network* – whom would you talk to when you don't know how to do something?
- *The strategic network* – whom would you ask for advice about your future?
- *The learning network* – whom would you talk to because they stimulate your thinking about the future and the way forward?
- *The decision network* – whom do you seek out to expedite a decision?

There are two key things to recognise about these networks. First, the title 'networks of trust' clearly indicates that they are social networks. These networks exist in an organisation in addition to, or in spite of, any other formal networks that might have been developed. Second, there are essentially networks of language – that is to say they are social interactions that depend upon individuals talking to one another. This reinforces the social relationships that underlie them. The existence of networks of trust is both deeply rooted and an essential part of the social organisation of human beings in whatever grouping, formal or informal, but they find themselves. Ignoring such networks is, organisationally, inept.

Nevertheless such networks often cut across the more formal structural hierarchies of organisations whether in the public or in the private sector. At best many of the informational, training, and team-building activity that takes place in modern organisations complements social networks that already exist; at worst they cut across and contradict existing social networks with the result that too often such formal organisational activity is neutralised. Many organisations have stories about team-building exercises that went disastrously wrong because they failed to recognise the existing pattern of social networking, and that the result was often deeper division rather than greater harmony – which was the ostensible objective. The inherent existence of networks in organisations also brings to the fore a dualistic pattern of human behaviour that we will come to later when we consider, in the next chapter, some of the implications of the networked organism type of organisation. Social relationships between animals that we observe, particularly those of apes and monkeys, which are closer to us on the evolutionary tree, indicate that sharing of resources is a key part of the group activity, and that it is often organised on two alternate bases. The first of these is that of a dominant animal – male or female (though it is very often male), and a pecking order of animals within the group with oversight of the fairness of food distribution. The second is a much more bonded arrangement of animals that operate equally and use social bonding as a stronger means of ensuring a fair distribution of resources. The first, a bounded hierarchy, might be seen to have a broad equivalence to a hierarchical bureaucracy under certain conditions. The second, a network organism type of organisation, corresponds more closely to the alternative paradigm that we are setting out here. Both exist, but the fairness of food distribution is an essential outcome from both. This particular issue of equality is picked up the book by Richard Wilkinson and Kate Pickett (Wilkinson and Pickett 2010), which we will return to in Chapter 10.

Much academic work has been done on the informal communications networks that exist in organisations (Stephenson 2000). Particularly in recent years tools began to be developed which begin by analysing the different roles played by individuals within a network and a mapping of that network by means of questions to individuals based on the seven social networks that have been identified and listed above. This work has been extended to go beyond organisational boundaries to consider the pattern of developing networks across organisations and throughout the community. As such it is particularly significant for the public sector whose raison d'être is the service of the community. Therefore, networks are capable of analysis, blocks and impediments can be identified and dealt with, and improvements can be made. What was sometimes seen as the soft side of management is in fact the hard stuff.

If a hierarchical bureaucracy chooses to ignore the social networks that exist in parallel within the organisation, then it can have adverse consequences. In the first place if there is not a good flow of information then the informal networks will have a tendency to fill in the gaps with fiction. Most organisations know the danger that rumour and conspiracy theories have in interpreting the action of senior management within the organisation at middle and front-line levels. In the absence of true information people will simply make something up and their speculations gain credence by repetition to become hard fact. The tendency of information to become distorted and lost in organisational 'noise' has already been remarked on in Chapter 6; the existence of social networks within an organisation simply gives the vehicle by which this is carried out. Second, human beings do have an ability for what Ben Page of MORI has called 'cognitive polyphasia' – that is the ability of individual to hold two apparently contradictory ideas as being true – simultaneously. This is largely because we know that an individual's behaviour is dependent upon the group situation in which they find themselves. So in one particular setting an individual may espouse one particular set of views, and in another setting a contradictory set of views. Individuals are broadly aware that their views are not consistent, and this tends to undermine their adherence to and belief in any particular one of them. Within a traditional hierarchical bureaucracy the official view can often be undermined by the views held by the various social networks which are quick to spot an inconsistency between espoused and actual behaviour in the organisation.

What does the networked organism type of organisation look like?

Given that the traditional formal hierarchical bureaucracy is so commonplace and pervasive, it is not always easy to spot organisations which operate according to the alternative paradigm, particularly within the public sector where many organisations have a statutory existence within the pre-existing hierarchy of political authority. So instead of trying to identify an organisation that might adhere to the new paradigm, it's worth trying to draw out the kind of characteristics that you would expect to see if an organisation was so organised. And, given that some of the underlying characteristics exist in organisations in any case, these features will often be only apparent in contrast to that which traditionally exists. We outline two groups of features – organisational and behavioural.

Organisational features

The networked organism will have a holistic approach to public sector issues. As a result it will not tend to deliver services in isolation from partners whose area of expertise bears on the issue being addressed. It will tend to use its networking capacity, measured and developed, as networks can be, to extend natural partnerships on a formal, or informal basis either long-term or task-orientated. This won't happen in every single case. When an organisation has the capacity and expertise to deal with an issue on a single organisation basis, then it will do so. However, it will have a tendency to reflect on the wider aspects of the issue, and its place within the community. This will tend to push it into partnerships more naturally and therefore a second feature will be its inherent participative nature. In particular, such organisations will tend to be more responsive to community need. They will be more aware of the variations that lead to service delivery demands, and the priorities that exist within the communities they serve. It will be natural for them to inform, consult, and delegate decision-making as a community, or at individual level. The current personalisation agenda will be a more natural part of their approach, rather than the 'add-on' which often appears to be in a more producer-orientated culture. We will see a little later how this fits into the more consumer-orientated 'demand pull' approach of systems thinking, which has become much more commonplace in private sector organisations. However, this participation will exist not only at community level, but also within the organisation. There will be a tendency to use and develop the inherent networks in order to bring a wider range of technical, social, and informational expertise to bear on a particular issue. In some cases this is likely to lead to extensive team working, in other cases the actual working relationships will be much more task group orientated. The organisation is therefore likely to have a more project-based and less rigid structure, and, put in traditional organisational language, is likely to exhibit more matrix management and a less hierarchical management. Some workgroups will have a relatively short shelf life while others may be inherently part of the organisation and have a long existence. A third developing future will be the apparent chaotic nature of the organisation. It simply won't stand still. It will appear to be constantly shifting with groups forming, delivering, and dispersing. One of its characteristics will tend to be a self-organising nature. Such groups generally won't establish themselves as a result of demands from a senior strategic level within the organisation; they will have the capacity and the implied delegative authority to be established without the need for any kind of prior authorisation. The self-organising capacity of such organisations is a complex feature. Whilst it might appear to be chaotic, in fact it can be highly tightly organised and the chances of groups existing for no particular purpose other than an historic one, or to fulfil a social function, which is a feature of hierarchical bureaucracies, will be significantly lessened. As a result, the empowerment, information reactivity, and flexible nature of organisation will tend to render such organisations more efficient than their traditional alternative. Because of the power and status structures of traditional hierarchies there is a tendency for groups to be packed with individuals who are there to observe, or represent, or to ensure that their status is recognised, without actually contributing to the solutions needed. Meetings are numerous, and are often attended by individuals who make no net contribution – a significant inefficiency. The more flexible working arrangements of the networked organisation will tend to dispense with such inefficiency. As a result of the higher delegative arrangement it is more likely that such organisations will also be more innovative. An ancient Japanese proverb runs 'none of us is as smart as all of us' which expresses the common observation that a group of people working on the problem will often come up with a solution that an individual may not reach. Nevertheless, there is always been a role for the individual maverick genius. Unfortunately, in traditional hierarchical bureaucracies such individuals are often deliberately sidelined and isolated because of their disruptive ideas. We will see in the next chapter how more modern thinking about organisations draws together the ability to individual reflection and teamwork to provide a better solution for innovative problem-solving in highly uncertain environments – an outcome that is particularly desirable in an age of austerity. We will also look at some of the current thinking about how apparently chaotic groupings are actually self-organising, and how they function.

Behaviours

We have seen how a traditional hierarchical bureaucracy can tolerate, or even promote, dysfunctional behaviours which detract from efficiency in delivery. Because of the more natural tendency of networked organism type organisations to 'go with the flow' – a very human pattern of social networking and technical expertise – behaviourally they exhibit less dysfunctional behaviour. That is not to say that dysfunctional behaviour may not exist within such organisations, but it is more generally due to individual dysfunction rather than organisationally generated. The underlying principle in McGregor's terms for the networked organism is 'Theory Y'. The general assumptions are that people can, and should, be trusted to do a good job; that they are generally motivated to do well; and that the degree of control that is necessary over their activities is slight. When we look at the issue of leadership of such organisations in Chapter 9, we will see that many of the features of leadership that are being developed by modern organisational thinkers build on the Theory Y approach. In any case, the participatory and delegative nature of the networked organism form often means that leadership is, as we have seen, related to the task, particular skills, or capacity of a group of individuals at any particular time. Leadership is not necessarily fixed, but can be a rotating arrangement. Recognising the value of this, some more traditional organisations have attempted to devise rules for self-organising groups within their structures based on rotating Chairs of task groups for example. Such rigid rules will only ape the real truth of rotating leadership which is driven by delivery and task, rather than any formal rule-based arrangement. In contrast with the traditional bureaucracy which aims at locating an individual in terms of status and position exactly within the organisation, the organic networked organisation, while not ignoring the role of individuals, will acknowledge that most people do not work individually but in teams. It will be around the team that the task and function and delivery of services are organised. It will be the social working within teams which is the focus of organisational efficiency effort. Finally, the participative and delegative nature of such organisations that 'go with the flow' of naturally occurring social networks will tend to give individuals and teams a greater control over their own working environment. The level of demands upon them will be just as difficult as that existing within a traditional hierarchical bureaucracy, even more so in some circumstances, but the greater controls individuals have over that will mean that one of the greatest stresses of individuals and organisations would be greatly lessened. With reductions in stress level come significant improvements in organisational health – mental and physical; the reduction of sickness absence, traditionally high in the public sector, and the consequent improvement in feelings of efficiency and fairness; and a significant improved level of behaviour and decision-making.

Supporting the new form of organisation

We have seen in the past how the paradigm which is the 'constellation of beliefs, values, techniques etc shared by members of a given community' represents either an understanding that it is the best model that describes a particular set of observations or experience and gives predictive capacity, or for some who take a more realism approach, it is seen as a description of objective truth. But whilst the central feature of the paradigm can often be very briefly explained, the definition recognises the fact that it is supported by a number of specific points of theory, experience, knowledge, myths and stories and beliefs, and understanding that add weight to it by being in themselves seen as the best model, or description of reality. It is this self-reinforcing, and mutually supportive, pattern of beliefs that gives a paradigm it's a long-term capacity and its persistence. Paradigms are resilient things which can often deal with contrary evidence by adjusting one or other of its supportive mechanisms in order to provide additional predictive capacity. The geocentric concept of the solar system was able to deal with contrary evidence by ever more complicated technical calculations that allowed the Ptolemaic system to persist for a great many years, before the altogether simpler and more elegant heliocentric proposals of Copernicus replaced it.

In shifting the supporting evidence, knowledge, and technical underpinnings the organisational model of hierarchical bureaucracy to one based not on a machine analogy, but one based on the natural world, we have to look at those elements that support the paradigm and which rely on the same basic underpinning thinking that we have drawn out from Quantum Theory and Chaos Theory and autonomous agents. We now identify two developing ideas in which this different kind of thinking has been applied that provides supporting weight to our proposed shift of paradigm within the public sector.

Firstly, we have seen how much the idea of a highly devolved organisation following the principles of decentralised control, distributed problem-solving, and multiple interactions of independent agents underpins much of the new type of organisation. The current political idea of the 'Big Society' is a key part of that debate. However, because of a certain lack of precision that idea is being stretched and in some cases distorted to cover other behavioural issues that are desired to change. We'll look at how the Big Society idea as it was originally proposed supports the paradigm shift that we are suggesting. Secondly, many of the ideas in the new organisational paradigm are consistent with the kind of modern systems thinking that was developed in the post-war world to deliver more flexibility, innovation, and lower costs in manufacturing industry, and which has been developed by extension into service industries and into the public services. We will briefly look at the way that this new thinking contrasts with the older 'command and control' organisational forms that it challenges.

Supporting ideas short of a full paradigm change

The Big Society

The 'Big Society' idea became part of the Coalition Government's principal policy for radical economic thinking as it began to develop its ideas for dealing with the public finance issue in an age of austerity. Lacking an absolutely clear definition, the term has often been hijacked by the media, commentators, and others to mean, as the Mock Turtle said, 'exactly what I want it to mean and no more'. Phillip Blond, of the think tank ResPublica, is largely credited with developing some of the thinking behind the Big Society concept. In his view the key point is about decentralisation of political and financial authority. The idea behind it was an attempt to solve the perceived failures of direct state provision of public services, and the equivalent monopolistic private sector contracted provision of public services to deliver flexible, quality, and consumer-responsive public services which recognised the principles of consumer choice. Instead, the recent history of the public sector involved increasingly 'nanny state' solutions with exhortation to behaviour change, and 'one size fits all' producer-led solutions – whether public or private sector delivered – that citizens and customers felt did not reflect their needs. The development of 'command and control' hierarchical arrangements to direct and deliver the services is widely seen to have created a public alienated from its public services, and undermined the wider aspects of the civil society of voluntary and third sector organisations that previously were seen to deliver local public services, so resulting a confrontational and dysfunctional legal claims culture.

The principal features of the Big Society idea are significant decentralisation of delivery, decision-making, and financial power; the development of mutualisation in the form of co-operatives, social welfare organisations, social enterprise, voluntary organisation provision, and worker owned and run organisations as an alternative to public sector direct provision and private sector market-based services. In many cases it is felt that the development of new technology on a common platform basis that is not 'owned' by any particular organisation – such as the Internet, social networking, and telecommunications – provides a physical environment within which these kind of local devolved arrangements can be established and run without the development of significant investment, or an inappropriate 'command and control' culture.

Systems thinking

Following the War the US Administration involved a leading management thinker W. Edwards Deeming in helping to restructuring Japanese industry in the post-war period. His views (Deeming 2000) were based on changing the arrangements for production from the traditional mass production, economies of scale, model to one which was based upon meeting customer demand variation by a systems-based approach. Subsequently the development of this new thinking became enshrined as the 'Toyota model' after the leading Japanese car manufacturer who adopted the new processes.

Although substantially developed within manufacturing industry these techniques have been later developed for service-based private sector industries and subsequently used as a model for public sector service organisations. John Seddon (Seddon 2003) has been particularly involved in this development.

The difference between organisations which are based on traditional bureaucratic hierarchies and those based on systems thinking is considerable. As we have seen within a hierarchy there is a difference between those who control and manage the organisation, setting budgets and targets, attempting to drive change from the top, and whose function is to manage and control budgets and people. A systems-based organisation turns all this on its head. The job of managers is to manage the system to make improvements for the front-line staff who work within it and who are responding to the legitimate demands of customers. The change process is essentially driven from the bottom in a number of small changes, rather than driven from the top through change programmes. The design of the system is not delivery through a particular function, but the analysis of demand, value, and flow through the system and the analysis of demand variation to identify and remove inefficiencies that arise from double work, non-value adding processes, and unnecessary repetitive functions. If the metaphor for a traditional hierarchy is a triangle, then the pattern of the systems organisation is concentric circles with the customer at the centre.

Some of the ideas behind the systems approach to manufacturing and service delivery have been particularly challenging to the traditional Western approach. The key is the introduction of the principle of 'demand pull', where the issue that the production process (whether for products or services) has to manage is the variation of customer demand, rather than the cost reduction by economies of scale in the traditional model. The systems-based approach recognises that fact and, within given parameters, the customer's individual product is built as the individual orders are received and the whole of the production process is designed around that principle – demand pull. However, a great many Western manufacturers dealt with the variation demanded by the customer by utilising the same mass production methods to provide batches of product in different configurations and then storing them until the customer demanded them. The efficiency of the systems-based approach was shown by the fact that good quality products built using manufacturers who use the 'Toyota model' can often be cheaper than those provided by traditional Western manufacturing approaches where quality was always an issue, and the cost of storage and rectification of damage and deterioration whilst the product was in storage, added to the cost base in what is defined under the systems approach as unproductive double working, which the systems-based approach aims to eliminate from the production process.

We've already seen how in the traditional model of public services delivery the producer-led 'one size fits all' approach to the delivery of public services has not met the demands and expectations of the modern citizen for choice or the variation of personal circumstances. Approaches in the 1990s and first decade of this century have aimed at reducing costs by outsourcing, off shoring, and the public services equivalent of economies of scale mass production, which, under a systems-based approach produces wasteful double working in many cases, and an inflexible response to citizen demands. Where it has been introduced successfully and properly system-based working within the public sector has often achieved significant reductions in overhead. With it's essentially highly devolved nature, and reversal of traditional roles and responsibilities within the command and control hierarchy, the system-based approach to public services delivery is consistent and supportive of the paradigm shift towards the highly responsive, information rich, and front-line-driven organisation, and forms an integral part of supporting the paradigm change.

Both of the above changes have, or could have, significant contributions to make to improved public services. However, they are both being undertaken within the existing paradigm of 'centralised command and control'. It is difficult to see how the Big Society approach requiring decentralisation of delivery, local decision-making, and devolved financial power can function in a paradigm comprising centralised planning, tight Treasury control, and micro-management from Westminster. Likewise the development of systems thinking while beneficial will probably wilt in an environment where the 'centre' tries to control every thing. Thus these are changes which could be beneficial to public services if supported by paradigm changes but they do not constitute paradigm change in themselves. In fact their degree of success is more likely to be inhibited by the continuation of the existing paradigm. The tragedy of the current paradigm is that the people at the centre (Ministers, MPs and civil servants) who have only experienced the centre just cannot see that it won't work and spend all their time tinkering.

There comes a time when a new model is needed as tinkering with the old model won't get it to work.

Some interim conclusions

Mrs Thatcher was once famous for declaring, when she introduced changes to meet the dramatically worsening economic environment in the 1980s, that 'there is no alternative'. Given the equally damaging economic and financial environment faced by public services in an age of austerity there is sometimes a natural tendency on behalf of public service bodies to suggest that the changes that are being proposed are ones where 'there is no alternative'. We have tried to show in this chapter is that there is a viable alternative approach in the delivery of public services which can both gain significant efficiency savings, and deal with many of the issues of unresponsiveness to public demand that have long been a point of criticism and separation between the public and the public sectors. However the magnitude of such a change is significant and it will have to be carried through on a consistent basis. It is not possible to adopt a new policy in a particular area such as the Big Society, for example, without also adopting the organisational forms, methodologies, and theoretical underpinnings that go with it. Where an attempt is made to make a change which is partial, then the inherent inconsistencies and incoherence will become clear, and the tendency of the policy will be to underperform or fail.

However, as we have seen from the history of public sector change in the UK, making wholesale revolutionary changes of H3 nature – and this would certainly count as such a change – is not something that has been done hitherto. Notwithstanding the unprecedented level of challenge to public sector services that we face, we recognise that the kind of changes that we are suggesting are 'a big ask' for the public sector organisations as they are currently configured. Making any kind of paradigm shift, even if it is seen as representing a better understanding of reality, is difficult. People want to see proof that it will be effective. However, this is not like the kind of change that we described in the Copernican revolution or the development of quantum mechanics. Those changes made certain predictions which were amenable to repeated experiments and observations, and where the basic paradigms were subsequently verified by those experiments and observations. Changes in public policy and public service delivery are not amenable to such experimentation. There is not the opportunity for testing one prediction against another. There is only one single stream of events that has to be interpreted, as a historian interprets, to see if, from the noise and confusion, an ordered pattern of understanding can be gained. Public sector commentators have to work on the basis of hypotheticals, asking themselves what would have been the outcomes if things were not as we thought they were. Decisions in such circumstances are a matter of judgement, rather than of proof.

So, in the next chapter we will take a look at some of the obstacles to effecting such a change even assuming that there was a desire to do so. We'll then go on to look at the history of public service development over the past 30 years and see if they might be interpreted in the light of what we now know about the public sector models, and try making an assessment of what might have been the case had the alternative paradigm been adopted. This is necessarily speculative in nature, but is the best that we can seek to achieve given the problem of measurement and uncertainty that we face. Finally, in the chapter we'll go on to look at how we might go forward with the new paradigm in the face of that uncertainty and the kind of approaches that we might take, and have in other contexts proved effective, to introduce a new way of thinking about public services.

9
Managing the Change – What Are the Implications?

Why change?

Why would anyone want to make the change? If the existing arrangements work well enough what would be the point? It's a valid observation. The traditional 'rational–legal' hierarchical bureaucracy was thought by Max Weber to represent the culmination of greatest efficiency from the personal charismatic leadership and traditional patronage type alternatives. It has substantially been the key vehicle from delivery of UK public services since the middle part of the 19th century. As we've seen, alternatives have been around at least since the end of the Second World War, and substantially developed for the past 30 or more years. Yet there has been little shift towards an alternative paradigm.

We've no doubt that the same point probably occurred to critics of Copernicus's first thoughts about the heliocentric planetary system. Its predecessor, the Ptolemaic system, had been around for decades and had a substantial amount of predictive and explanatory capacity. The reason ultimately that it was overthrown is that Copernicus's solution was a simpler and better explanation of observed reality, and had better predictive capacity, which subsequently be ratified by direct observation. Yet the question about whether it was true remained essentially a philosophical one. Like the later development of quantum mechanics there remains the debate about whether or not it represents an improved empirical methodology for practical use, or whether it represents a true description of what is experienced.

So, in looking at the question of whether or not the current state of public services demands a full-scale paradigm shift, as we believe, we have to ask whether adopting this different paradigm would have given us different outcomes in explaining our current circumstances. We believe that it does and in this chapter will turn first to look at an explanation for the changes that we've experienced in UK public services over the past 30 years, and drawing on that experience we will look at what the alternative might have been. Inevitably, since this is not a laboratory scientific experiment, but an interpretation of recent political and economic history, our conclusions will not be absolute, but will represent what we think is the most reasonable and credible explanation of outcomes.

The past 30 years in public services – an explanatory account

We begin by looking at a key difference between current economic thinking and the new economics – the distribution of income in the economy. Figure 9.1 shows the way that income inequality has risen over the past 30 years using the Gini coefficient measure, based on 1974=100.

With the substantial deregulation of the economy in the late 1980s there was a significant rise in income inequality under the Governments led by Mrs Thatcher. This stabilised somewhat under the administration of John Major and the first administration of Tony Blair, but the significant shift of income inequality was not challenged by the New Labour Administrations who were of the view that 'they didn't mind if people became filthy rich'. The implications of unequal distribution of income on the body politic have been set out in 'The Spirit Level' by Richard Wilkinson and Kate Pickett (Wilkinson and Pickett 2010).

In this book they show that whilst increasing income levels are associated with better community well-being for developing countries, once countries have reached a certain level of income the well-being of the country does not significantly improve with increased GDP growth. Instead it substantially levels out. This thinking has been picked up by some economists who felt the GDP is too crude measure for community well-being, and suggested a wider range of alternative measures. Although the development of this kind of work has often attracted significant criticism from those wedded to a fully functioning market economy, it is borne out by survey work. Organisations such as MORI have demonstrated that despite increasing

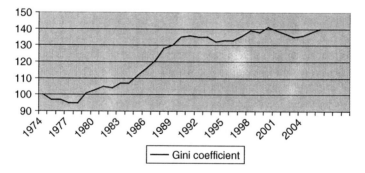

Figure 9.1   Issues of inequality

levels of personal wealth over the past few decades people report that they do not feel any happier as a result. It is further supported by psychologists who have looked at what makes people happy and who find that provided basic levels of financial security are met, additional wealth does not bring happiness, instead it is to be found in close personal relationships and in belief that lies beyond an individual's personal satisfactions.

Most critically, across a wide range of political, social, and economic outcomes, more unequal societies incur higher costs and greater problems. On issues related to community life and social relations; mental health and drug use; physical health and life expectancy; obesity; educational performance; teenage pregnancies; violent behaviour; imprisonment and punishment; and social mobility, more unequal societies have a higher incidence of personal and community dysfunctional behaviour that demands public service responses. The underlying driver for these problems is essentially the stress reactions of individuals faced with a society where the aspirations, often exacerbated by advertising and the media, remained frustratingly unmet for a significant number of individuals. People see that there is a desired level of material well-being, status enhancing and socially desirable over-consumption to which they aspire, but poor social mobility means that they will never attain. The stress created as a result of the gap between desired outcome and probable attainment creates a series of personal health and social problems. The authors, using their basic medical background, trace the physical and mental impacts on human beings of prolonged and unresolved stress. But there are also social implications. People faced with this kind of unresolved stress can also become alienated from wider society, which they see as providing unattainable goals. They become excessively narcissistic about their own position, demanding 'respect' from others which is backed up by violence or threat of violence, associated with increased levels of criminality. Since the greatest single driver of income inequality is long-term worklessness, then the operation of the unregulated market economy places unreasonable work demands on many, who are employed, whilst ensuring that significant numbers of people remain unemployed adds to the chronic stress.

In the light of this the drivers for some of the increases in public services in the past 30 years or so, since the major worsening of income inequality become clear. In order to combat inequality driven by worklessness, particularly in an economy which has shifted away from direct manufacturing to a more service-based pattern (which has been described as the 'weightless' economy because of the insubstantial nature of much of income generation) there has been increased pressure on a greater individual knowledge-based skills in order to improve employability. It was not a simple personal whim that led to Tony Blair's famous 'education, education, education' mantra for public service delivery. At the same time the impact on personal health, both physical and mental, and the equal rise in obesity (which historically was related to diseases of the wealthy, but is now inversely related to wealth as a disease of the poor – with the ideal body shape, particularly for young women, being that of an almost anorexic slimness), has given rise to a significant increase in health costs. Over the long period the pattern of public and personal health expenditure provided by the public services has shifted. In Victorian times it was the community impact of public health improvements necessary as a result of increasing urbanisation and poverty that drove the increasing costs of health provision. In the 20th century it was a substantial attack on the bacteriologically driven infections, often significantly increased as a result of poverty, which drove health costs. Post-Beveridge it was thought that the introduction of the NHS, whilst initially costly, would actually steadily reduce health costs as the issues of poverty and want, which were part of the 'five ills' that Beveridge wished to abolish, were dealt with. Instead, we have seen how costs are consistently driven up by illnesses which are associated with lifestyle and which are considerably exacerbated by a more unequal distribution of income. The impact of lack of social cohesion, alienation (particularly amongst young men, but more recently extending to young women), violence and criminality have become key drivers in the increased costs of policing, justice, and imprisonment and punishment arrangements.

Not all the increased costs of UK public services have been driven by the unequal distribution of income, however. Continued improvements in technical health care have meant that increased life expectancy overall (albeit unevenly experienced, also poverty related) have continued to drive up the demographic costs of health and social care for the old. Climate change and the impact on the environment, as we have seen in Chapter 2, continue to provide a significant threat and cost pressure for public service delivery. And the UK's position as a residual 'Great Power' in the interwar period because of the isolation of the US and USSR as the new 'Great Powers' – as described in Kennedy's book *The Rise and Fall the Great Powers* (Kennedy 1989) – has led to a continuing demand for military and defence expenditure beyond that required for a country of our stature, also driven by the continuing association with the leading military power of United States through alliances in the post–Second World War world.

Against this pattern of increased demand for public services how has the traditional bureaucratic hierarchy coped? In a word – badly. To begin with the bureaucratic hierarchy model is a stressor in its own right – both of those working within it, and for those to whom its services are delivered. We've already examined the efficiency and behavioural consequences of the 'command and control' structure in terms of its internal workings. We've seen that it leads to a pattern of producer culture that is at odds with the personalisation and consumer choice agendas that have been developed in public services. As the size and extent of public services grew over the past 30 years, so these internal and external frustrations have grown. People perceive an increasing mismatch between the declared objectives of public service organisations and political leadership and what is actually delivered on the ground. They find dealing with public service organisations to be a frustrating and time-consuming exercise, with a great deal of repeat work as the same information is given over and over again, and individuals are passed up and down the communication chain of the organisation to reach the right point at which a query can be dealt with, a service requested, or a complaint made. Not surprisingly people find dealing with bureaucratic hierarchies, whether public or private, stressful. Given that, for a number of services, contact is often a point when the individual is already feeling stress as a result of accident, illness, criminal activity, or antisocial behaviour, the fact that the public service organisation adds to the stress is hardly a recommendation.

The increased demand for public services, driven by an increased level of inequality, led to attempts to improve the level of public service organisation efficiency and service delivery by the increasing use of market-based methods. This has tied the pattern of public service organisations into the very pattern of economic thinking which is responsible for the generation of a significant part of its problems. This interrelationship has created a spiralling negative feedback as public service organisations struggle to cope with increasing levels of demand, and the increasing use of market and quasi-market solutions for the delivery of those services that, through an unequal distribution of employment and income, has meant that many public organisation workers find themselves faced with increased levels of personal demands, and increased cost pressures, at the same time as the same economic system is driving up service volumes.

In the face of this spiral of increased demand the 'command and control' approach has generated three bureaucratic responses:

1. *Blame cultures and avoidance of key issues* – As the pressures created by an unequal society have impinged on public service delivery there has been a tendency for bureaucratic organisations to attempt to shift the blame for the increased criminality, or ill-health, or lack of educational attainment, onto the service user and away from the service provider. Single-parent motherhood, teenage gangs, binge drinking, and poor personal discipline and social responsibility have all featured in the blame game. There has been a tendency to avoid dealing directly with the key issues of poverty, and an unregulated market economy. It is much easier to blame binge drinkers, for example, than to question the availability of cheap alcohol as a loss leader in late-night supermarkets. Young single mothers can be criticised for having children in an irresponsible way which become a burden on the State as a means of gaining some element of adult status, rather than address the issue of why people in a modern market economy might feel that this element of personal control is

the only way that they have against impersonal market forces that seem against them.

2. *Record instead of act* – public service organisations process and record the situation rather than address the issues. A cogent criticism of police and social care activity is its excessive reliance on documenting and recording aspects of dysfunctional behaviour, rather than spending time attempting to address the issue. It has been estimated that up to 50% of police officers' time is spent in recording crime, rather than crime prevention, or addressing criminality directly. Similarly, in reports following the recent headline cases of child protection, it's been clear that anything up to 35% of the social workers time is taken up in recording and discussing actions, rather than undertaking them. This is not to criticise the individual police officer or social care worker. It is, however, to criticise the bureaucratic arrangements within which they were compelled to work which requires them to record activity rather than directly address the issues.

3. *Ineffectual behaviour change policies* – organisations make ineffectual attempts at modifying behaviour – leading to the development of the so-called Nanny State. Instead of dealing with some of the key drivers behind obesity, for example, attempts are made to get people to individually modify their behaviour by exhortation. The extent of this attempt to deal directly with people's behaviour has been considerable. There is an increasing level of criticism about the extent to which Government seem to wish to influence the behaviour of citizens to keep down costs, and the relative inefficiency of creating significant behavioural changes. Although it is quite possible that some campaigns to change behaviour might have had individual effects, or if supported by more direct interventions might have been successful, it is generally unlikely that people's behaviour will change whilst the stresses which gave rise to that behaviour continue, and the system within which that behaviour is exhibited remains unchanged.

Faced with a seemingly inexorable rise in the demands for public service delivery as a result of the stresses and strains created within the public sector paradigm of the past 30 years, the financial consequences have been clear. Rather than address the issues around employment, and income inequality, there's been an increasing tendency to rely on welfare payments to offset income inequality, and address its social consequences. The burgeoning welfare payments bill has created a significant future burden that the current economic crisis has rendered unsupportable. The bill for the level of welfare payments that was created by an unequal economy was met from increasing growth which increasing levels of income and taxation could not support when the recession reduced incomes, and tax receipts. And as increased money was pumped into the public sector to provide more and more services because of the increasing pressure of the cost drivers, so it was clear that public sector productivity, far from increasing, actually plateaued. After a significant early improvement in educational outcomes from additional educational expenditure, the improvement for subsequent tranches of expenditure was significantly less. Money that was spent on the health service, though it initially increased the quantity of patient throughput, did not show a significant improvement in overall productivity. Indeed, when measured conventionally the significant increase in public services expenditure in the first decade of the millennium showed an absolute decline in public services productivity. The complexity of dealing with increased volumes increased level of management required under the command-and-control approach, so effectively increased the overhead of public service provision, and produced a significant cost base level that will prove difficult to bring down in an age of austerity. Finally, in an attempt to increase productivity, privatisation, and the introduction of private sector tenderers into service delivery of the public sector has not significantly increased the competitive element that it was assumed would drive down public service delivery costs. Instead of there being a large market base of companies involved in the public sector the number of organisations in the private sector now delivering public sector services has decreased to the extent that public service monopolies have, to a very large extent, been replaced by private sector monopolies.

Nor is the prognosis for the public services during an age of austerity particularly positive. The current proposed changes seem unlikely to improve the situation. Rapid cutting of public services will tend to increase worklessness and the unequal income distribution that goes with that. With no more buoyancy from taxation to pay for increasing costs, the reductions in welfare payments, and the loss of key services that control the social implications, will worsen the social environment. In due course Governments may find it necessary to reverse some of the reductions as the social implications become unacceptable, but this will only serve to distort, rather than deal with, the underlying issues. Finally, the approach of looking at individual services and seeking to downscale those services may well not reduce the level of overhead proportionate to the reduction of service. Overhead costs may actually rise because of the failure to link overhead and direct service costs and a lack of overall systems thinking.

If the past 30 years experience can be seen as a result of the interaction of unregulated market economy, public services demand, and a market efficiency approached to the delivery of those services, and that outcome is widely felt to be unsatisfactory, then we should ask whether adopting the alternative paradigm that we are suggesting would have had a different outcome. We think it would.

The alternative that we are suggesting does not represent some utopian vision. As Figure 9.2 shows, the UK, along with the US, is at the more

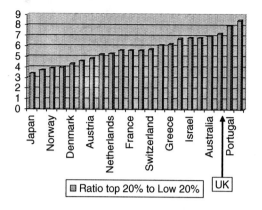

Figure 9.2   Inequalities between countries

unequal end of the distribution of income of developed Western countries, which represents broad comparators on the international scale of developing and developed economies.

Countries which are at the lower end of income inequality have achieved that position by one of two means: they have either started out with a community ethic that does not support substantial differentials in income levels or used to taxation to lower unequal pre-tax income levels to a more acceptable post-tax equality. Japan is an example of the former, and many of the Scandinavian countries are examples of the latter approach. So it is possible to adopt policies which seek to address directly the inequality of income, even within the existing economic orthodoxy. We are of the view that the approach of the new economics, with its greater emphasis on empirical findings away from theoretical suppositions, would find that either the direct or fiscal approaches would be consistent with policies aimed at a more managed and regulated economy, avoiding the repeated periodic economic crises of the unregulated market economy. Wilkinson and Pickett (Wilkinson and Pickett 2010) in their evaluation of the impact of income inequality on key social and economic outcomes have estimated what would have been the impact in the UK had we had outcomes consistent with the four countries – largely Scandinavian – that are at the more equal end of national distribution of income. They suggest that the inherent level of trust which underpins much of community and social cohesion would rise by 75%, with consequent impacts on the need for public interventions in communities. Rates of mental illness and obesity might be cut by almost 2/3, and the teenage birth-rate could be halved. Prison populations might fall by up to 75%, life expectancy might rise by up to one year (with consequent impact on acute healthcare being offset perhaps by impact on social care in old age), and the rebalancing of overwork and unemployment could gain people the equivalent of seven weeks in which to undertake the personal or community activities which are so often squeezed out under the current arrangement. Whilst these are the result of the application of regression analysis results to the overall pattern of impacts with respect to the distribution of income, and therefore may not be reproduced with such mathematical precision in reality, we think the outcome would still show four significant differences:

1. First, there would probably have been slower growth in the economy overall, and a slower growth of public service delivery. However, through a more even distribution of income that would have also resulted in less demand for public services to deal with the social and personal dysfunctional consequences. Based on the outcomes from other economies which are less unequal in terms of income distribution, it is clear that there would have been significantly less demand in terms of health, policing, and welfare payments as a result.
2. Second, there is a greater likelihood that we would have had communities which in John Major's words were 'at ease with themselves', that is in exchange for less conspicuous over-consumption there should have been a greater level of community involvement, feeling that people with more control of their lives, and a greater social and community coherence and linkage to political activity.
3. Third, a greater degree of regulation, particularly in the financial sector, would have resulted in less damaging impact from the banking collapse of 2007. This was what was experienced in Canada where the financial sector had less deregulation than implied in the adoption of the Anglo-American model. The chances are that recession would not have passed the UK by, but some of its impacts in terms of overall debt could have been avoided.
4. Fourth, instead of being driven by the financial imperatives of debt and its perception in financial markets in determining public sector expenditure, there would have been a greater chance that a slower rate of overall growth long-term, and a more stable pattern of sustainable public finance, which would have given a chance to address at a more steady pace the longer-term cost drivers of demographic change and climate driven environmental impact.

The decision to change

So far we have argued that the recent history of the public services in the UK would have been substantially different had decisions being taken 30 or more years ago to follow the new paradigm that was then being developed. We believe overall that the current crisis in public finances might have been significantly reduced, and perhaps avoided, had the alternative approach been adopted. Yet to some extent the power of the new way of thinking about organisations and the public services has already taken hold, albeit on a partial and sometimes uncertain basis. There have been a number of developments which would be in line with the new way of thinking. The current development of ideas around the 'Big Society' is a case in point, as is the current Coalition Government's insistence that it wishes to devolve responsibility to operational units for decision-making. From as long ago as 20 years, the development of Local Management of Schools could be seen as an approach that encouraged devolved decision-making in the Education service. When the Customs and Excise and the Inland Revenue were brought together to form HM Revenue and Customs, the use of systems-based thinking was widely trumpeted as an approach which had led to greater efficiencies. There are a number of examples, often at local authority level, where worker cooperatives or local management buyouts have continued to provide levels of services on a contract basis rather than though direct employment. Increasingly, in a time of austerity, local authorities are seeking to consult more widely with community leaders and others about the pattern of inevitable reductions so as to seek a consensus, which in some part could be seen as seeking an overall vision for the community (Local Government Association 2010). In the development of Local Strategic Partnerships in the recent past there have been attempts to bring together community leaders to gain a greater understanding of how the various partners contribute to public service well-being in an area, and to encourage greater cooperation. The development of the 'Total Place' pilots (HM Treasury 2010) was seen as a way of improving partnership working which had the key by-product of creating greater efficiency in the delivery of public services in an area. These examples can be multiplied but seem to fit into the organisational pattern of the new paradigm which emphasises shared vision, free flow of information and responsiveness, delegation to the front line, and the use of existing networks as its key components.

However, these initiatives have generally been dogged by the persistence of the traditional command and control hierarchical bureaucratic approach. The delegation of responsibility to the school level has been within the framework of a principal and agent relationship, and within the strictly determined guidelines of the National Curriculum. There are clear signs that the current Coalition Government wishes to give greater delegated authority, but it will be instructive to see how the central government departments react if an individual school chose to exercise that delegation in an unusual or innovative way. The Total Place initiative, though substantially about relationships, networks, and better partnerships, experienced considerable diversion of their objectives which were translated into simple cost-saving initiatives. Public consultations have often been less than ideal, as the public have been unable to express views outside an analytical straitjacket imposed from above. And there has been considerable criticism of the

HMRC reorganisation on the grounds that it adopted a 'sheep dip' approach to systems thinking aimed at grinding out financial efficiencies at a cost to staff morale and numbers. Overall, although there have been a number of pilots which can be seen to be in line with the new paradigm, more often or not are set within the traditional framework and have been less than successful as a result.

This has not stopped a number of organisations, however, from claiming that they have embraced the new thinking. Consultants and others who are involved with these organisations are acutely aware that there is often a significant gap between statements of values and organisational practices. Two key questions, which rely on people repeating some of the myths, stories, and legends of an organisation, can give some very telling responses which can tell you much about how an organisation actually operates. Ask 'tell me about something that happened here that went well and what it was like' and 'tell me about something that went wrong and what happened', and you will garner key information about how an organisation actually operates rather than how it says it operates. In the adoption of the new paradigm we generally find that organisations are capable of self-deception, not for malicious or fraudulent reasons, but because they genuinely believe their own marketing messages.

So we find that there are very few cases, if any, of organisations which have adopted the new paradigm in its entirety as their approach. And stepping aside from the possibility of self-deception, we believe that there have been significant blockages in getting to the first base of making a change – the wish to actually make the change. The traditional approach inevitably has a strong level of support from those who fear that they will be disadvantaged if it were to change. Wilkinson and Pickett identify two key centres of resistance – the corporate and political worlds. The corporate world is for the most part committed to a deregulated market economy, which allows it the greatest flexibility to make surpluses and remain in existence. Whenever there is a suggestion of moving to a more equal distribution of income, or regulating some part of economic behaviour, then there is a substantial body of lobbying opinion from the corporate world that seeks to persuade Government not to undertake that course of action. However, there is equal resistance within the political world where the hierarchies of political parties, and the status and influence that comes through an 'command and control' approach, are often justified on the basis that political parties cannot deliver their mandate to the electorate unless they have tightly acting and efficient 'levers of power'. In our experience these blockages to change extend further. It is not just the controlling political party, but also opposition parties, trade unions, and even radical revolutionary groups, who feel that they have a stake in the inherent confrontation in traditional arrangements, and fear the loss of power and authority that would come from adopting a more diverse networked approach.

These 'blockers' are often able to exert a disproportionate influence, not simply because of their controlling position within the existing traditional hierarchies, but also because those working in and through those hierarchies, despite their unhappiness and stress, are concerned that if there was a move to a more devolved, networked and visibly locally led arrangement then they would lose overnight the value of all the technical experience that they have gained at how to work within hierarchical bureaucracies. They often express real worries that the outcomes of more network working would be chaotic and uncertain, and wide-open to abuse and fraud of public money. Despite the fact that evidence from elsewhere shows that networks are self-organising, take rational decisions, and self-correct for adverse environmental change and potential collapse, they continue to insist that a change which utilised such networks would be a disaster. This is maintained despite the fact that the market economy itself represents a largely self-organising network, a fact that was observed very early on as Adam Smith's 'Invisible Hand' which guided the market towards rational, efficient, and beneficial solutions. Writing in 2005, Margaret Wheatley (Wheatley 2005) commented that despite the 'destructive impact of command and control' and the fact that 'we know how to create smart resilient organisations' organisations continue to take a great leap backwards into the familiar territory of command and control. She puts this down to fear; when confronted with the unknown, humans have a tendency to default to what they do know, even though they know it is not very efficient. It is this inertia that those who have something to lose can rely on to support them in blocking changes which would benefit the public and the public service organisations.

Assuming, therefore, that there was a willingness to want to make a change to an improved organisational paradigm to deliver public services, how would we go about doing this given that we have few markers to indicate the way; have no real examples to follow; and will be undertaking significant innovation against a hostile environment? It is to this question that we now turn.

The process for change

We've already seen how the nature of paradigm change creates uncertainty. Adopting a new approach not only provides explanatory power for the existing circumstances, but also has predictive capacity and may suggest outcomes and implications that have not even been thought of. When our minds are programmed to only consider one set of possibilities, then it can be difficult to see alternatives. Any new approach implies that there will be innovation and the realisation of as yet unimagined futures. There is often an initial period of experimentation rapid development, followed by a period of consolidation and 'tweaking' of the original concept, providing less radical second-order improvements.

What we are practically concerned with here are the issues around how we search for, and implement the innovation implied in the new organisational paradigms. By its very nature we cannot rely on past history or experience; the nature of innovation is to provide new insights, new technologies and new methodologies for us to deal with current situations. The stereotype of the innovator has been that of the lone hero, working in straitened circumstances with minimal support, finally triumphing in some 'Eureka' moment when the hunch that he or she has been backing for all these years, in the face of scorn and derision from colleagues, is finally vindicated. Actually, the reality of innovation does not appear like that at all. In his book *Where Good Ideas Come From*, Stephen Johnson evaluates around 200 significant innovations of the past 600 years (Johnson 2010). The evaluation is based on a Boston square which looks to distinguish between two sets of two alternatives:

1. Innovations which are the result of the individual 'hero innovator'; and those which have resulted from the open networking of groups of individuals, or which have utilised communications networks in order to develop them.
2. Innovations which had been driven by the competitiveness of the market economy in its drive towards the unique selling proposition which distinguishes one trading organisation from another; and those which have come through nonmarket, non-competitive situations such as open source platforms that are provided for free and outside individual control or institutions, like universities for example, where shared learning is seen as a non-competitive objective.

Figure 9.3 sets out in the form of a stacked bar chart the four sets of possible outcomes (individual market/individual nonmarket/network market/networked nonmarket) for innovations over time.

The results turn the conventional stereotype on its head. In particular it shows that:

1. the networked approach to innovation is more significant than the individual approach whatever the period under consideration. People find innovation develops best in teams working on the same issue, or in cross collaboration between individuals trying out ideas on each other, than it comes from the inspiration of a single person.
2. over time the pace of innovation has increased almost exponentially. One explanation might be that as the market economy began to develop so the competitive pressures pushed companies into innovation. It is certainly true the development of the market economy went along with a major switch of attitude between the traditional and respect for the old, and the future and the desirability of novelty. In preindustrial societies

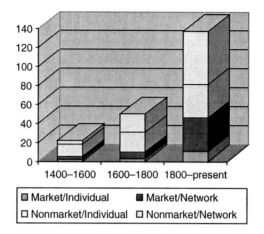

Figure 9.3 Analysis of innovations

the wisdom of the elder is often paramount, and the traditional way of doing things is passed down as the best way of doing things. In modern industrial society it is precisely the reverse. It is the new which is always deemed to be better, and the market drives the development of novelty. However when looking at the pattern of innovation it seems clearer that this simple explanation is inadequate. It is not only the collaboration between individuals in a network which is a key driver of innovative capacity; it is also the application of open systems in a non-competitive, nonmarket situation that gives the greatest number of significant innovations. The rapid development of modern communications might therefore provide a stronger, alternative, explanation of the rapid rise in the number of innovations. The communications networks, particularly those associated with the digital age, providing an open platform which individuals can populate with content seem more likely to provide innovation for the future.

This analysis shows that the new organisational paradigm, with its emphasis on information flow in open systems, delegation to teams, and the use of networking provides a better environment for undertaking innovation than does the traditional hierarchical bureaucracy. Indeed, we have already remarked on the apparently stultifying effect of bureaucracies on the change process which, as Georgiades and Phillimore express in their seminal paper (Georgiades and Phillimore 1975), 'eat hero innovators for breakfast'. We might also add that bureaucracies, since it's unlikely a hero-innovator would in reality have the original idea on their own, are also likely to eat hero innovating teams for breakfast as well – marginalising them, and bringing to bear organisational pressures to ensure that their radical ideas do not get implemented. Given that the nature of innovation is often based on hunches, backed up with experimentation and failed prototypes, it is relatively easy for bureaucracies to kill off innovative ideas on the grounds that they are not well argued, and that there is no 'proof' of their final success.

Nevertheless there are questions that need to be addressed, particularly in the public sector. In the face of an extremely hostile financial environment is it not irresponsible to simply go round backing hunches and taking risks which may result in substantial waste of public money and make matters worse? It's perfectly okay for private sector organisation to pump some of the shareholders capital into a risky venture, because taking risks is inherent in the decision to put money behind private sector ventures, but doesn't public sector money, raised through taxation, need to be handled more carefully? It might be fine to say that the new organisational paradigm provides a better environment for innovation to take place, but can we have any confidence that such innovation might be successful? Is there a process, and probable outcomes, that suggests we are not simply backing some wild and wacky idea. Isn't better to 'play it safe'?

The work of two individuals helps, we think, to give some confidence that the better environment provided by new organisational paradigm for innovation might also give greater confidence that innovation would also be successful. The first is from the work of Stuart Kauffmann (Kauffman 2000, Kauffman 2008, Kauffman 2003) who is interested in the way that animals and species adapt in environmentally difficult circumstances and establish an ecological niche. He suggests two principles which are material to our consideration of how whole organisational systems might function efficiently – the adjacent possible, and stretching the envelope of possibilities.

1. The adjacent possible represents a step-by-step approach to making systematic changes. It is rare that innovation makes a massive step to something which is totally unconnected with existing arrangements. As Johnson (Johnson 2010) points out in his book *Where Good Ideas Come from* very often innovation involves what he calls exaptation – that is the application of a commonly understood technique or idea into a totally different environmental setting, which allows for a completely new realm of possibilities to develop. The adjacent possible imagines the concept of being in a room with a number of doors. By selecting a single door it opens out into another room with another series of possibilities, and so step-by-step changes of great significance can be made. What is not clear is the endpoint of all these changes. In the same way innovation takes place against a future which is unknown, and is only the step-by-step approach, including significant prototyping and trial and error, that is available. Again, Johnson remarks in his book on the importance of

error, backing hunches, and the adjacent possible examining how innovations develop.

2. Simply selecting at random one of the adjacent possibles does not necessarily lead to a successful outcome. To some extent backtracking may be necessary when it becomes clear that the change is leading up a blind alley. But Kauffmann suggests that those animals which successfully adapt to environmental pressures are ones that will stretch the possibilities that they have to the point when the safety of order is in danger of becoming chaotic. Successful animals tend to stretch the boundaries of what is possible as far as they will go. In this way they are able to adapt quickly and take a significant number of steps towards a completely innovative solution, adapting to an otherwise hostile environment.

These ideas may not necessarily seem immediately relevant to the organisational problems that the public sector faces. However, both are talking about changes made in the face of significant environmental stress, much like an age of austerity. Both are talking about making changes by a series of gradual step-by-step amendments to existing arrangements in the face of future uncertainty, analogous to the situation faced by the public sector. However, there is also the need to stretch the boundary as far as it will go. Making small steps may be the way to go, but the steps have to be repeated and the progress continuous if significant changes going to be made. Going as far as you can, as quickly as you can, is much more likely to make the innovation successful than hesitantly pausing and checking each individual step. If it is, as Darwin suggested, a survival of the fittest, then the pattern of evolutionary change has always been that of rapid adjustments followed by a period of equilibrium – the so-called process of 'punctuated equilibrium' – the kind of change implied in the phase shifting, Chaos Theory approach.

The second set of ideas concerns the kind of process and individuals, leaders, and organisations need to go through if they are to create the possibility of that maximum stretch that is important for survival. It builds on the work of C. Otto Scharmer in his idea of 'Theory U' (Scharmer 2009) that identifies four types of listening:

1. *Downloading* – this is listening which confirms habitual judgements. The typical response to the information is 'yeah, I know that already'.
2. *Factual* – this is a more scientific form of learning in which you do not make immediate judgements; you listen to what is being said, and observe the information as it unfolds, before coming to a judgement on what you observe. You're typically surprised by what you hear 'oh, just look at that'.
3. *Empathetic* – this move is listening away from focusing on things the 'it world' to focusing on the self, and others 'you world'. It involves an intense form of really listening, and a preparedness to be silent, rather

than to interject or come to view. Typically the outcome would be 'oh yes, I know exactly how you feel'.

4. *Generative* – this is a listening which is deeply quiet and self-reflective. It is an intense form of listening when individuals typically feel connected to a greater reality. The extent of this listening is such that typically people might say 'I can't express what I'm feeling in words, but I am in touch with something greater than myself.'

These four patterns of listening are intended to draw your attention to different areas of reality, which Sharmer describes as fields. Downloading is typically choosing to operate in a world which is based on current understandings and very much centred on the self (field one). Factual listening is based on exploring the world of things – an 'it world' as it is experienced at present (field two). Empathetic listening focuses away from things and onto relationships as they are currently expressed – moving from an 'it world' to 'you world' (field three). The generative listening is operating from the point of consciousness in which the possibilities of future worlds can begin to emerge (field four). The U process, as Sharmer expresses it, consists of moving from essentially reactive pattern based on downloading and factual listening (field one and field two) to one which is based on empathetic and generative listening (field three and field four). He describes the process as moving down the shape of a 'U' towards the generative experience before utilising the possibilities revealed in that fourth stage of listening to create the possibilities of something innovative and substantially different. This pattern of change operates not only at an individual level, but within a group, if effectively led by an individual who wishes this 'U' process to emerge and lead to significant alternatives that can be prototyped and then comprehensively introduced.

This clever conceptual thinking can sound woolly and almost narcissistic, but nevertheless is widely used in a range of organisations to try and develop new thinking through collective group activity. Within a sporting context the use of this inner reflection to put a sports man or woman 'in the zone' is seen as a way of exacting at the highest level of performance from them and getting them to do some things which they otherwise might find unachievable. By seeking to get someone to imagine a positive outcome encourages the individual to produce that positive outcome, a process that is sometimes referred to as actualisation. The same sort of idea lies behind cognitive behaviour therapy, which has been effective in dealing with people with mild depressive disorders by getting them to reflect on what would be a favourable future outcome for them when they are facing personal circumstances in their environment which would otherwise prevent them from shaking off the depressive effect. The actualisation process enables people to 'talk themselves round' to a more positive attitude where simple exhortations to 'pull yourself together' are patently unsuccessful. People are then able to cope with adverse changes to their life and effectively realise their dreams. In the same way the U process, skilfully led, can produce significant new insights about a range of possibilities. It allows an organisation, or group of individuals, to establish what the range of adjacent possibles might be, and to see which of them is going to stretch the organisation to adapt most effectively to the future.

Using this developing area of thinking about the way in which change can be effected gives us some of the basic building blocks for introducing the new organisational paradigm which we have outlined. However, in practical terms these conceptual ideas need to be grounded in a programme for change that meets the immediate needs of the public service facing the current crisis. It is this to practical programme that we now turn.

A practical programme for change

In Chapter 4 we introduced the strategic framework of H1/H2/and H3 as a basis for analysing the current policies in the public sector to deal with the challenging financial environment of an age of austerity. We noted there that H1 type changes – coping strategies – were useful in the short-term, but were unable to sustain the weight of a long-term change in the financial environment, let alone the permanent change of a paradigm shift. However, the H3 approach – a paradigm shift – typically takes so long to introduce this is unlikely to be successful strategy on its own. So in looking at a practical change which involves an H3 strategic approach, it's essential that it needs to be backed up with H1 or H2 type changes so that the organisation can begin to adjust in the short-term to the new environment, whilst the longer-term change is being effected. The short-term changes represent the 'adjacent possibles' for an organisation, whilst the longer-term H3 type of change typically lends itself to a 'theory U' approach aimed at actualising a permanent future vision. So in looking for a practical programme of change we need to introduce elements which are familiar, together with elements which are stretching. If this programme is to have a name, then we would call it 'zero-based budgeting plus'.

Organisations that wish to make significant changes often find themselves stuck with a budget that no longer matches the pattern of their ambitions; which has become restricted to lack of resources; or where there are significant opportunities for increased efficiencies by the application of new technologies and innovation which they wish to grasp. A common technique that is recommended is that of zero-based budgeting. However, this title is commonly misapplied to a number of approaches to structural budget changes that fall far short of the rigour of a zero-based budget approach. Such approaches, which often take selected parts of the budget and look at them in some detail, are better described as base budget reviews, rather than zero-based budgeting. As a widely recognised technique zero-based budgeting has the characteristics of an adjacent possible for most organisations, giving them the opportunity to explore significantly greater options for change. However in the approach that we are commending here the initial steps of zero-based budgeting are taken a stage further by the introduction of the theory U concept to involve a wider group of people in imagining future possibilities, and thus using the information gained as part of a more traditional zero-based budgeting exercise to be used to prototype and build a new organisational future. Faced with the significant changes that most public sector organisations will see in the next decade, we see this combination that brings together the H1/H2/H3 strategic approach; the development of adjacent possibles; and the process of theory U, as a way practically affecting the paradigm shift that we set out in Chapter 9. 'Zero-based budgeting plus' is broadly a four stage process. The key stages are:

1. Information gathering
2. Key questioning of existing activities
3. Building alternative scenarios
4. Scenario-testing and decision-making

Organisations that simply want to cut the budget to meet available or desired resource levels often stop after the second stage. However, this misses a real opportunity to innovate in the way that the budget is created. Using zero-based budgeting approaches simply to cut the budget often creates a pattern of H1 style reductions that can be dispiriting and demoralising. This can be particularly the case if the traditional zero-based approach, which typically should be a once through project, is in fact used repeatedly to meet successive annual budget reductions. The zero-based approach does give the opportunity for developing some H2 and, in some circumstances an H3 style approach, but at these higher levels it is much more demanding. Figure 9.4 sets out the overall 'zero-based budgeting plus' approach diagrammatically, drawing on material used by International Futures Forum.

Stage 1: Information gathering

Good quality information is essential to an effective zero-based approach to whatever standard, and attempts to cut corners at this stage will be a mistake. There are three key steps to collecting information needed:

1. *Define the services provided.* This is not a trivial activity. Properly defined services ought to have the citizen initiating the service request and the service being delivered to a citizen. Approaching services with this in mind is much more likely to align them towards the 'demand pull', systems-based thinking, which is inherent in the new paradigm. The person requesting and the person to whom the services are delivered need not necessarily be the same, but commonly they will. The service request

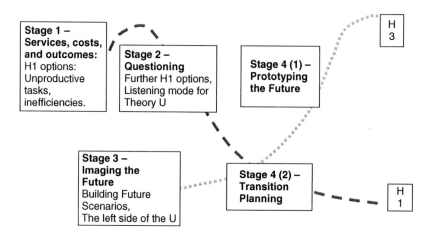

Figure 9.4 Zero-based budgeting plus approach

may not be a voluntary action. Where regulatory services are involved the request may be completely involuntary, but required in statute. Not every activity an organisation undertakes will be a service. However, at this stage, the organisation should flush out those activities that do not contribute to a service. Such activities need to be closely questioned as to whether they are adding any value to the organisation's activities. If they are not, then they constitute an H1 opportunity for change.

2. *Define the cost of providing the service.* These costs should include the variable costs associated with delivering services at a particular level, and also the apportioned overheads of the organisation that go to support that service delivery. It is essential that as far as possible all overheads are properly apportioned to service levels, and that they are carefully designated between those which are volume related – i.e. they are scalable and if volume is reduced, costs should proportionately be reduced – and those which are related to service delivery but are genuinely fixed, in the sense that the organisation might need capital equipment to provide one unit or 100 units. However, it is highly likely that the organisation will discover that overhead costs which are apportioned are not directly scalable but go in steps so that if a service is reduced below a particular level savings can be made, but if the reduction is not to a particular level then no overhead costs are saved, and therefore the overhead ratio to direct service provision cost rises. Eventually you should be left with a small residual of overhead cost which should represent the cost of being in business – i.e. the unavoidable costs the organisation existing in the first place – and these cost may include the cost of an organisation's decision-making and

key statutory support. Some organisations doing zero-based budgeting define some parts of what are seemingly unavoidable costs as a service provision – things like the mayor's office or civic representation – others leave these as the cost of organisational existence. It matters little, but an organisation should find that its costs of existence are significantly less than its cost of service provision. If the ratio is too high questions need to be asked, providing further H1 opportunities for change.

3. *Define the outcomes from service provision.* This will be particularly challenging in the public sector. Most service managers will be able to give an account of throughput, but it will be much more difficult in some circumstances to define the outcomes in terms of improvement in individual or community well-being. Nevertheless it's important to strive to get both statements of what you get for the money that is being applied to the service in terms of physical output, and also an estimate of what effect that has on the community.

Steps 1 and 2 will often be very challenging for public sector organisations. In one of its final publications before its abolition the Audit Commission (Audit Commission 2010) looked at strategic financial plans a number of local authorities, and discovered that over 60% of them did not apportion fixed and variable costs accurately, or at all, and well over 50% gave no indication of outcomes or outputs in their financial plans for the future. This suggests a significant area of weakness, which if repeated elsewhere in the public sector, which suggests there may be significant problems in handling future change, and leaves these organisations wide open to populist attacks on 'bureaucracy' which failed to relate the direct costs of service provision with the indirect costs.

Stage 2: Questioning existing activities

Whilst the decision-makers in an organisation can rely on the professional and technical support that they've hired to produce much of the information in stage one, it will be important to check that the quality of the information that is being provided is adequate. An assurance function therefore needs to be applied to the data. However, in stage two when activities are questioned it is essential that the decision-takers are in the lead, and this time-consuming activity needs to have sufficient resources applied to it otherwise a great deal of information will be collected, which may be valuable for future budget construction, but it will fall short of zero-based budgeting.

The Canadian Government's five key questions (Scratch 2010) represent a good standard against which to undertake this stage. It is important in any zero-based budgeting approach to resist the call to protect certain budget areas.

The five key questions are:

- Is the service core to the community? – Does it need to be done at all?
- If it is core, does this public authority have to do it? – Do others also provide the service, and could they do it?
- If another organisation can do it, does it need external support in order to do this? – Could another organisation do it more cheaply?
- If we have to do it, can we do it better? – Are there different technologies or innovative approaches, or do other people do it better than we do and if so how?
- Even if we can do it better, can we afford to do it at a level that affects the community's well-being? – Even if it's an important service, is there a point at which it's not worth doing it because we can't do it well enough to make a difference?

At the end of this stage it should be possible to build up a so-called balanced scorecard or playing card description of each of the services with all the relevant information pulled together. This gives the essential building blocks for reconstructing a budget. One of the key outcomes from the second stage, as well as challenge to the individual services, should be a sense about the nature of those services which are scalable – i.e. can be delivered at different levels – and the implications of scaling. It should also be possible to start seeing some of the key linkages which are an essential part of the third stage.

It will be possible to call a halt to the zero-based budgeting approach at this stage. Sufficient opportunities will have been presented for H1 and H2 changes to allow budget to be reconstructed within a different resource envelope, or to take advantage of significant efficiencies and innovations which are already available to the organisation to implement. However, such an approach will only have explored the most immediate adjacent possibles, and it is unlikely that it will have stretched an organisation in terms of making sufficiently significant changes to allow it to adapt long-term to a different financial environment. It would meet the first, but not the second Stuart Kauffmann's basic principles, and only at the lowest level of change. Similarly, within the pattern of Sharmer's theory U this represents at best a field one and field two level activities involving 'downloading' and 'factual' listening. It is only by moving beyond this stage that the possibilities of significant innovation become possible, and the challenges of moving to a new organisational paradigm can be practically delivered.

Stage 3: Building scenarios

Stage 3 will have two key elements:

- *Key element one* – the community vision in terms of aspiration for the shape of the community in the future. Although this can be developed by the decision-takers, it is best if this approach involves wider community debate from leading community representatives and decision-takers. This is not just representatives of individual groups of service users, but will also involve other agencies, significant private and civil society representatives who are doing work in the area, and members of the public. There are approaches and methodologies for bringing together the key players in the event or series of events which allows them to bounce views about the kind of area that they would wish to see for the future. Not all the leaders and community representatives will have complementary or coherent views, and part of the action of decision-takers, in the last resort, will be to apply their political judgement in undertaking key political decisions, rather than the kind of managerial decisions into which they are customarily forced.

- *Key element two* – the pattern of services that would go to support that vision in terms of overall priorities now needs to be brought together. Some services will have a natural synergy, or may even be directly related, so it is not possible to treat them as being independent of each other. For some services doing them together may give a greater impact than if one or other of them was done alone. Some of the results from key element one (vision) may give some surprising results when the pattern of services is looked at. In Canada, for example, where public consultation of this nature did take place as part of the arrangement, some service spending was actually increased, because it more closely matched the aspirations of the community, whilst some services that politicians had felt were likely to get priority were actually proposed for quite significant cuts or, in some cases, elimination altogether. The important aspects of key element two are to bring together the technical interrelationships of services, the vision that they serve, to form a scenario which patterns the services in a budget envelope for the future.

The processes involved at stage three will follow the pattern of Theory U. Moving beyond the downloading and factual basis of listening, the movement is towards more empathetic and generative listening approaches. Within the pattern of the 'U' diagram the organisation would be moving towards the deeper reflective area of presencing. It would be then begin to establish future possibilities in scenarios as a means of taking this forward. It would be unlikely that this would be achieved through a single event, it is much more likely that to develop the scenarios in any meaningful sense would require individuals to meet together, to understand the situation (factual listening), and then to reflect on it in groups (listening empathetically), and individually before coming together again to share in empathetic listening the reflective experiences that come from the generative process.

It's unlikely the single scenario will emerge from this stage of the zero-based budgeting analysis. More likely there will be some alternatives that fit within the budget envelope. The scenarios may indicate a starting pattern of services which changes over time. If part of the overall planning for the scenario is the introduction of a major shift of technology, or a major new innovative initiative, then the budget may start off with one pattern of services and migrate to a second pattern of services as the project's or activities to deliver the innovation begin to mature. This builds into the overall approach and H3 type element and suggests that the outcome of zero-based budgeting will not be a once for all shift in the budget, but a pattern of changes over a period of time that would constitute a medium-term financial strategy.

Stage 4: Decision-making between scenarios

At the final stage there will be two sets of choices to be made by the key decision-takers using the authority they have through the democratic process:

1. *Choice between scenarios.* From the scenarios that will have emerged at stage three the decision-making group may need to come to view as to which one of them will constitute the core approach for the change of the budget. Unless it is the decision of the democratic representatives to pass the actual decision-making over to the community representatives, this is a function that they will need to retain themselves.
2. *Transition choices.* Even when a single scenario has been agreed to be the pattern of the budget for the future there will need to be transition arrangements between the current budget pattern and the new budget pattern as set out in the scenario.

Though they are leading through this fourth stage, the delegative and inclusive nature of the new paradigm would demand that the organisation utilises the remaining steps of the theory U process of community-led innovation, strategically delivered change and democratic renewal. The essential pattern would create a number of key insights that need future development, but where it would remain uncertain as to their success. As stage four proceeds there may be a number of intermediate solutions, sometimes in the form of H2 projects, which have relatively short shelf life, and a number of innovations which may prove totally or partially unsuccessful. A period of experimentation risk-taking becomes an inherent part of this final stage particularly in dealing with the transition arrangements. It is highly unlikely that a single scenario, with obvious transitional steps will emerge. It is much more likely that as the move is being made to the desired outcome or scenario, that the organisation and the community will effectively explore a number of adjacent possibles that move it towards final success.

Achieving these final two stages is not a straightforward task. In bringing together a significant number of stakeholders, community leaders, and individuals there is a danger that in moving through the theory U process there will be significant blockages. Individuals will find that as they move down the left side of the U they need to open up and deal with the resistance that they experience in thought, emotion and will. The enemies of this change will be the ever-present voice of judgement, the voice of cynicism, and the voice of fear (as Sharmer describes them) within themselves. As they move up the right-hand side of the U then essentially they are experiencing the reintegration of the intelligence of the head and the emotions towards positive action. Even in this actualising process there will be a danger of taking instinctive and ill-considered reactions without thinking about them; the danger of endlessly analysing alternatives without ever being able to come to a decision to act on them – paralysis analysis; and endlessly talking without connecting the conclusions to action.

However to fail in the attempt is, in our opinion, to risk something more significantly serious. There is another U-shaped curve that psychologist tell us we experience whenever we face a shock or grief. Figure 9.5 sets out the pattern of reaction to a shock. As you descend the left-hand side of the U so you go through denial and anger towards depression, in a process that we choose to call awfulisation – a depressive state that imagines the very worst that could happen, and, because we act on that belief, can sometimes ensure that the worst will happen. Only after a period of time, psychologists tell us, do we recover the point of acceptance and making the best of the situation to something which is more positive – more adapted to the changed circumstances. This process is, if led positively, becomes actualisation, but if

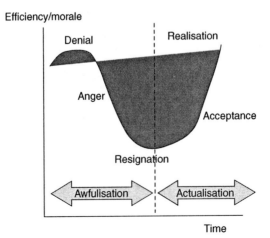

Figure 9.5 Reactions to shock

not led at all can result in a drifting into a new set of circumstances without proper regard to the outcomes.

At the present time it seems that, despite all the media coverage and concentration upon the issue of the credit crunch and its aftermath, the public are still 'in denial' about the changes that are to come in public services. A survey carried out immediately after the announcement of the Government's Comprehensive Spending Review in October 2010 (Dash. com 2010) found that 13% of adults expected that their local public service organisation would have more money to spend in the following fiscal year, with 50% believing that there were not likely to be cuts in local public service funding. This finding came despite the fact that over 60% of adult said that they felt that they were well-informed by local public service organisations. As the major changes in public services which are inevitable as current proposals are implemented then it seems likely that the public mood will change from denial to anger, the more so since the same survey shows that around half of adults did not trust local public sector organisations to make 'the right decisions'.

So getting the public involved in a more positive experience of envisioning and building a changed future seems to be essential if public service organisations are not to find themselves implementing simply a string of H1 type cuts in the teeth of public opposition and anger. It is therefore worth spending time and effort working in innovative ways to achieve an outcome which has so far eluded most public service organisations.

Leadership

As we moved through this brief explanation of the 'zero-based budgeting plus' approach we've touched a couple of times on the key issue of democratic leadership in such circumstances. Clearly the idea within the new paradigm of a significant delegation to the front line, and the principle of using networks as part of a self-organising system, might imply that there is no place for leadership. This is not the case. As we have seen with the changing managerial task under the systems-based thinking for the delivery of public services, there remains a place for leadership, but it is one which is very different from the traditional model. In replacement of a 'command and control' approach the managerial leadership in a systems based model is to support and improve the efficiency of the system to maximise the outcomes of the controlling front-line in meeting the variations in customer demand. In an analogous way, there is a change of leadership approach for the democratic function of public services. It moves away from the policy command and control model towards one which is about enabling communities to realise their potential. This change is in line with a move away from the managerial straitjacket into which many political leaders have been forced over the past 30 years and towards a reassertion

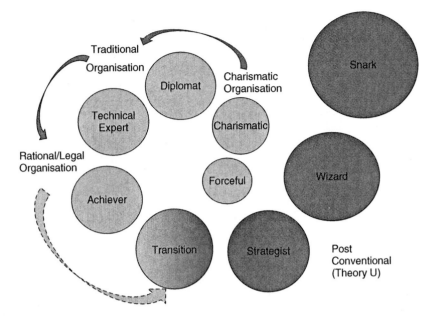

Figure 9.6 Changing characteristics of leadership

of the value-based trust relationship which underlies genuine political decision-making (Wheatley 2007).

The nature of this change is illustrated in Figure 9.6. It shows the changing characteristics of leadership as we move away from the very traditional heroic model of the leader who asserts leadership authority by reason of force in a physical or psychological way, through the form of charismatic leadership, and onwards towards the diplomatic, technical, and achievement-led leadership which dominates the current approach to public sector organisational leadership. This tracking change is in line with Max Weber's thinking about the change of organisations away from those built around the heroic leader; through to traditional form of organisation built around status and respect for a charismatic leader; towards the rational/legal bureaucracy which he saw as the epitome of the most efficient modern type of organisation.

In making the paradigm shift we are arguing that this traditional pattern of organisational leadership itself needs to change again towards a post-conventional arrangement, which is more closely aligned with the thinking of theory U. Many organisations are recognising that the conventional patterns of leadership increasingly need to be 'softened' to include a wider range of skills involving influencing and motivating the organisation, rather than instructing it. Going beyond this transitional phase we believe that the ideas of theory U require the leader to develop high-level strategic approach, rather than a more detailed tactical approach to service delivery, which we argue is best left to systems-based front-line responsive part of the organisation, and then to move on through two characteristics which we call the Wizard and the Snark:

1. Typically wizards are individuals who turned the dreams of the people into reality, by incanting magic spells over them. Whilst we are not suggesting that leadership consists of discovering a book of magic spells (though in some cases we could argue that accountants fulfil a similar function in the way that they use national and international accounting standards!), it does involve taking people's dreams and finding ways in which they can be turned into reality. This leadership involves enabling people to envision and realise that vision. This scenario-building in decision-making that we set out in 'zero-based budgeting plus', stages three and four, is typically the role of the Wizard.

2. The Snark is leadership which has reached virtually the point of invisibility. When Lewis Carroll wrote his epic poem 'The Hunting of the Snark' he suggested that his intrepid travellers were afraid that they would find that the Snark was a Boojum, in which case they would mysteriously and quietly vanish away as they found it. What we are speaking of here is leadership which is so integrated with the organisation and the community that people lead without seemingly exercising leadership. It is leadership at its greatest point of influence, and its lowest point of directive activity.

In the development of theory U Sharmer utilises the U diagram to bring out seven key characteristics of a leader who follows the approach set out above that he describes as a new social technology. Figure 9.7 describes the characteristics of leadership at each part of the new process.

The first word in the boxes represents the role that the leader plays at each stage of the development of the 'U' process. The second represents the function or task that the leader undertakes. As you move down the left-hand side of the 'U' so the function of the leader is essentially an enabling one that allows others the opportunity to learn and reflect and express their deepest principles and visions; as we move up the right-hand side of the 'U' so the role of the leader is to enable that deep reflection to create the 'adjacent possibles' that lead to innovative actions against an emergent future and to enable change take place against a background of uncertainty.

This kind of Snark type leadership pattern has found its expression in earlier thinking. In the words of the Tao te Ching (Lao T'su):

To lead people, walk beside them ... As for the best leaders, the people do not notice their existence. The next best, the people honour and praise.

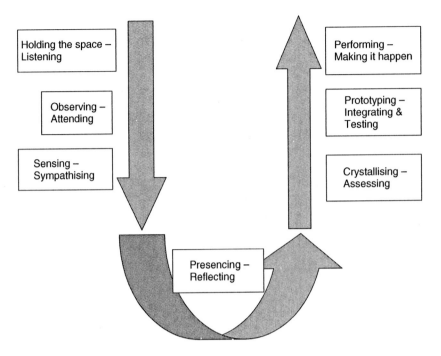

Figure 9.7 Characteristics of leadership

The next, the people fear; and the next, the people hate ... When the best leader's work is done the people say, 'We did it ourselves!'

Some concluding words

This chapter aimed to demonstrate that the new paradigm for organisations is not just a theoretical construct, it is both practical and possible, though it can also be blocked by those who do not wish it and who are committed to the traditional model.

The environment for the new paradigm sets out conditions which are consistent with innovative change; sets out the ways in which the process of searching for an available option is achievable; and the process by which the change can be discovered and collectively implemented. We've taken an existing and well known financial reconstruction technique – zero-based budgeting – and overlaid it with the new paradigm changes to show how a programme of change could be practically implemented. We've drawn out the key changes to the leadership model that adopting such an approach would imply.

As we move towards the overall conclusion of our work we are left with two questions:

- Looking at the current situation, and setting it in its wider global context, it is likely that the conditions are such to either compel or significantly enhance the paradigm shift?
- If the conditions are ripe for a change, are there sufficient signs that we are moving towards the new approach, or does more need to be done?

10
The Wider View

A risky venture

Niels Bohr, the quantum physicist, is reputed to have said that 'predictions were difficult to make, especially about the future'! Although his remark made sense in context, I've no doubt that it has been reproduced repeatedly as clear evidence of a confusion of mind. A similar fate awaited Donald Rumsfeld when he famously talked about 'known unknowns, and unknown unknowns etc'. What both of them were aiming to get across was the inevitability of genuine uncertainty about the future path for any system or society with imperfect knowledge. So, it is with some trepidation that we now embark on the final chapters and begin to draw together the threads and thinking that we have laid out in the past 9 chapters to see if we can come up with some prognosis and predictions the likely trajectory of public policy and public services in the age of austerity that confronts us.

A great deal of this book has been taken up by a comparison of two paradigms – the traditional paradigms and it's alternate. Discussion of these paradigms has been dominated by two key elements – the underlying economic theory, and the organisational pattern for public services. This is not just because these two elements happen to have a particular obsession for us. They are closely tied together and although supported, as we saw from our discussion of paradigms in Chapter 4, by a whole host of beliefs, behaviours, legends, myths, and stories which set out the worldview for any particular organisation, they are the key elements. The economic thinking and theory provides explanation, predictive capacity, options analysis, and policy direction which the organisational form interprets, evaluates, and acts on as an autonomous agent. One represents the why of public policy, the other represents the how.

- **Paradigm A** – represents the traditional orthodoxy of public service policy and delivery. It is driven by the post-neoclassical growth theory of economics and the hierarchical command and control bureaucracy. It is underpinned by a reductionist; deterministic; scientific method; post-Enlightenment philosophy, which leads to a so-called scientific 'positive' approach that describes facts and events in terms of what is, and following the example of the Enlightenment philosopher David Hume, does not seek to interpret what is into what ought to be, and is thus stripped of value judgements. The approach is broadly linear; monotonic; simple; with a tendency to equilibrium, and is delivered through behaviourally independent autonomous agents who operate without reference to each other and to maximise their personal utility without regard for the social consequences.

- **Paradigm B** – represents an approach of organic networks and the new economics. The economic principles are broadly a neo-Keynesian, Ricardian, radical critique which remains still somewhat disparate in its nature and has yet to be formulated into a single coherent alternative. The organisational pattern is one of the networks best described by the use of organic metaphors such as herds and flocks but one which is nevertheless driven by five key elements of vision; high levels of devolution; empowerment by information; self-organisation; and is holistic. The thinking that underpins it is based on holistic, whole system thinking of a complex nature, and is generally non-linear, cyclical, and in which equilibrium positions are never reached as a result of 'strange attractors'. Being organic in nature the patterns are not deterministic but emergent and uncertain and can only be seen and interpreted forwards in time, not backwards. The paradigm is value laden and exists for a reason or purpose which seeks to be achieved, with autonomous agents recognising their interdependency, their capacity for self-organisation, and group activity and objectives.

While we have set out these in more detail in previous chapters what we have summarised here as the two paradigms, we have not been indifferent between them. We consider that Paradigm A is internally conflicted. It accepts the existence of a self-organising market economy, but theoretically excludes it by its underpinnings. It seeks 'positive' value-free outcomes but is, organisationally, objectives and values driven. Its rigid hierarchies overlay natural forms that exist in the pattern of group activity within organisations and dysfunctional behaviours and inefficiencies follow. The system is rigid and deterministic, but seeks innovation and novelty. Paradigm B, by comparison, operates under consistent principles but is still very novel and relatively untried in both public and private sectors, but especially in the public sector. The practice of some of the approaches is emergent, but has not yet been completed or evaluated. Nevertheless we believe that it more closely matches experience, reality, and the observed behaviours of the public sector and public sector agencies.

We set out in earlier chapters some of the implications of adopting a new approach to public service delivery. We've identified the improvements in outcomes that could result, whilst identifying the self-defeating nature of much of the public service demand and delivery over the past two decades which has been the consequence of an orthodox economics driving an uneven distribution of income. The question we sought to answer in Chapter 9 was why there would be any compulsion to make a change from the traditional and orthodox approach to the radical, but as yet completely untried, new approach? In this chapter we want to look beyond that to the question as to 'what will make the change happen?' We are looking at the way in which the age of austerity is compelling an environment for change in public services. We are looking from 'why?' to 'what?' It is the difference between deciding to change, and being compelled to do so.

Analysis for a changing world

We use an analysis which doesn't decide between the underlying paradigms, but is sufficiently flexible to allow for the more complex analysis, the inherent uncertainty in the system, and the fact that outcomes may not simply be measured by GNP, but by a whole complex of factors which comprise a 'space state'. Figure 10.1 tries to set this out diagrammatically.

It contrasts increasing levels of activity with increasing levels of variability, broadly making an assumption that there is a relationship between

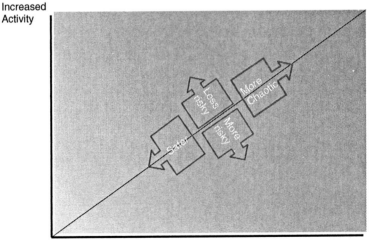

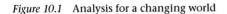

Figure 10.1   Analysis for a changing world

these two which statisticians would call heteroskedastic – that is increasing levels of activity tend to be associated with increasing levels of variability. So taking the point which is on the 45° line drawn up from the origin we can determine four directions of movement which indicate the particular relationship between activity level and variability. As we move further away from the origin so we get into increasing levels of chaotic activity, as we get closer to the origins so we get to increasing levels of stability. By stability we don't need to imply that the system will be static. The economy and pattern of public services may well oscillate between different space states anywhere in the quadrant. However, places closer to the origin it is likely that they will exhibit a consistent and repeated pattern so much so that it enables there to be some level of predictability as to what will happen next. So, for example, the economy may oscillate between a boom and bust condition in the normal pattern of economic cycle but we are able to recognise when the economy is in a boom or a recession, and predict outcomes accordingly because that pattern is well-established. There is change, but it is stable. As we move further away from origin so these patterns become increasingly difficult to discern and high levels of activity and variability the path of economic change may appear to be so completely unpredictable that we might term it random, even though the underlying elements of Chaos Theory are essentially deterministic.

If we move at right angles to the 45° line then as we moved downwards so increased levels of activity are associated with more than proportionate increases in variability. Moving upwards from the line there is increased level of activity without there being a proportionate increase in variability. If the object of the exercise is to get 'more bangs for the buck' then we may consider that increased levels of activity which are not accompanied by increasing variability are more efficient than the reverse. It's a sort of input/output ratio, but we treat the words efficient and inefficient with some caution, because a great deal would depend on society's tolerance for ambiguity. However, in general terms, we believe that people prefer to see things which are more predictable and more stable is being conducive to greater well-being.

Figure 10.2 takes this basic analysis and moves it on a bit by looking at how we might place the two paradigms within the quadrant of possibilities that we set up. However, as we do so we've introduced a third element, degrees of freedom – that of a feasible set of space states enclosed within an ellipse. We hasten to add that this diagram is not intended to be mathematically or scientifically formulated, it simply gives a visual interpretation to make it easier for the reader to follow the thinking. Within the range of possible states we recognise that individuals, organisations, communities, societies, and states are bound by constraints on action. With high degrees of freedom there is a greater ability to choose, as degrees of freedom are constrained so the level of possibilities that we can choose for our activity

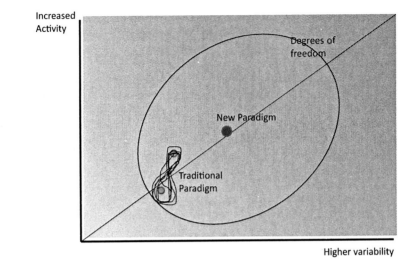

Figure 10.2 Analysis for a changing world with new paradigms

states are equally constrained. The ellipse indicates the degrees of freedom for the public sector in this case.

Within this diagram we would place the traditional orthodox paradigm as being closer to the stable and safe end of the range of possibilities compared to the alternative paradigm which whilst it might have higher levels of activity and greater efficiencies, comes at a price of moving towards the more chaotic end of the spectrum with higher degrees of uncertainty and variability. Given what we have said elsewhere in the book we think this is a fair representation.

If we now look at this in the context of an age of austerity we see a diminution of the degrees of freedom available to the UK public sector over time. Much of the book has outlined the increasing constraints in detail so we summarise here the key findings.

- Chapter 2 set out the domestic challenges that we face in terms of the economy and some of the significant challenges for our society as a result of demographic changes and the impact of climate change in the future.
- In Chapter 3 we looked at some of the ways in which other countries have faced similar constrictions in their degrees of freedom in financial restructuring terms during the past two decades. We've seen how the restructuring now facing the UK, but also a significant number of other economies in the Eurozone, and the United States have been at the high end of what has been achieved so far, and how countries who are held up as having successfully made the transition – such as Canada and Sweden – have

been only able to do so against an international economic environment which was considerably more favourable than that which now confronts the UK. Where countries have begun to address this issue and are ahead of the UK on the learning curve, so to speak, such as Ireland and Iceland, the difficulties that they are now facing is not encouraging.

- We've seen how current policies and approaches based on the traditional paradigm have shown an underlying strategic uncertainty, and are taking on a high level of downside risk.
- Over the past two decades the adoption of a more market-driven approach to public services delivery and an economic policy consistent with a more 'monetarist' approach has resulted in a position which has increased the demand for public services delivery at the same time as increasing the level of growth and taxation, in a self-defeating spiral of activity.
- The substantial lifestyle and behaviour driven demands on public services have led governments into increasingly ineffective behaviour modification policies, and how the recessionary impact on demands for financial restructuring have undermined the stability of public services delivery at the very point at which the pattern of induced demand is undiminished and even increased.

The repeated attempts that have been made to reform and improve the efficiency of public service delivery and policy and organisations have been unsuccessful in shifting significantly the efficiency of the public services, or increasing the effectiveness of their outcomes. Yet adopting radical alternatives has not been a model of change in public services, instead an adaptive approach has been taken. We've seen how the constitutional weaknesses in the UK governance arrangements have added to these problems

Figure 10.3 tries to encapsulate these are key findings in the diagram. Compared to Figure 10.2 the degrees of freedom are now considerably reduced for public services as a result of the factors that we summarise above.

We envisage that there are two possible responses, which we set out in terms of the paradigm shift, the details of which we've considered in the last few chapters. We noted in those chapters that Margaret Wheatley (Wheatley 2005 and 2007) saw in the first decade of this millennium a tendency for organisations to revert to the more traditional orthodoxy, even when faced with knowledge of a possible and better alternative. We believe that this tendency which we've illustrated as a move towards the more stable, more certain world closer to the origin of the quadrant as a 'flight to safety'. We think there is ample evidence that this is what is being carried through at the present time across a wide number of sectors. Faced with increasing restriction organisations are plumping for the safe alternative. In the financial sector banks are now infinitely more cautious and lend less, even though this damages business organisations by denial of credit and investment.

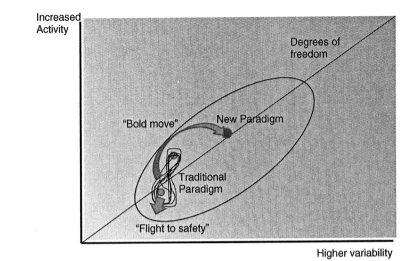

Figure 10.3   Analysis for a changing world with reduced degrees of freedom

The stability of the housing market is undermined by an increasingly cautious approach to new mortgage lending. Public sector organisations faced with increased restrictions are tending to go for service by service reductions across the board. Concerned with the potential impact of future debt financing, Governments have gone for earlier and larger financial restructuring packages to avoid a sovereign debt crisis.

What this book is suggesting is that the bolder stroke is actually to go in the opposite direction and the head for higher level of activity and efficiency but at the risk of a higher level of uncertainty and variability. It is the counter intuitive move that might rescue the situation. But, given the unprecedented nature of the current fiscal restructuring crisis and its impact public services it easy to see why this might not be seen favourably.

Yet, might the time be ripe for such a change? An analogy drawn from physical and biological systems might help here. Imagine a situation where grains of sand and dropped onto a surface. Steadily they will build up to create a small pyramid of sand particles each held by the relative friction between particles and between the heap and the surface. From time to time an added particle will cause itself and a few other particles to roll down the pyramid edge. Very occasionally the added particle will trigger a set of conditions which will cause the whole side of the pyramid to collapse in an avalanche. Such environments are very common. Clearly there are physical examples, like snow accumulation in mountains, which are directly analogous to a heap of sand particles. But there are also other more biological processes that show a similar pattern. Take for example the evolution of species. Generally there is a steady change which is relatively small-scale in species development. But from time to time, the process 'punctuated equilibrium' shows there are disastrous 'avalanches' when significantly changing environmental conditions create the circumstances for a major extinction of species. Similarly, there are circumstances in which innovation in the economy follows a similar 'power curve' pattern. Generally changes which are made to products or the range of products are small-scale, but from time to time there are major technological shifts which result in the economic equivalent of an avalanche. Whole industries are swept away to be replaced by new ones. This was the essence of Schumpeter's analysis of technological change and the process of 'creative destruction'.

The analogy leads us to a broader conclusion. The small-scale changes and incremental pattern of growth of the public services that we have seen is now facing significant challenge given the scale of the issues. The domestic environment is now such that as the degrees of freedom for public services begins to be squeezed it is the bolder, more chaotic, more highly variable, but more active move towards the alternative radical paradigm that may ultimately prove more successful. The environment is set for an avalanche, but the concern must be that in line with Schumpeter's 'creative destruction' there is an inevitable period of turmoil to be gone through before improvements are delivered.

Longer-term issues and external factors

The squeeze in terms of degrees of freedom of the public sector is not just determined by the domestic pressures of financial restructuring. Chapter 2 outlined key larger demographic and environmental pressures which impinge not only on the UK public sector but also on the public sectors of other economies. The degrees of freedom for the UK public sector are equally under pressure from changes in the balance of world economies that have accelerated as a result of economic recession. There is now the emergence of new world powers, or rather the re-emergence in some cases, as the Western economies falter. Consideration of the future of UK public services cannot be considered in isolation of these changes.

The impact of these global changes on public policy and public services in the UK comes through four factors.

- Firstly, over the past 20–30 years the impact of the globalisation of the world economy has meant that the competition for resources, employment, and economic activity can no longer be limited to a single country, but has to be seen in the context of the whole world economy. So, for example, the UK's very open economy has meant that significant elements of community services in the former public utilities, and significant parts of UK employment are controlled by international companies that are no longer local to the source of their labour and raw materials, and increasingly take a global view in their pursuit of cost minimisation. Conventional economic theory holds that this is a natural consequence of relative economic advantage, but the advent of globalisation has led to a position where the key resource required for the modern economy – oil – is concentrated in the hands of a relatively small number of largely Islamic states; and the comparative advantage in manufacturing has led to a position of absolute advantage with the Far East, particularly China, has become the lowest cost manufacturing provider, while other key developing countries, like India, have become a lowest cost service provider. UK public service providers therefore find important drivers of public services in the terms of employment, or lack of employment, income are in the hands of forces and organisations that no longer have a local loyalty. Additionally, the increasing accretion of world surpluses that have followed the comparative and absolute economic advantages have meant that substantial portions of Western assets are now in the hands of sovereign funds – from football clubs to Government bonds.

- Secondly, with the globalisation of the world economy and increasing ease of communication and travel there has been an increasing tendency to diversity in communities. Partly based on a colonial past, but also driven by significant economic forces, the UK, in common with many countries in the West, has seen increasing levels of migration. The impact of significantly different worldviews that are carried by migrant communities on social cohesion, and on the provision of public service is considerable and increasing. The dangers that arise from fundamentalism within these differing worldviews can threaten the stability of the State.

- Thirdly, the impact of changes in the global economy and the shift of power have further impacts on the cost of public services through increasing competition for vital resources. As economies elsewhere in the world begin to develop and exercise their full potential, and as the impact of climate change begins to affect resources of water, food, and raw materials, so there is a strong possibility of increasing escalation in the cost of these materials with consequent impact for local economies. It is widely predicted that the era of cheap food has come to an end, and the consequences, in the absence of significant redistribution of income, will be to increase absolute and relative poverty levels. We have already seen how these drive the demand for public services, whilst the same factors of cost escalation are already acknowledged to increase the cost of delivery of public services – it has long been understood that the inflation rate experienced by public service providers is generally two or three percentage points greater than that experienced by average households.

- Finally, the differential impact of the recession on the world economy has two further implications for the overall viability of UK public services, along with other Western economies. For the first part the relatively sluggish growth of Western economies contrasts with a much more rapid growth of developing economies particularly in the Indian subcontinent, South America, Russia, and China. Over a period of time the differential that has previously existed between higher income Western economies and developing economies will rapidly close, and as it does so the impact the ability of Western economies to impose their worldview internationally will diminish. Second, the internal strength of many of these developing economies who have a large latent internal demand does not necessarily mean that the growth of those economies will lead to a growth in the internationally traded world economy on a proportional basis. Many Western economies are relying on significant export led manufacturing growth to recover their economies. Given that the public and domestic sectors are struggling to recover from an over indebted position, and many internal services have been significantly weakened, with the possible exception of financial services, these two characteristics mean that the strong economic recovery which is the key to public fiscal restructuring does not lie within the gift of Western governments, and the growth and influence of the more rapidly developing economies may significantly restrict the degrees of freedom and scope for policy action in the UK and elsewhere.

Given the importance, therefore, of these international changes in limiting the scope for public services delivery in the future and the scope of public policy it's worth spending a little time in looking at how the shifting balance of international economic power might restrict public policy choices in the age of austerity. From what we have already said there are three contrasting worldviews that tend to dominate the debate – the West; Islam; and China. These worldviews tend to act rather like paradigms, they affect attitudes and behaviours, and, analogous to the geocentric view of the universe, each worldview tends to put itself at the centre and to treat its interaction with others as being people who are 'out there' and who are not 'one of us'. These individual worldviews are not internally uniform however - the events of history have not uniformly affected behaviours, beliefs, and values – there is also diversity within them to deal with. In the figures that follow this internal diversity is indicated by connecting boxes that indicate some of the variety of attitudes that have been driven by historical events.

Figure 10.4 tries to pick out from the recent development and history of the West some of the significant events that have begun to dominate our Western worldview.

Although grossly simplistic we pick up five historical events or movements that have underpinned our worldview:

- The emergence of the Renaissance and Protestant Reformation began to launch the West on its path of economic growth. The key issues of the

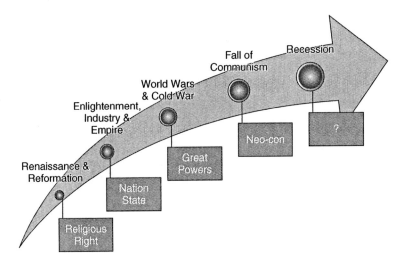

Figure 10.4 Trajectory of the West

Reformation still underpins some of the mindset of the religious right in the US and elsewhere.

- Following on from this the period of the Enlightenment was associated with development of industrial and economic growth in the Industrial Revolution is and the securing of vital raw material sources with the establishment of colonial empires. During this period the concept of the 'nation-state' began to develop away from earlier views of polity, and with it the association of representative democracy with economic development and the market economy.

- Within the West the development of nation-states and empires led to the inevitable clashes to decide who would be master and the earlier part of the 20th century was dominated by two world wars, followed later by the Cold War between the Great Powers as they struggled for hegemony. This led to the development of the Great Power mentality as the mantle shifted initially from Great Britain towards the competition between the Soviet Union and America and latterly to America alone.

- With the collapse of communism in the late 1980s it looked as if the Western free-market economy had triumphed, and as Lanchester comments it was the existence of the competition between the two polities that helped to restrain some of the wilder elements of free-market economics. When these restrictions were lost the past 20 years have seen what apparently was the worldwide adoption of the capitalist market economy, and with it the development of the neoconservative view that assumed automatically that as this pattern of economic activity spread the associated worldviews of the nation-state, representative democracy, and Great Power responsibility would also spread.

- Our last key marker on this trajectory of Western expansion and development was the recent economic recession, which we see as a key turning point and one which may be seen in future time as changing and challenging the historic dominance of the Western worldview. How that will happen, and its impact public services, has been part of the purpose of this book, and we leave as uncertain any predictions of the final outcome.

Figure 10.5 looks at the trajectory of growth of Islam and its worldview, and again in a grossly simplistic manner tries to draw out key historical events or movements that underpinned the Islamic viewpoint, and the diversity of attitudes and behaviours that result (Ansary 2010).

- The development of Islam as a major world religious movement drawing together in a single society – the Umma – the disparate and fragmented nature of the Arabian tribes has given it a key core set of beliefs that are referred to by elements of Islam that are associated with jihadist fundamentalism. At the same time the Sunni/Shia split in Islam remains a key source of political and religious division.
- The rapid expansion of Islam from its core area has led to a view that what is commonly called the Middle East actually represents the world centre and the eastward and westward expansion is part of a pan Islamic movement that seeks to bring the whole world under the Islamic worldview.

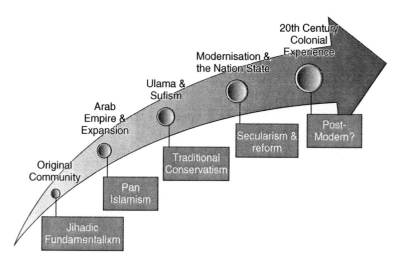

Figure 10.5   Trajectory of Islam

- The development subsequently of the intellectual roots of Islam through Sufism and councils of scholars in the Ulama has created within Islam a core traditional conservatism that has historically restricted the ability of Islam to respond to the kind of economic growth and industrial and economic revolution experienced in the West and elsewhere.
- The development of greater secularism within Islam separating the religious and secular states and the desire for reform has created a number of key Islamic states – such as Turkey or Egypt – that have sought to develop a more modernised, westernised, and nation-state approach but yet within the Islamic framework. This tension in Islamic states between fundamentalism and conservatism is a continuing political dilemma.
- As the West sought to secure through colonial activity the key oil resources found within Islamic states, so many fairly conservative and economically undeveloped Islamic states experienced some of the worst elements of the Western colonial arrogance which created a significant backlash and tension. Nevertheless, the increasing powers of Islamic states in terms of acquisition of Western assets from sovereign wealth funds has implications for the way that the broader group of Islamic states sees itself getting back on track after a period of Western interruption as the dominant worldview.

Figure 10.6 looks at the trajectory and the growth of worldview from the Chinese perspective. Again, it is grossly simplistic, but four key events and movements are identified.

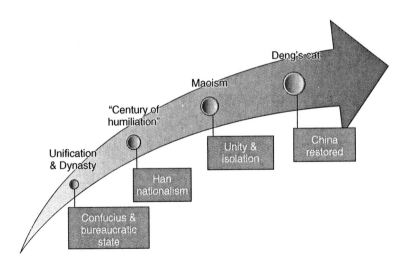

Figure 10.6   Trajectory of China

- China represents one of the world's oldest and most continuous civilisations. Its history to modern times has been dominated by the development of a unified bureaucratic state and whenever forces divided China the pressure to pull back to the unified Chinese state was seen as desirable, whatever the social and political consequences. Unification and dynastic rule are central and the continuing influence of Confucianism and neo-Confucianism and the unified bureaucratic state are a powerful legacy. For a substantial period of its history China developed the world's most substantial economy, without it feeling any need to engage in international trade, and provide a magnet for Europeans and others to trade with it substantially driving the voyages of discovery from the West.

- The rapid growth in Western economies in the early modern era led to a greater level of interaction with China and the establishment of Western colonial dominance in some parts of the Chinese state which led to a period in Chinese history referred to as the 'century of humiliation'. The result of arrogant and insensitive European intervention in particular (including Japanese intervention once that country had decided, following the Mejii Restoration, to virtually adopt Western economic and social practices), led to a resurgence of Chinese nationalism based around the social, political, and racial concept of the Han people.

- The period of confusion that followed the breakup of the old dynastic state was finally concluded with the victory of the Communist Party and the establishment of the People's Republic. A period of isolation and essential reunification of the Chinese state under Maoism re-cemented Chinese worldviews about the significance and importance of their place in history, but restricted the speed of economic development.

- Following the death of Mao Tse-tung, there was a shift of power towards a more pragmatic rule under Deng Xiaoping. The pragmatic Deng commented that it didn't matter whether the cat was black or white provided it caught the mice. Subsequently, China has been restored in its own view to its former position as the world's leading power through the rapid growth under a market economy, but it would be a mistake to assume, as some Western neoconservatives have done, that this would automatically shift the long-standing worldview towards a more democratic state.

Table 10.1 tries to draw together the worldviews of these three – the West, Islam, and China in a table.

We accept that such a summary is at best partial, however the important point is the significant differences between and within the worldviews of these three existing and emergent world power centres. In particular the West can no longer assume that its worldview will prevail. There are three areas which seemed to us to provide the greatest challenge:

Firstly, the assumption in the West that representative democracy is automatically associated with economic development and market economy

Table 10.1 World Views

	The 'West'	Islam	China
Unit of Focus	Individual	The Umma	'Han' community
Government	Democracy	Shared Autocracy	State Autocracy
Economics	Free market	Controlled market	State capitalism
Philosophy	Secularism	Monotheistic	Syncretic 'Tao'
State	Nation-states	Theocratic states	Civilisation state
Legal framework	Contractual	Civil society patronage	State bureaucracy
Knowledge base	Scientific reductionist	Shared science and Shar'ia	Holistic empiricism
Minorities	Politically correct tolerance	Tolerant indifference	Hierarchical racism

will be significantly challenged by the substantially autocratic nature of the Chinese and Islamic worldviews. Secondly, the continuing pattern of economic growth fuelled by debt in a self-perpetuating feedback cycle will be challenged by the impossibility of all world economies operating such an approach within the total resources available on the planet. The more managed approach of China, and the more communal approach of Islamic finance will challenge Western assumptions. Lastly, the West's emphasis on individual consumerism and unrestrained growth will be challenged by the more communitarian and equality driven attitudes of China and Islam.

China, and to a lesser extent Islam, are already asserting their influence based on their worldviews and there is a significant danger that if the reaction to this is a retreat into nationalistic fundamentalism then the scope for conflict and further restriction of the freedom of individual states to act seems inevitable. These worldviews will begin to dominate debate over key issues such as climate change and how the impact of that should be dealt with. If the existing degrees of freedom are not to become increasingly more limited by conflicts between worldviews, a means of dialogue has to be found building on the more pragmatic and tolerant interpretations of them which may allow for a mutually beneficial modus vivendi, but which are likely to fall far short of a syncretic common worldview, or the dominance of any one of them.

In this section we turn again to Figure 10.3. The economic and social circumstances in which UK public services find themselves has significantly squeezed the degrees of freedom that we have at national or individual organisational level to adopt a particular strategy. At international level the impact of globalisation, the recession, and the shifting balance of world power has created circumstances which will further squeeze the degrees of freedom, and have created challenges to the normal assumption of world-view that we have in the UK and elsewhere in the West. In the circumstances there is the greatest danger of an insular reaction, a defensive assertion of long-held attitudes, and a fundamentalist response (restated as a return to core values) that pushes the policy choices towards the 'flight to safety'. The dangers of having a closed mind and closed attitudes loom large. However, as we have tried to show, there are viable alternatives.

Opportunities and threats, risks and rewards

When we looked at the practical ways in which the alternative programme could be implemented in Chapter 9 we drew together threads of thought from Stuart Kauffmann and Otto Sharmer. Stuart Kauffmann's analysis and critique of the prevalent post-Enlightenment scientific thinking (Kauffman 2000 and 2008) leads to a conclusion that in going forward individuals, organisations, communities, and states will find that opportunities and events are emergent, rather than determined by some rigid application of scientific principles and laws; that the emergent reality will be beset by inherent uncertainties, rather than be deterministic; and that it will be driven by values and choices rather than being seen as unavoidable events. Progress will be by way of the 'adjacent possible', looking for the next best alternative amongst a range of alternatives, and the forward passage of time will mean that it would not be possible to go back and retrace what might have been. Otto Sharmer's contribution was to propose a process of thinking which he described as based on 'open minds, open heart, and open will' in which the individual, group, community, or organisation is open to a range of alternatives, is prepared to engage empathetically with others, and is prepared to find solutions which are not based in analysis of what has been, but in discovering and exploring the possibilities of the future as it emerges. While Kauffmann provides the philosophical background to understanding our experience of change, Sharmer provides us with a process to explore it.

Presently, public services are very much located in the area of centralised bureaucracy. The centre of focus is at the centre of the organisation looking outwards. Sharmer envisages a process which leads through deeper and deeper understanding and community, partnership, and environmental involvement down the left-hand side of the U, towards a collective understanding and developing alternatives of collective decisions, innovation, strategic delivery shift and democratic renewal on the right-hand side of the U. As you begin to move through this process so the centre of focus moves from the centralised bureaucracy to a much more decentralised arrangement. The focus moves from the centre of the organisation towards its periphery and its interface with customers. Many of the developments in the public sector over the past 20 or 30 years have aimed at making this move. The reforms that have been undertaken in attempting to set up 'Next

Steps Agencies', decentralisation of activities, and the introduction of market forces and market factors have been aimed at shifting the centre of focus towards the periphery and the interface with the customer, citizen, or client of public services. The proposals of the current Coalition Government move solidly in this direction, but fail to go far enough. Simply replacing public sector providers with market-orientated private sector companies in a system of public sector 'privatisation' does not necessarily lead to the kind of decentralisation and closer linkage with the customer. The best private sector organisations are much more heavily customer-orientated than the public sector. But this is not universally the case. Some large private sector organisations – utilities or banks or large service companies – are every bit a centralised bureaucracy as the traditional public sector organisation. They lack the close interlinking and understanding of their customer base. Simply replacing public sector monopoly providers with private sector monopoly providers will not give the necessary interlinkages shown by this second level of decentralisation. It was this critique that led Phillip Blond of ResPublica to propose the ideas of the 'Big Society' as we saw earlier. Moving beyond this decentralised position to the next level is part of what the 'Big Society' idea is about, and moves us, as we have seen, out of the realms of Paradigm A in the first two levels towards the increasingly Paradigm B world.

The first critical area is around the increasing understanding of the networked organisation and interlinkages to civil society, thus introducing the third key element of the now widely understood tripartite public, private, and civil society sectors of the body politic. The point of focus now places the organisation as being linked much more closely into all the networks that support and depend on it. The best private sector organisations, adopting the system-based thinking typified in the Toyota model, are operating in this key area and are linked to supply networks, distribution and customer networks, and exercise their social responsibility to a wider group of stakeholders. This is a new and key area for public sector organisations to move into, learning from that best practice.

When individual decisions are taken about individual levels of services in a decentralised assessment under financial pressure, there is a real danger that no one is looking at the networked effects of these individual decisions. As public services become squeezed down, so they lose any redundant capacity they have to cope with unexpected changes, and with increasing levels of interdependence between services, and the organisations that provide them, there is greater chance that resilience is lost and conditions will prevail where the whole public service system teeters on the brink of instability. A significant and unexpected event – such as emergency flood, health epidemic, or adverse weather conditions – can then create the circumstances that bring down wider areas of public services for a significant period of time. It is only by moving to the next stage and engaging the wider range of stakeholders in civic society in understanding the implications of public service changes that there is a chance that sufficient redundancy can be made available to make sure the system remains stable, and the complex interaction of events can be best understood.

Moving beyond this level of networking into a situation where the organisation is interacting with its environment, and the environment with it, creates the most profound and open change that is at the very depths of Paradigm B. This is where the exploration within the community of the adjacent possibles and the emergent future really begins, and where people begin to realise the real power of their common and shared values for the community and society which strengthens the possibility of addressing the big issues. The boundary of the organisation has effectively become porous, and the organisation of public services is very much more one of permanent or semi-permanent partnership organisations which exist to deliver values and outcomes, rather than existing for itself. It is at this point that the community, and its community organisations and collective groups begin to cooperate in addressing the big issues that confront public policy and public service delivery. It is from these that, moving up the right-hand side of the U, we begin to develop experiments and prototypes that are community-led. Some will be successful, others will not. Most will need to be adapted and changed using some of the kind of techniques of project management. From these there is the chance of bringing together the more successful elements in a major strategic delivery shift which is the desired outcome from the outset in making the kind of fiscal and activity adjustments which underlie the ambitions of political and community groupings. From these the possibility of developing a new and renewed democratic engagement of the community becomes real.

The ambitions of collectively addressing big issues; community-led prototyping of innovations; ultimately leading to a strategic delivery shift and renewed democracy, on the right-hand side of the U represent the final outcomes of a much deeper process. However, there is always the temptation to shortcut across the levels without going down to the deeper and deeper engagement between decision-makers and the community that is implied in following the new pathway. Politicians look for validation of activities for a renewed and engaged democracy but fail to engage individual consumers or communities or the wider stakeholder environment. Such reforms where they have been attempted, have generally been partial, and improvements trivial, and have failed to achieve effective outcomes. Similarly the introduction of market type practices in an attempt to engage public sector organisations with their citizen and customer base, but which have not engaged the wider representation of civic society, or encouraged the openness and seeking of common values and principles, have often reduced such initiatives to a system of marketing and propaganda in which organisations, traditionally using performance measurement, seek to persuade a disillusioned, disengaged, and distrustful public that they really have improved and are more efficient. Such approaches within Paradigm A only serve to enhance public cynicism and it is only by going deeper into the elements of Paradigm B, and getting around the full 'U' path instead of trying to cut across it, that it is likely that the public will begin to support and understand changes which may be necessary as the degrees of freedom are squeezed and options are reduced.

Going through the U process implies a move away from the 'flight to safety' into making the bolder paradigm shift. However, given the nature of the restriction in degrees of freedom internally and externally there is another, and more dangerous and destructive path that is suggested by Sharmer in his work. He calls the movement through the bottom part of the U the process of 'presencing'. By contrast there is the alternative of 'absencing'. In a metaphor drawn from quantum mechanics this path represents antimatter as opposed to matter. Whilst the path of presencing requires approaching it with 'open mind, open heart, open will', the path of absencing envisages the closing of such openness and the limiting of thinking to one approach, one organisation, and one internalised focus. Sharmer draws examples from a number of political and company narratives to illustrate the disastrous consequences of this negative approach. He speaks of business organisations such as Enron, which could only see one view, and were only interested in the well-being of the one organisation, irrespective of the damage they did elsewhere, or of the violation of norms of ethical business behaviour, and describes how they moved through a one-view approach to a point where they were deliberately putting out disinformation and the company had become divorced from reality to the point where it faced destruction. Similarly a 'one viewpoint and a one approach' path was taken by Hitler and the Nazis in Germany and, as time progressed, they became increasingly dissociated from reality and society and failed to see the imminence of their own destruction, or the damage that they had wrought on the world. But this negative view is not just an example of recent history. Barbara Tuchman (Tuchman 1984) describes a number of historical events where organisations or states pursued policies contrary to self-interest in the face of known alternatives.

We've seen how the pressures on the squeezing of the degrees of freedom from global changes bring into sharp relief the forces of intense conservatism and fundamentalism across all three emerging worldviews. We suggested that an open-minded dialogue might be a way – moving through the bottom part of the U – for the world to collectively address some of the big issues which we were concerned would be missed out of the equation for public sector changes as the West became increasingly obsessed with fiscal restructuring. The path of 'absencing' represents for us one of the most significant threats to public polity and public service as we face the age of austerity. If rigid thinking based on old conservative orthodoxies, and fundamentalism based on some harking back to mythical golden ages, or unyielding assertions of basic principles, intolerant of other views and understandings, is allowed to dominate then there is a real danger that politics in the public sector will become increasingly divorced from the reality of what is happening to the communities that they seek to serve with disastrous consequences.

If we stick to the traditional approach and 'flight to safety' we are concerned that we may see:

- an enfeebled state that is unable to meet the challenge of big changes. Simply going as far as decentralisation will not be enough and there will be a danger of the loss of political control to private sector suppliers, and the divorce between the experience of the citizen as customer and the citizen as elector. Failing to take it to at least the next level of considering networks and the impact on civil society may leave it open to reductionist approach to solving the fiscal restructuring which runs the risk of systemic failures;

- an alienated electorate as those leading within the centralised bureaucracies become increasingly divorced from the reality of what is happening in communities. *The Economist* (*The Economist* 2010b) reporting on the announcements that were made following the Comprehensive Spending Review drew attention to the fact that although the Government was emphasising strongly it's decentralising approach, in fact it could be seen as dumping the consequences of larger financial decisions on lower-level public sector organisations, unknowing and unconcerned about the implications. If the centralising tendencies of the UK public sector continue and there is a severe danger of a mismatch between centralised bureaucratic pronouncements and what happens on the ground. Public sector managers, local politicians, the boards of public entities, and the public will not be convinced that there is scope for local decisions as alleged by central government when it is obvious that the resources necessary to support that local decision-making have been withdrawn;

- a greater inequality than that seen over the past decade as the impact of global changes in costs, the loss of tax revenue and support infrastructure in public sector services, and increasing levels of unemployment in a low growth economy, create increased levels of public service latent demand, but prevent the delivery of public services to ameliorate or mitigate the consequences of that inequality. This is likely to have a differential impact. As we have seen from Chapter 2 there is already a norm of standing geographical and sectoral inequality in economic well-being. It is likely that this will get worse, and it is highly unlikely that migration of either economic activity or human migration will significantly ameliorate the situation.

In such circumstances we would be concerned that people's sense of fairness and equity would be outraged by the implications of what is actually occurring. Support for the changes will begin to falter as the consequences become apparent, and there will be no path for dialogue. Already we have seen significant radicalisation of young people, and this inter-generational radicalisation against government and politics and against capitalism and business could rise, destabilising social cohesion and the State. Anatole Kaletsky, writing in the *Times* in November 2010 drew attention to the threats to democracy that such inequalities created. Referring to the work by Will Hutton and Michael Portillo, he suggested that the Coalition Governments' attempt at a Fair Pay Review would need to address some critical issues if this danger were to be avoided (Kaletsky 2010b).

Concluding remarks

If this represents a threat, then the real opportunity is to go further into the bottom two layers of the U, adopting the thinking behind Paradigm B. It better places the community to meet the new environment and the big issues that need to be faced collectively. It gives the opportunity to expand the degrees of freedom by joint action, but requires a positive action of will and intent by pragmatists and moderates to overcome the rhetoric of the fundamentalists. By moving in this way it is much more likely we will end up with a more equal, but perhaps not as collectively wealthy society, but it gives a real opportunity of long-term stability. Moving in this direction will be out of the comfort zone for many. Instead of looking to the past for examples and guidance, it will have to embrace the uncertainty of an emergent future. Rather than hold onto political power it will require individuals and organisations to learn that they need to give up the power in order to gain the support that is needed. And it will require us to give up the myth of 'unavoidable consequences' of what is for a clearer restatement and dialogue about the values and outcomes that we collectively seek to achieve. It is an uncomfortable and uncertain area, but we believe that it is the way forward to meet the challenges that the public sector faces in an age of austerity.

11
Postscript – Not Far Enough

'A price you cannot afford'

Shelby Foote in his monumental work on the American Civil War (Foote 1958–1974) relates a conversation after Gettysburg between a British Army military observer to the Confederate States and some Confederate commanders. The observer remarked: 'Cannot you see that your system feeds upon itself? Your men do wonders, but each time it is at a price that you cannot afford.' By this he meant the attritional damage to Southern Confederate society not only from the loss of men and material, but particularly from the impact on the younger generation who provided many of its junior officers. It was this disparity in resources that President Abraham Lincoln called 'the arithmetic'. The North, with its significantly more dynamic economy, and larger resources of raw materials and manpower, could absorb losses even on a more proportional scale than that of the Confederate South, and would still end up with more than enough to win the war in the long-term. And although history has tended to romanticise the significant military achievements and superiority of Confederate forces over their Union opponents, in truth the South was fighting for hopelessly bad cause. It was fighting to maintain the dominance of an economic system that was in decline; that was supported by a substantially hierarchical society that was at odds with the 'American Dream' of personal achievement and social mobility; that was sustained by the morally indefensible practice of slavery; and which, in the long-term, by deforestation and agricultural monoculture, was stripping the fragile physical environment and creating the conditions for subsequent ecological disasters. Daniel Burstein in his trilogy 'The Americans' describes how the seeds of the Civil War conflict were sown years before during the very founding of modern America by Western Europeans. Even then there was a north–south split. In the South the colonisation was commercial, mirrored the hierarchy of European society, and was largely exploitative in the pursuit of profit. In the North colonisation was, by religious and political dissidents, substantially built around trying to develop a new society, and struggled in the poor agricultural land and climate initially for survival, and subsequently for sustainability. At least at first the political weight of the newly formed United States of America lay in the South, with its economic advantage, but over time the North, with more conducive Protestant ethical values, and natural raw materials, became the more dominant economic force. The South could see a steady loss of power, and at some point conflict seemed inevitable as eventually the South – fearing the loss of its substantial cost advantage through the abolition of slavery – sought to maintain a prominence that the emerging situation denied it.

The phrase 'as a price you cannot afford' seems to us to sum up in many respects the current situation. It seems to us that the Western economies are seeing an overall loss of their economic power that they are struggling to overcome. We are trying to maintain a position globally that we are steadily losing, and one where the nature of globalisation and environmental impact means that the credibility of any kind of separate development is about as credible as secession was to the Confederacy. We are seeking to maintain old patterns of hierarchy in our political and organisational systems, and we are maintaining our machinelike attitudes towards organisations and the economic system that are less conducive to our future than adopting new approaches – much as the Southern States were doing in the Civil War period. We are attempting to maintain an old pattern of values – or rather a valueless economic system that tries to assert itself as a scientific deterministic enterprise in the traditional post-Enlightenment tradition – rather than seeing and adopting a more value laden, and more equitable system that might give us longer-term sustainability. Finally, our approaches to the current situation may achieve significant results, and even achieve a successful fiscal restructuring, but it might be at a reduction of the resources of the people, and particularly the damage done to future generations that becomes 'a price we cannot afford'. In short, our current policies and approaches, however badly defined, may be successful but the suffering to achieve them may be unacceptable.

Why stories?

The reader will have noticed our use of stories within this book, not just here in this postscript, but elsewhere. We have not confined ourselves to numerical descriptions, but have drawn on information from the physical world, the natural world, and from history in support of our arguments. We make no apologies for this. We find that such stories not only resonate with people by providing an analogy to the current situation that they find helpful, if sometimes disturbing, but also impart a level of understanding which is more comprehensive than a dry recitation of facts. But there is also a more cogent, philosophical, reason for our use of stories. We have argued strongly in this book of the need to move beyond the traditional paradigm which regards organisations and the economy as a machine. We have argued that a move to a new paradigm is what is required. What we have suggested is a two-stage process – first using the understandings and insights given by Chaos Theory and Quantum Theory to give more complex, but more realistic, explanations of reality and to introduce the fundamental issue of uncertainty. Second, we suggested that it is by moving to adopt an approach based not on machines, but on living entities, organisms, and biological, rather than physical, thinking that we begin to understand our political, economic, and organisational systems as they actually are. In moving to this second stage we begin to see that our political, social, and economic environment is not valueless but value laden, and does not need the heavy hand of 'command and control' to manage it because it is substantially self-organising. But with it comes two other features. First, the pattern of our social, political, and economic environment is not predetermined and predictable in some physical machinelike sense, but is emergent, the consequence of the independent decisions and choices of thousands of autonomous agents each of which acts and is acted upon by the environment which they co-create. Second, the pattern is fraught with uncertainty – not just in a quantum sense – but in the that the emerging future in a biological sense, in which Time's arrow points one way only, is unique and unrepeatable. These two elements mean that our social, political, and economic environment is not predictable – we cannot define even the universe of possible outcomes within which a particular future path is set – and we face a genuinely unique set of circumstances in that whilst there might be discernible patterns, we cannot go back and repeat and experience at some future time that we had experienced in the past.

In such circumstances it is only by reflecting on what has happened, and by the stories of historical analysis that we gain insight into the future. Stories therefore become an integral part of how we relate to our universe, and how we understand the 'adjacent possibles' of our future. So we have used examples from history in order to try and explain current circumstances, and future trajectories, for public services in an age of austerity, whilst recognising that our current circumstances are really unique. In our introduction we could identify only two periods in the history of modern public services from the beginning of the 20th century in which there had been an absolute decline in the level of public service expenditure. Those two periods of absolute reduction occurred in a transition from a wartime to a peacetime economy related to the two great conflicts of the 20th century, the First and Second World Wars. Of those two periods we felt that the post–First World War Geddes reductions set out a more appropriate model for our current circumstances. The economic background was one of the traditional neoclassical model rather than the more mixed managed market economic model that emerged as the post–Second World War consensus and that finally collapsed in the Smithsonian Agreement of 1971.

The society against which the Geddes cuts were addressed was decidedly an unequal one, in comparison to that produced by the post-Beveridge drive against poverty and want that emerged after the Second World War. The goal of restructuring was one of 'sound money' and to attempt to reintroduce the economic and monetary systems that had existed before the First World War, even though it was recognised at the time that this was wholly inappropriate. Post–Second World War there was a greater attempt to manage exchange rates, and to use international agencies to achieve this, rather than the post–First World War reliance on the market system. So for all of these reasons we felt that the Geddes reforms gave us a more appropriate model to a current circumstances, albeit that the economic consequences, social consequences, and political consequences were fairly disastrous, contributing as it did to waves of industrial unrest, culminating in the General Strike; and sustained economic hardship. This was prolonged throughout the 1930s when given a particular financial twist by the 1929 Wall Street collapse; and the rise of fascism as a political force with its emphasis on factionalism, racism, nationalism, and its disastrous ethical consequences that we described as part of the 'absencing' process.

By looking at more modern examples from other countries we set out in Chapter 3 a number of other stories drawn from modern Western economies that had coped with, or were coping with, similar circumstances. However in all of this we didn't lose sight of the unique nature of the UK's current position. Looking at fiscal restructurings from the 1970s as analysed by OECD, we found our current situation well outside the range of previous experience, and the more successful restructurings of modern times in Sweden and Canada were set against an economic environment that was substantially more favourable. The stories we found to tell gave us pointers, but did not provide a blueprint.

'Too little, too late'

Because of the unpredictability and inherent uncertainty with which an emergent future presents itself it is not at all surprising that what we have observed in the past has been a tendency to an innate conservatism or an approach of 'muddling through'. Like an individual in a darkened room trying to find the door, the tendency of leaders is to take hesitant steps, feeling the way against known and imagined dangers and only proceeding by increments. Certainly this is the path of history for public services, with a tendency to only address issues when they had become an issue of considerable crisis, and then to adopt partial and adaptive approaches in an evolution of change, rather than more radical solutions. The general criticism here is therefore that the politicians and leaders usually engage in 'too little, too late'. It was reported that a junior intern in the incoming Obama Administration was shocked to realise that the timescale within which he was expected to give his advice on the environment was dominated by concerns about to what would be important issues in the media within the next 90 days. The timescale did not even extend as far as the next elections! So it is perhaps unsurprising that our more general criticism of the approach currently being adopted to manage change in the public sector in an age of austerity is that it does not go far enough. Some examples should suffice to demonstrate what we mean:

- We are concerned that by sticking to the traditional paradigm we will experience a situation that we described above, we may achieve a financial restructuring but at 'a price we cannot afford'. The traditional paradigm does not go far enough. If we adopted the alternative that we have set out, the total demand for public services in a more equal society could be in the order of 30–40% less than we currently experience, and there would be greater scope for more preventative rather than immediate, expedient policies. At the same time the more efficient type of organisation has been shown to deliver outcomes which are 30–40% more efficient. Taking the two together, and allowing for an element of double counting, suggests that adopting the new paradigm might mean we could provide the same level of public services for 50% of the current resources, given sufficient time to make the change. That would be more than sufficient to meet the needs of financial restructuring.
- The strategies currently being adopted are, to use the taxonomy that we introduced earlier, strictly of the H1/H2 category with very little devoted to H3 type changes. We are of the view that this does not go far enough. The kind of shift that we think the current situation calls for requires us to make the paradigm shifting H3 type of change. As we said such a change needs H1 and H2 changes to provide the interim coping strategies and transitional measures, but it needs a full-scale commitment to major change to gain the benefits long-term that come from an H3 approach.
- We commented how the strategy is being developed without a clear vision as to what the final shape of the public sector will be. We've noted how of the four, strategic visions that form part of the general discussion and debate seem to centre around a reformed public service versus a smaller State, although this might provide a pole of contention within the current Coalition arrangements with 'small state conservatism' only being prepared to accept the principles of 'reformed public sector' in as far as it leads to a reduced level of State activity. While we would feel that the 'no change' approach of assuming current circumstances as a temporary phenomenon is unrealistic, there are clear aspects of the 'reformed capitalism' approach that need to be embraced if the circumstances which gave rise to the collapse of economic activity are not to be repeated. Without this there is a danger that the disparities between economic sectors, parts of the country, communities, and between individuals will be continued to

our long-term disadvantage. There needs to be a more ambitious vision – the current one, in as much as it is articulated – does not go far enough.

- We took some time in our early chapters to set out the range of issues being faced by the public sector in the UK, as elsewhere. At the present time the concentration of debate and attention is on the single issue of economic recovery and financial restructuring. We described this earlier as a 'hygiene factor' – a necessary condition that has to be met if other issues are to be dealt with. However, we are concerned that the almost obsessive concentration on this single issue means that other critical issues, which are more long-term and which we described as 'cold water frog', remain unaddressed. The current range of policy is necessary, but it does not go far enough. We remain concerned that it is these longer-term 'cold water' issues that have been shown historically to be fatal to the sustainability of individual civilisations and ignoring them does not make them go away.

- One of the supporting elements of a move to a new paradigm that we commended was the thinking about 'Big Society'. The approach to a wider platform of service provision, in particular to a greater devolution of responsibility to local bodies has much to commend it, but it does not go far enough. We described, using Sharmer's 'Theory U' process, how the current intentions of Big Society appear only to go as far as creating a more market-based mixture of provider arrangements for public services. This took it one step down the U process, but there were significant other steps to be taken in getting to a much more user-orientated approach by involving citizens, service providers, and key stakeholders in a real debate about what really matters to them, and what the basic principles were that they shared in wanting to deliver better public services. Only by going through the slow and greater involvement part of the U process designated as 'presencing' will the advantages and benefits of innovation and prototyping, and a new engagement and democracy, likely be delivered. Without them there must be a significant danger that attempting to shortcut across the U will prove unsatisfactory, impermanent, and ineffective. The partial approach is one which simply creates a wider range of service providers and who are financially the clients of the still centralised 'command and control' Executive will not address key issues of legitimacy and effective service delivery.

- The current rush to achieve a quick financial restructuring is perhaps driven by an electoral cycle or even shorter political timescale. However, by making rapid adjustments, without allowing the space for new approaches to embed themselves and start delivering outcomes, may well mean that we close off these long-term opportunities for short-term gain. Curiously by concentrating too much on a short scale we will not go far enough and take into account the long-term implications of short-term actions. So for example proposals are being made to deal with the increasing cost of public sector pensions which bring them more in line with the rapid downscaling of pension provision already seen in the private sector. The long-term implications of doing this, along with private sector pensions under-provision may simply be to create a position in 20 or 30 years time when there is substantial absolute poverty amongst those who are reaching the end of their working life. The pressure to then supplement future incomes by increasing direct State provision will be significant and will create a future problem. The long-term cycle approach to evaluating outcomes is in danger of being ignored, and the short-term approach on its own does not go far enough. If we do not allow sufficient time for the creation of innovative change, then we are in danger of suffering the short-term consequences of Schumpeter's 'creative destruction' without gaining the long-term benefits.

Cutting down the last tree

We find it difficult to believe that any of the points that we are making here are not properly understood. But there is the key question of attitudes to change. Jared Diamond (Diamond 2005) describes how in presenting his analysis of the collapse of civilisations to students and commentators he asked them to consider the factors that led the last tree on Easter Island being cut down, thus ensuring the final environmental damage which condemned the islanders to conflict and poverty, whilst at the same time depriving them of the only means of escaping. He was surprised when his audience said that the key question for them was 'What was that person thinking of? He cut down the last tree'! How could anybody do so, uncaring of the consequences? In answering that question he provided four key points about attitudes of those exercising choices in the kind of critical situation that we now face:

- First, ignorance – people simply didn't know the consequences. However, such an excuse is not valid today. For example, it may have been true in the past when the longer-term consequences of economic activity on climate change were unknown but the extensive debate and discussion that has taken place about the current set of circumstances, their cause, their history, and the range of issues to be addressed means it's highly unlikely that decision-makers, or the public, could claim that they felt uninformed. Nevertheless, even though well-informed, people might still make the wrong judgement call.
- Second, SEP – someone else's problem. The person who cut the tree down might have felt that the consequences were not ones that he or she would bear. In such circumstances there is a lack of engagement and a lack of regard for the consequences. That might be one of the emerging current issues, as one generation creates significant consequences for another, in

the knowledge that it is someone else's problem. However, given the fact that many of the significant environmental issues, as well as the economic issues, are now highly interrelated in a globalised world, and we can't avoid the consequences because there is simply nowhere else to go to avoid them, means that someone else's problem is our problem and vice versa. It's misjudgement to think that anything is 'someone else's problem'.

- Third, the tragedy of the commons. There are common resources that nobody owns individually, and everyone therefore feels that they are able to exploit. However there is nothing to stop an overexploitation in such circumstances, because no one is prepared to forego their own personal interest for the greater common interest. The assumption is that 'if I don't benefit from doing this, someone else will'. This remains a very strong common attitude particularly on environmental issues, but also with regard to economic opportunities. So the pursuit of personal profit that drove the economic situation was predicated on the fact that if there was a profit to be made, and I refused to act for whatever ethical grounds there might be, then I was simply giving up that profit to someone else.
- Finally, TINA – there is no alternative. In a world based on machinelike thinking and its concentration on 'facts', values play second place. Not surprisingly when things need to be done and there is only a 'one view' approach then we approach issues with 'closed minds/close hearts/closed wills' and the consequence is that instead of going through the process of 'presencing' we go down the route of 'absencing', believing that there is nothing that we should do, because there's only one thing that we can do.

These underpinning attitudes give rise to the possibility of undertaking acts of folly, even with the understanding that alternatives exist which are viable. Essentially they are attitudes driven by sectional or factional interest, and in the absence of a genuine engagement with the wider community interest. The alternative approach is one of cooperation, learning, listening, and dialogue. It is the approach of 'presencing' which develops understanding, innovates, and allows experimentation to reach new solutions. It requires the space to do so at community, national, and international levels. The hardest thing that will get in the way of achieving a paradigm shift is the simple act of changing our minds. And the simplest way that we can begin that process is by opening a conversation, telling ourselves stories, and generating a genuine dialogue. We have seen this book as one step in that direction. We hope that it will stimulate a debate, but one which is not driven by defence of set positions, but a real one that engages us as stakeholders in a better future.

References

Ahamed, L., (2009), Lords of Finance, Penguin.

Ansary, T. (2010), Destiny Disrupted – A history of the World through Islamic eyes, Public Affairs.

Appleby J. Dixon, J. (2004), Patient choice in the NHS, British Medical Journal, 329, 61–62.

Appleby, J. (2007), NHS: Where's the money gone, BBC January 2007, http://www.bbc.co.uk/radio4/today/reports/politics/nhs_cake_20070118.shtml.

Audit Commission (2010), Strategic management in councils, Audit Commission.

Baumol, W. (1982), Contestable Markets and the Theory of Industry Structure, Harcourt Brace Jovanovich.

BBC (2005), Home Alone, British Broadcasting Corporation, http://news.bbc.co.uk/1/hi/magazine/4375030.stm.

Beveridge, W. (1942), Report of the Inter-Departmental Committee on Social Insurance and Allied Services, HMSO.

Boyle, D. and Simms, A. (2009), The New Economics – A Bigger Picture, Earthscan.

BP (2007), Statistical Review of World Energy, http://www.bp.com/liveassets/bp_internet/globalbp/globalbp_uk_english/reports_and_publications/statistical_energy_review_2008/STAGING/local_assets/downloads/pdf/statistical_review_of_world_energy_full_review_2008.pdf.

Bundred, S., (2009), Our public debt is hitting Armageddon levels, Times online, 27 February 2009, http://www.timesonline.co.uk/tol/comment/columnists/guest_contributors/article5811186.ece.

Cabinet Office (2001), Satisfaction with public services, Cabinet Office 2001, http://www.cabinetoffice.gov.uk/media/cabinetoffice/strategy/assets/satisfaction.pdf.

Cabinet Office (1945), Memorandum by the Minister of Health to the Cabinet, 5 October 1945, Public Records Office, CAB 129/3.

Centre for Social Justice (2011), Outcome Based Government: How to improve spending decisions across government.

Coyle, D. (2009), The Soulful Science – What Economists Do and Why It Matters, Princeton University Press.

Crosland, A. (1975), Speech in Manchester Town Hall, 9 May, 1975, http://en.wikiquote.org/wiki/Anthony_Crosland.

Dash.com (2010), http://www.24dash.com/news/communities/201 0–1 0–18-Nearly-50-of-adults-dont-expect-council-cuts.

Deeming, W.E. (2000), Out of the crisis, MIT Press.

Diamond, J. (2005), Collapse: How Societies Choose to Fail or Survive, Allen Lane.

Drucker, P. (1989), The New Realities, Harper and Row.

The Economist (2010a), Radical Britain: The Unlikely Revolutionary, Aug 2010.

The Economist (2010b), Careful What You Wish for, December 2010.

EIU (2007), Heading for the Rocks: Will Financial Turmoil Sink the World Economy?, Economist Intelligence Unit.

ESRC (undated), A level briefing, Economic and Social Research Council, http://www.esrcsocietytoday.ac.uk/ESRCInfoCentre/Images/families_a-level_tcm6–11450.pdf.

Financial Times (2007), Extra cash for schools badly used, says ONS, September 2007, http://www.ft.com/cms/s/0/4b0f62c4–5b4a-11dc-8c32–0000779fd2ac.html#axzz1luKobsGw.

Foote, S. (1958–1974), The Civil War: A Narrative, Vintage Books.

Fulton (1968), Report of the Committee into the Civil Service chaired by Lord Fulton, HMSO.

Galbraith, J.K. (1954), The Great Crash 1929, Hamish Hamilton 1955.

Georgiades, N. and Phillimore, L. (1975), The Myth of the Hero-Innovator, Associated Scientific Publishers.

Goleman, D. (1996), Emotional Intelligence, Bloomsbury.

Guardian (2002), Cook: Britain is most centralised state in Europe, http://www.guardian.co.uk/politics/2002/nov/03/uk.constitution.

Hague, W. (2005), William Pitt the Younger, Harper Perennial.

Handy C. (1989), The Age of Unreason, Hutchinson Business.

Heclo, H. and Wildavsky, A. (1974), The Private Government of Public Money, Macmillan.

HM Government (2010), The Coalition: Our Programme for Government, HMSO.

HM Treasury (2010), Total Place: A Whole Area Approach to Public Services, HMSO.

House of Commons (2009), Report of the Treasury Committee on the impact of the failure of the Icelandic banks, HMSO.

House of Commons (2011), Public Accounts Committee Report on the Management of NHS hospital productivity, HMSO 9 March 2011, http://news.icm.ac.uk/business/government-debt-overtakes-nhs-budget/3564/.

Hutton, W (1995), The 30/30/40 Labour Market, The Jobs Letter No.30 / 15 December 1995.

IFS (2008), NHS spending – What Does the Future Hold, Institute of Fiscal Studies, October 2008.

Institute of Commercial Management (2009), http://news.icm.ac.uk/business/government-debt-overtakes-nhs-budget/3564/.

Jansen, P. (2009), Forum on the Future of Higher Education, McKinsey and Co, June 2009.

Jay, A. (1988), Management and Machiavelli, Hutchinson.

Johnson, S. (2010), Where Good Ideas Come from, Allen Lane.

Kaletsky A. (2010a), If interest rates rise, our prospects plummet, The Times 11 March 2010, http://www.timesonline.co.uk/tol/comment/columnists/anatole_kaletsky/article7057327.ece.

Kaletsky, A. (2010b), The pay gap is putting democracy in danger, The Times November 2010.

Kauffman, S. (2000), Interpretations, Oxford University Press.

Kauffman, S. (2004), The Adjacent Possible, http://www.edge.org/3rd_culture/kauffman03/kauffman_index.html.

Kauffman, S. (2008), Reinventing the Sacred, Basic Books.

Kennedy, P. (1989), The Rise and Fall of the Great Powers, Fontana.

Keynes, J.M. (1925), The Economic Consequences of Mr. Churchill, Hogarth Press.

Keynes, J.M. (1935), The General Theory of Employment, Interest and Money, Harcourt, Brace and Company.

Klein, R. and Buxton, M. (1978), Allocating Health Resources: A commentary on the report of the Resource Allocation Working Party, Research Paper Number 3 of the Royal Commission on the NHS, HMSO.

Kumar, M. (2009), Quantum, Icon Books.

Lao T'su (2003), Tao te Ching, Hackett Publishing.

Latham R. and Prowle M.J. (2010), Double Trouble, Public Finance, April 2010.

Local Government Association (2010), Place Based Budgets, LGA.

Lowth, G., Prowle, M.J. and Zhang, M. (2010), The impact of economic recession on business strategy planning in UK companies, Research executive summary series Volume 6, Issue 9, CIMA.

Lubit, R. (2003), Coping with Toxic Managers, Subordinates and Other Difficult People, Prentice Hall.

Machiavelli, N. (1532), The Prince, Penguin Books Edition 2003.

Marshall, A. (1890), Principles of Economics, Cosimo Inc 2009.

Maslow, A.H. (1943), A theory of human motivation, Psychological Review, 50, 370–396.

Miller, P. (2010), Smart Swarm, Collins.

Mladovsky P., Allin S., Masseria C., Hernandez-Quevedo C., McDaid D. and Mossialos E. (2009), Health in the European Union: Trends and Analysis, European Observatory on Health Systems and Policies.

Morris, J. (2001), The Age of Arthur, Phoenix Books.

Musgrave R.A. and Peacock, A.T. (1958), Classics in the Theory of Public Finance, Macmillan.

NAO (2008), NHS Pay Modernisation: New contracts for general practice services in England, National Audit Office.

OBR (2010a), Budget forecast and Budget 2010, HMSO 2010.

OBR (2010b), Pre-Budget forecast, Office for Budget Responsibility.

OECD (2007), Economic Outlook.

OECD (2009), PISA 2009 Results, http://www.spectator.co.uk/coffeehouse/5247793/leaked-slides-connected-to-grays-defence-procurement-report-are-very-damning.thtml.

ONS (2002), Trends in Female Employment, Office for National Statistics 2002.

ONS (2008a) , Social Trends Report, Office for National Statistics.

ONS (2008b), Work and Family, Office for National Statistics,.

Ormerod P. (2008), Butterfly Economics, Basic Books.

Ormerod, P. (1997), the Death of Economics, John Wiley.

Parris, M. (2010), Tories do have ideology – and they'll need it, The Times, October 2010.

Pensions Commission (2010), Interim Report, Independent Public Service.

Polkinghorne, J. (2002), Quantum Theory – A very short introduction, Oxford University Press.

Powell, J. (2010), The New Machiavelli, Bodley Head.

Prowle, M.J. (2008) Developing Contestability in the Delivery of Public Services, Public Money and Management.

Public Finance (2009), Governments Should Think Twice about Rearranging Whitehall, warns O'Donnell, 30 October 2009.

Pugh, D. and Hickson, D. (2007), Writers on Organisations, Penguin.

Rawnsley, A. (2010), The End of the Party, Penguin.

Reiss, G. (2007), Project Management Demystified, Taylor and Francis.

Ruskin, J. (1860), Unto This Last, Cornhill Magazine.

Santayana, G. (1951), The Life of Reason: Volume 1, Common Sense, Prometheus Books.

Scharmer, C.O. (2009), Theory U – Leading from the Future as it emerges, Berrett Koehler.

Schumpeter, J. (1934), The Theory of Economic Development, Oxford University Press 1969.

Scratch, L. (2010), Public Service Reductions in the 1990s, Library of Parliament – Canada.

Seddon, J. (2003), Freedom from Command and Control: a Better Way to Make the Work Work, Vanguard Press.

Sennett, R. (1999), The Corrosion of Character, Norton.

Sennett, R. (2003), The Corrosion of Character: Personal Consequences of Work in the New Capitalism, W.W. Norton & Company.

Smith, L. (2007), Chaos – A Very Short Introduction, Oxford University Press.

Spectator (2009), Leaked slides connected to Gray's defence procurement report are very damning, 6 August 2009, http://www.spectator.co.uk/coffeehouse/5247793/leaked-slides-connected-to-grays-defence-procurement-report-are-very-damning.thtml.

Sraffa, P. (1972), The Production of Commodities by means of Commodities, Cambridge University Press.

Stephenson, K. (2000), Case Study 10: Understanding the Role Informal Networks Play in Community Innovation, Netform SNA.

Stern, N. (2006), The Stern Review on the Economics of Climate Change, HM Treasury.

Talbot C. (2009), Public domain: Mandarin-tinted glasses, Public Finance, 27 February 2009.

Tuchman, B. (1984), The March of Folly: From Troy to Vietnam, Ballantine Books.

United Nations (2007), Climate Change 2007: The Fourth Assessment Report of the United Nations Intergovernmental Panel on Climate Change (IPCC).

Veblen, T. (1899), Theory of the Leisure Class: An Economic Study of Institutions, Dover 1994.

Walras, L. (1874), Elements of Pure Economics, Routledge 2003.

Wheatley, M. (1997), Goodbye, Command and Control, Leader to Leader.

Wheatley, M. (2001), Leadership and the New science, Berrett Koehler.

Wheatley, M. (2005), How is your leadership changing?, http://www.margaretwheatley.com/articles/howisyourleadership.html.

Wheatley, M. (2007), Finding Our Way – Leadership for An Uncertain Time, Berrett Koehler.

Wikipedia a, http://en.wikipedia.org/wiki/Recruitment_to_the_British_Army_during_World_War_I.

Wikipedia b, http://en.wikipedia.org/w/index.php?title=Heliocentrism.

Wikipedia c, http://en.wikipedia.org/wiki/John_Ruskin .

Wikipedia d, http://en.wikipedia.org/w/index.php?title=David_Ricardo.

Wilkinson, R. and Pickett, K. (2010), The Spirit Level. Why Equality is Better for Everyone, Penguin 2010.

Suggested Reading

6, P. (2002), Towards Holistic Governance: The New Reform Agenda, Macmillan.

Ahamed, L. (2009), Lords of Finance, Penguin.

Aldred, J. (2009), The Sceptical Economist, Earthscan.

Amable, B. (2009), The Diversity of Modern Capitalism, Oxford University Press.

Berry, S. (2006), Strategies of the Serengeti.

Bickers, R. (2011), The Scramble for China, Allen Lane.

Cardini, F. (2001), Europe and Islam, Blackwell.

Christensen, T. and Laegreid, P. (2007), Transcending New Public Management, Ashgate Publishing.

Collins, P. and Byrne, L. (eds) (2004), Reinventing Government Again, London: The Social Market Foundation.

Coyle, D. (2009), The Soulful Science – What Economists Do and Why It Matters, Princeton University Press.

Deeming, W.E. (2000), Out of the crisis, MIT Press.

Diamond, J (2005), Guns, Germs and Steel, Vintage.

Diamond, J. (2005), Collapse: How Societies Choose to Fail or Survive, Allen Lane,.

Foley, M. (2010), The Age of Absurdity, Simon and Schuster.

Foote, S. (1958–1974), The Civil War: A Narrative, New York: Vintage Books.

Friedman, T. (2005), The World Is Flat – A Brief History of the Globalised World of the 21st Century, Penguin.

Galbraith, J.K. (1954), The Great Crash 1929, Hamish Hamilton 1955.

Georgiades, N. and Phillimore, L. (1975), The Myth of the Hero-Innovator, Associated Scientific Publishers.

Gladwell, M. (2000), The Tipping Point, Abacus.

Glynn, A. (2006), Capitalism Unleashed, Oxford University Press.

Goleman, D. (1996), Emotional Intelligence, Bloomsbury.

Hague, W. (2005), William Pitt the Younger, Harper Perennial, London.

Handy C. (1989), The Age of Unreason, Hutchinson Business.

Heclo, H. and Wildavsky, A. (1975), The Private Government of Public Money, Macmillan.

Heeks, R. (2001), Reinventing Government in the Information Age, Routledge.

Hofstede, G., Hofstede, G.J. and Minkoff, M. (2010), Cultures and Organisations, McGraw-Hill.

Hourani, A. (1991), A History of the Arab Peoples, Faber and Faber.

Hutton, W. (1996), The State We're in, Vintage.

Hutton, W. (2002), The World We're in, Vintage.

Jay, A. (1988), Management and Machiavelli, Hutchinson.

Johnson, S. (2010), Where Good Ideas Come from, Allen Lane.

Kauffman, S. (2000), Interpretations, Oxford University Press.

Kauffman, S. (2008), Reinventing the Sacred, Basic Books.

Kennedy, P. (1989), The Rise and Fall of the Great Powers, Fontana.

Kettl, D.F. (2000), Global Public Management Revolution: A report on the Transformation of Governance. Washington D.C:.Brookings Institution.

Keynes, J.M. (1925), The Economic Consequences of Mr. Churchill, Hogarth Press.

Keynes, J.M. (1935), The General Theory of Employment, Interest and Money, Harcourt, Brace and Company.

King, S. (2010), Losing Control – The Emerging Threats to Western Prosperity, Yale University Press.

Krugman, P. (2008), The Return of Depression Economics, Penguin.

Küng, Hans. (2007), Islam, World Oxford.

Lubit, R. (2003), Coping with Toxic Managers, Subordinates and Other Difficult People, Prentice Hall.

Machiavelli, N. (1532), The Prince, Penguin Books Edition 2003.

Malloch-Brown, M. (2011), The Unfinished Global Revolution, Allen Lane.

Miller, P. (2010), Smart Swarm, Collins.

Milner, E. and Joyce, P. (2005) Lessons in Leadership: Meeting the Challenges of Public Services Management. Routledge.

Ormerod P. (2008), Butterfly Economics, Basic Books.

Ormerod, P. (1997), The Death of Economics, John Wiley.

Osborne,D. and Gaebler, D (1992), Reinventing Government; How the entrepreneurial Spirit is Transforming the Public Sector, Addison Wesley.

Parris, M. (2010), Tories do have ideology – and they'll need it, The Times October 2010.

Pollitt, C. and Bouckaert, G. (2004), Public Management Reform: A comparative analysis, Oxford University Press.

Powell, J. (2010), The New Machiavelli, Bodley Head.

Prowle, M.J. (2000), The Changing Public Sector: A Practical Management Guide, Gower Publishing.

Prowle, M.J. (2010), Managing and Reforming Modern Public Services: The Financial Management Dimension, Pearsons.

Public Management and Policy Association (2005), Why Are We So Badly Governed?

Pugh, D. and Hickson, D. (2007), Writers on Organisations, Penguin.

Rawnsley, A. (2010), The End of the Party, Penguin.

Scharmer, C.O. (2009), Theory U – Leading from the Future as It Emerges, Berrett Koehler.

Sennett, R. (2003), The Corrosion of Character: Personal Consequences of Work in the New Capitalism, W.W. Norton & Company.

Tuchman, B. (1984), The March of Folly: From Troy to Vietnam, Ballantine Books.

Wheatley, M. (1997), Goodbye, Command and Control, Leader to Leader.

Wheatley, M. (2001), Leadership and the New science, Berrett Koehler.

Wheatley, M. (2007), Finding Our Way – Leadership for An Uncertain Time, Berrett Koehler.

Wilkinson, R. and Pickett, K. (2010), The Spirit Level, Penguin.

Zalasiewicz, J. (2008), The Earth after Us, Oxford University Press.

Index